The Enlightenment

𝔅

THE MAKING OF EUROPE

Series Editor: Jacques Le Goff

The Making of Europe series is the result of a unique collaboration between five European publishers – Beck in Germany, Blackwell in Great Britain and the United States, Critica in Spain, Laterza in Italy and le Seuil in France. Each book will be published in all five languages. The scope of the series is broad, encompassing the history of ideas as well as and including their interaction with the history of societies, nations and states, to produce informative, readable, and provocative treatments of central themes in the history of the European peoples and their cultures.

The Enlightenment

Ulrich Im Hof

Translated from the German
by
William E. Yuill

BLACKWELL
Oxford UK & Cambridge USA

Copyright © Ulrich Im Hof 1994

English translation copyright © Basil Blackwell Ltd 1994

First published in 1994 by Blackwell Publishers and by four other publishers:
© 1993 Beck, Munich (German); © 1993 Critica, Barcelona (Spanish); © 1993
Editions du Seuil, Paris (French); © 1993 Laterza, Rome and Bari (Italian).

First published 1994

Blackwell Publishers
108 Cowley Road
Oxford OX4 1JF
UK

238 Main Street
Cambridge, Massachusetts 02142
USA

British Library Cataloguing in Publication Data
A CIP catalogue record for this book is available from the British Library.

Library of Congress Cataloging-in-Publication Data
Im Hof, Ulrich.
[Europa der Aufklärung. English]
The Enlightenment / Ulrich Im Hof; translated from the
German by William E. Yuill.
    p.   cm.—(The Making of Europe)
Translation of: Das Europa der Aufklärung.
Includes bibliographical references and index.
ISBN 0–631–17591–1
    1. Enlightenment—Europe.   2. Europe—Intellectual life—
18th century.   I. Title.   II. Series.
B802.I4 1994   93–46872
940.2′53—dc20   CIP

Typeset in 11.5 on 13 pt Garamond by
Pure Tech Corporation, Pondicherry, India
Printed in Great Britain by
T.J. Press Ltd, Padstow, Cornwall
This book is printed on acid-free paper

Contents

PART VI
A Window Opened to a Wider World

PART VII
Emancipation – A Release from Age-old Restraints

PART VIII
For and Against Radicalization of the Enlightenment

Part IX
The Way Ahead into the Nineteenth Century

Series Editor's Preface

Europe is in the making. It is founded on great hopes. But these hopes will not be realized if we neglect history. A Europe lacking history would have neither a past nor a future. For today stems from yesterday, and tomorrow comes from all that has gone before. What is past, however, ought not to paralyse the future, but enable it, whatever it may choose to preserve, to assume new and progressive shape. Our European continent, situated between the Atlantic, Asia and Africa, has long existed as shown on our maps and as it has been shaped by history ever since the Greeks gave it the name it still bears today. The future must be built on this heritage which has enabled Europe since classical – indeed since prehistoric – times, precisely because of its unity in diversity, to develop such a wealth of culture and such extraordinary creative power.

The series, *The Making of Europe*, which has been launched as a joint venture by five publishers of different nationalities and languages is designed to throw light on the shaping of Europe and on its not inconsiderable potential for successful integration, without disguising the problems it has inherited. The series does not mean to conceal the fact that this continent, in its striving for unity, has had to overcome so many conflicts, so much that divides the nations, so much that is contradictory; for anyone who embarks on the European enterprise must be familiar with the continent's past and fully aware of its future prospects. This explains the 'active' title of our series. It does not seem to us, in fact, that the time is yet ripe for the compiling of a definitive universal history of Europe. We wish to encompass our subject in a series of essays by the most able contemporary historians, irrespective of whether they are Europeans or non-Europeans, whether they are established authorities or as yet scarcely known. They will deal with the essential themes of European history in the fields of economics, politics, sociology, religion and culture, drawing on the long tradition of historical writing founded by Herodotus, but also on the new ideas that have fundamentally changed the writing of history in the twentieth century, and especially during the last decades. They will endeavour to make the issues clear, so that they may be understood by all.

Our aim is to provide those involved in the building and development of Europe, as well as interested individuals throughout the world, with evidence and material to answer the fundamental questions: Who are we? Where did we come from? Where are we going?

Jacques Le Goff

Part I

The Age

1

Enlightenment and Fresh Light

Enlightenment is the title of an engraving by Daniel Chodowiecki, that most prolific of German artists of the eighteenth century. In the foreground of his picture a horse-drawn cart is being driven behind a pedestrian and a horseman along a highway in the shadow of a dense wood. All three travellers are making their way towards a kind of manor-house, of which two towers, one taller than the other, can be glimpsed behind the trees. The building is already bathed in the radiant light of the sun, which is just emerging beyond a distant range of hills. It is the early morning sun which sends its rays far into the still overcast sky and which is about to disperse the mist that still shrouds the village.

Chodowiecki comments as follows on his representation of the Enlightenment:

> Perhaps because the phenomenon itself is still a novelty, the supreme achievement of reason has not yet been accorded a generally acknowledged allegorical emblem other than the rising sun. And no doubt it will long remain the most fitting image on account of the fumes that will constantly rise from swamps, censers and burnt offerings on pagan altars and that are so apt to obscure the light. But as long as the sun continues to rise, mists do not matter.[1]

As a further comment on this engraving with the sun of the Enlightenment we might single out another statement from

3

this period which refers to the contemporary reform movement. 'We have ever been convinced that it is, above all, light – often light that heralds the chill of dawn – which will ultimately bring congenial warmth.' And once this warmth had indeed been engendered, we might quote a metaphor from England in which reason is likened to the sun, 'of which the light is constant, uniform and lasting'. It was in the eighteenth century that the idea of light acquired a new status. Light is now invoked over and over again when reason, liberty or happiness are mentioned. It is a light that is reflected in the ideas that characterize that century.

The English term, Enlightenment, does not, in fact, make its appearance until the nineteenth century, when it vies with the expression the Age of Reason. During the eighteenth century the philosopher Berkeley, for instance, speaks of 'that ocean of light, which has broke in and made his way, in spite of slavery and superstition', while another Englishman remarks that the century 'is enlighten'd beyond the hopes and imaginations of former times'. The poet Alexander Pope, pointing proudly to the grand philosophical and scientific syntheses of the age, declares:

Nature and Nature's laws lay hid in night.
God said, let Newton be! and all was light.[2]

From that point on, it might well be said: *Ex occidente lux!* The light no longer came from the East, but from the West, not only from a democratic Britain, but also from France, which was beginning to free itself from the fetters of absolutism.

Lumières was the French expression. Lumière, light, implies understanding, knowledge and perspicuity. *Lumières* was to become a specific notion of the age:

Les seules lumières de la raison naturelle sont capables de conduire les hommes à la perfection de la science et de la sagesse humaine.

Only the light of natural reason is able to lead man to the perfection of knowledge and human wisdom.
The same message may be found in poetic form:

Et ce qu'avait produit l'ignorance grossière Disparait au grand jour d'un siècle de lumière.

And may those things gross ignorance has born
Be banished in the light of our new age's dawn.

Most statements of this kind are of a later date than those from
England. This is no mere chance: over the coffin of Louis XIV
the great preacher Massillon had proclaimed, 'God alone is
great', and it was not until the echo of those words had died
away that there began to emerge all those ideas that a monarchy
'by the grace of God' had tried to suppress. Europe, which had
begun by copying French elegance, French manners and the
French language, was now inundated from the same source by a
light that was at times disconcertingly chilly and that found its
way into every dark nook and cranny. The most outrageously
wicked remarks were liable to be made in emulation of the
French and in the French language by the mistress of some
German princeling or other, or even by an Italian *abbé*.

The German expression, *Aufklärung*, which, to begin with,
had merely meteorological connotations, was first used in the
sense of *erleuchten* ('illuminate') and had various related verbal
forms. It was understood as applying to a historical era only
from the 1780s onwards: *das Zeitalter der Aufklärung* – the Age
of the Enlightenment. It was not widely accepted, however,
until the nineteenth century.

We find the idea of light in a number of parallel combinations: *Aufklärung und Licht, Freiheit und Licht* – 'Enlightenment
and Light, Liberty and Light'. 'Enlightenment means removing
those veils and screens that obstruct our sight, making way for
light to enter our hearts and minds to illuminate the former and
warm the latter and hence make its way into those realms of
truth and order where man's destiny and happiness hold sway.'
Wieland speaks of freedom of thought and freedom of the press,
'which are to the mind what light is to the eyes'. When the
young Herder seeks to characterize the age in which he lived, he
calls it 'our enlightened age, the brightest of centuries'.

The Italian term *Illuminismo* is relatively recent in this form
and did not become current usage until the twentieth century.
In the eighteenth century the phrase commonly used was *luce, i
lumi, illuminato*, which sounds like a translation from French.

'*Un secolo così illuminato come il nostro*' — 'a century as enlightened as ours'; or '*La legislazione, il commercio, la pubblica gloria e sicurezza dipendono da' lumi delle nazioni . . .*' — 'Legislation, trade, public reputation and security depend on the enlightenment of the nations'. May we rank Italy along with England, France and Germany in this century of enlightenment and reason? It should be borne in mind that Italian was still a language that the educated European might be expected to know and to have a better command of than, say, English. In Italy the freedom of the Renaissance had still not faded from people's memories!

In Spain the more modern term *Ilustración* had replaced the older *Iluminismo*. Throughout Europe Spain had the reputation of being a backward country, but it had important representatives of the Enlightenment and intelligent administrators in the service of the Bourbon monarchy, who were doing their best to stimulate reform. A Spaniard of the time nevertheless felt obliged to say of the situation in which intellectuals found themselves, 'que . . . estudian a Newton en su cuarto y explican a Aristóteles en su catedra'[3] — they used Newton's methods in private study, but in their public function as teachers they went on expounding Aristotle in order not to find themselves in trouble with the authorities. This was a situation that obtained in a good many Catholic countries. Rousseau notes, however, that, compared with the French, the English and the Germans, 'the Spaniard is the only one of these four who brings back home with him sundry useful observations concerning what he has seen abroad'.

The Enlightenment, the light of reason, spread through other linguistic areas, of course. It even reached the Portugal of the Marquis de Pombal, and this was the first country to bring charges against the Jesuits. We might mention the Swiss, who brought into play rational reforming tendencies from both French and German sources; or the Dutch, who, even earlier than the English, had known a world of intellectual freedom. We ought also to mention the Nordic kingdoms, which adapted French and German suggestions to their own indigenous forms; Poland, which was much under Masonic influence; and the Russia of Catherine II. Nor should we forget the two Americas, where the radiance of the Enlightenment was beginning to spread abroad in its Spanish, Portuguese and Anglo-Saxon versions.

We are dealing with the world of white men, which was founded on Christianity and on the culture of the classical age, and which had been modified in national and confessional terms over a good many centuries.

It was now a matter of removing all manner of 'veils and screens'. The new light was to get rid of 'slavery and superstition' and dispel the 'shadows'. There were, however, fanatics, the anticlerical Italian writer Pilati claims, 'who mean to preserve darkness, blindness and ignorance, and who detest the coming of light'.

If we look back on the period preceding the eighteenth century, it seems as if this light had in fact been lacking in previous ages. The history of the human race now seemed to be a gradual progression from primitive beginnings to an existence that grew ever more complex: it was no longer seen as a predetermined path leading to the Apocalypse and the Last Judgement. Around the middle of the century Voltaire, Ferguson and Iselin attempted to sketch a historical view of human progress. They stand at the beginning of a long series of similar undertakings with the same purpose which extends via Wieland, Home, Herder, Lessing, Mably and Kant to Condorcet.

But it was not merely the intellectual concepts of the century that were to be illuminated by this new light; it was to penetrate every sphere of human activity. We have already quoted the Italian opinion that legislation, trade and public safety depended on the *lumi* of the nations. In the same vein Wieland extols every contribution that casts some light 'on political economy, politics, the civil and military constitution, religion, morals, public education, the sciences, arts and crafts and husbandry in any part of our common fatherland'. In this way Wieland reviews all the fields in which light might be shed to advantage.

The allegorical emblem which Chodowiecki identifies with the atmosphere of the dawning day had already delighted Montesquieu: 'I wake up in the morning with a secret joy in the light of day. I behold that light with a kind of rapture and feel at peace for the rest of the day.'[4]

2

The Eighteenth Century as the
Background to the Enlightenment

The Enlightenment is associated with a specific historical period. Every movement of this kind must come to terms with the realities of its historical era which may run counter to it: humanism, for instance, had to cope with a universal church and its religious ideas, liberalism with a powerful upsurge of militaristic and nationalistic forces, and the Enlightenment with deeply rooted traditions of secular and spiritual government.

And yet it was the Enlightenment that set the seal on the character of its century. People spoke and wrote differently from the way in which they had spoken and written hitherto, and they would go on speaking and writing like that for some time to come. Any monarch, however despotic, found it worth while to masquerade as an enlightened ruler, to behave more like a schoolteacher than a tyrant.

It was the Enlightenment that effected the transition from theory to practice, from mere criticism to action designed to improve and reform education and husbandry, social intercourse and political life. It gave birth to enlightened absolutism and also to two great republics – in France and in North America.

Enlightenment was a reaction against the baroque, against orthodoxy and the Counter-Reformation. The persistent undercurrents of the humanism epitomized in Erasmus, of plain speaking and writing, of criticism on the classical model once again found their way to the surface – as expressed in a phrase coined by Albrecht von Haller: 'A man who thinks freely, is thinking well.'

The Enlightenment imparted an uncommonly powerful impulse to the traditional and ossified shape of things. People began to look forward, and not back – or, if they did look back, it was to the exemplary innovative age of the Renaissance and of a classical Greece that was now on the point of being rediscovered; they even looked back to the blissful idyll of the 'noble savage'.

But people were also looking for a new stability following the crises of the seventeenth century – the last plague epidemics or the last expulsions of religious dissidents.

> The search for a new stability begins – a stability founded on rational arrangements in social and political life that would embrace both individual morality and the relations between entire states. The measures that were recommended, planned or implemented to this end, however, were not always explicitly envisaged as elements in a programme of Enlightenment; they were undertaken more in an attempt at better understanding or as a form of criticism of existing traditions. It was in fact the multiplicity and diversity of such measures and the tension between them and their divergent motives that formed the driving force of the process we know as Enlightenment.[5]

The ideas, the style, the attitudes of the enlightened age were expressed, of course, not only in the writing of the day, in its ideological and literary slogans; they may be seen – and heard, too – in the arts of the period. The music of that period is still very much alive – more so, in fact, than ever before: musical scores from the eighteenth century are still regularly being unearthed in one library or another – works by Corelli, Vivaldi, Albinoni, Handel, Bach and his sons, Telemann, Rameau, Stamitz, Haydn, Mozart, Gluck and Boccherini, to mention but a few of the composers of the day. It is through the symphony, the minuet and the concerto, with their straightforward lilting melodies and lucid structure, that we may most easily discover the special magic of the age.

The painting of that time might be seen as a prelude to the Impressionists, whether it be in a still life by Chardin or in portraits by Lawrence, Gainsborough, Latour or Graff, or in the whimsical precision of the landscapes and cheerful scenes of a Watteau or Fragonard. The world they show us is no longer dim and mysterious, overwhelmingly larger than life, as in the paintings of the baroque. At the same time, rococo taste transformed architecture, retaining no more than the trimmings of the baroque style. The interior of the churches adheres to the same basic plan, but the general effect is more luminous, with colours reminiscent of a perpetual sunny evening sky unmarred by sombre masses of cloud. And the little putti cavort ever more nimbly and boldly round the gilded cornices, toying idly with book, trumpet or harp — even with the princely insignia of crown and sceptre.

Part II

A Changing Society

1

The World of the Monarchs

The Kings

For as long as anyone could remember it was with crown and
sceptre that kings had ruled the destinies of the world. They
had always been there; God's governors, appointed to manage
matters on earth; in the final analysis, heirs to the ancient
Roman emperors.[1]

In the eighteenth century Europe was dominated by crowns.
A dozen monarchs wore royal, or even imperial, crowns. For
more than half a century Louis XIV of France had been the most
successful of them all in personifying the royal power and glory
– and in making his influence felt by the exercise of real political
authority. He and his court in Versailles had become the model
for almost all the monarchs of the age. His rule came to an end
at the beginning of the century. He was succeeded by Louis XV,
who himself reigned for a good half century. When he died and
was succeeded by Louis XVI, a great many things had changed
and France was no longer the sole leading power in Europe.

Louis XIV had been able to ensure that his House, the House
of Bourbon, reigned over a realm greater than just France itself.
The Bourbons had replaced the House of Habsburg in Spain
(1700–14). Philip V was succeeded by Ferdinand VI, Charles III
and Charles IV. It is the rule of the last-named that is reflected
in the work of Goya. The might of the Bourbons in Spain was
duplicated in overseas viceregal regimes in Mexico, Peru, New

Granada, La Plata and the Philippines. Apart from all this, the Bourbons had a claim through a secondary line of succession to the kingdom of the Two Sicilies, with the royal courts of Charles III and Ferdinand IV in Naples.

Until the beginning of the eighteenth century the Habsburgs in Vienna had controlled a large part of the world; even at this stage a Habsburg monarch in Vienna still basked in the ancient splendour of his House as the ruler of the Holy Roman Empire of the German Nation. As emperor he was the prime ruler, taking precedence over all others, although the kings no longer took serious account of this ancient dignity. The emperor still wore the royal crowns of Germany, Burgundy and Italy, even though Burgundy had been firmly in the grasp of the King of France for a century or more, and no more than remnants of imperial rule had survived in Italy. The titles of King of Hungary and King of Bohemia still represented something real and tangible, as did the emperor's rule over the southern Netherlands, present-day Belgium. In Vienna, where the elaborate Spanish court ceremonial still obtained, strenuous efforts were being made to preserve Charles VI's patrimony and, above all, to secure the succession of his daughter, Maria Theresa. In 1740 an event took place which the Habsburgs had long feared: another German prince, the Elector of Bavaria, became emperor as Charles VII (1742–5). After his death, however, the imperial crown reverted once more to the Habsburgs in the person of Maria Theresa's consort, the Emperor Francis I. Maria Theresa herself maintained her position in her own realm and was destined, as empress, to restore the paramount importance of Vienna.

Paris and Vienna were indisputably the great courts of mighty states. Along with them there ranked a number of other courts, some of them of greater antiquity. In London there reigned a king who wore the crowns of England, Ireland and Scotland. Since 1714, following the end of the Protestant Stuart line, the throne had been occupied by the Georges from the House of Hanover. In the case of London, in fact, the commercial City was of more interest and importance than the royal palace of St James.

In Copenhagen the Danish kings, who were also kings of

Norway – Frederick IV, Frederick V, Christian VI and Christian VII – were beginning to recuperate from past heroic exploits, as were the Swedish monarchs in Stockholm – Queen Ulrike Eleonora, Frederick and Adolphus Frederick. In both these capitals the monarchs had managed to foster an elegant Nordic version of French courtly culture.

Ever since 1640, following sixty years of government from Madrid, Lisbon had boasted a courtly culture of its own under monarchs from the House of Braganza: during the eighteenth century the rulers were John V, Joseph V and Queen Mary. The eighteenth century had actually created two new kings: the Elector of Brandenburg had become king of Prussia (1701), and the Duke of Savoy had become king of Sardinia (1720), so that there were now royal courts in Berlin and Turin.

And, finally, there was still a king in Poland – during the first half of the century the monarchs had come from the House of Wettin, the Electors of Saxony (1697–1763), so that an appropriately regal lifestyle was adopted in Dresden. And in the remote north-east the Russian emperor, the Tsar, was gradually becoming a force in Europe.

Of all these emperors and kings four have achieved the appellation of 'Great'; they are known above all because they broke away from the traditional image of the absolute ruler by the grace of God in the manner of Louis XIV and were determined to rule effectively in their own person, and not through their ministers. The others were outshone by the 'upstart', Frederick II (1740–86) the 'Great' of Prussia, the 'philosopher of Sanssouci' with his palace in Potsdam, which was more of a cabinet office than a court. He was wont to deride traditional monarchical pomp and courtly circumstance. It was said of him that 'The king was not fond of hunting or of any other extravagant pursuit.' He considered himself 'the first servant of the state' and was in fact his own prime minister. 'His theology is reason, and his canon law is lodged in his armouries.'[2] He was also his own Field Marshal. The Empress Maria Theresa (1740–80) was also capable, in an analogous manner, of running her realm in a style that was just as different from that of Louis XIV. She was the matriarch of her country in a traditional sense, which did not prevent her from introducing sensible innovations. Her son, the 'crowned revolutionary' Joseph II (1765–90), a curious mixture of authoritarianism and 'democratic' posturing, was a hard worker, like Frederick II, but he was prone to introduce precipitate and premature reforms, something which the Prussian king was careful not to do. Finally, Princess Sophie von Anhalt-Zerbst ought to be mentioned: from a tiny German principality she found her way to St Petersburg, where she married Tsar Peter III and, during her reign as Catherine II (1762–96), astonished Europe with a policy of enlightenment that was unmatched anywhere else on the Continent.

The four monarchs we have mentioned ruled *in person*: the princes of the House of Savoy (Victor Amadeus and Charles Emanuel III, at least) tried to follow suit in Turin, but they adopted a more plainly patriarchal approach. Stanislaus Augustus of Poland and Gustav III of Sweden also pursued relatively enlightened policies, but without much success. At the start of his reign, George III of Great Britain (1760–1820) also set out to rule in person. Ever since the Glorious Revolution of 1688, however, the British had been wont to see the crown *in* Parliament and not *above* Parliament, so that the third member of the Hanoverian dynasty was doomed to failure with his policy of the 'king's friends'.

Most monarchs were content to leave the business of government to prime ministers of varying degrees of competence, or even to their mistresses, or the latters' favourites. This was particularly obvious in the France of Louis XV, where one could well speak of the reign of Madame de Pompadour. From 1745 until her death Jeanne-Antoinette Poisson – a woman of plebeian origins – guided the destinies of France as *Maitresse en titre*. She was succeeded by Madame Du Barry, who was politically less ambitious.

It is noteworthy that during the century women achieved power in a number of monarchies simply through the accident of succession. This applied not only to the two empresses, Maria Theresa and Catherine II: the century had opened with Queen Anne (1702–14) in Great Britain and with Queen Ulrike Eleonora (1718–20) in Sweden. It closed with Queen Maria in

Portugal (1777–1816). Even before the time of Catherine II women had occupied influential positions in Russia – for instance, Peter the Great's successors, Catherine I, Anna and Elizabeth. Then there are the influential consorts of male monarchs who deserve mention: Elizabeth Farnese, for example, the wife of the Spanish king, Philip V; Caroline Mathilda in Denmark, the wife of Christian IV, who was unfit to rule; or Maria Caroline in the Naples of Ferdinand IV. Women had, in fact, always played an important part in monarchies as the consorts of kings, as their mistresses, or as dowagers, but the eighteenth century, in which the emancipation of women began, seems to have been particularly auspicious for women at court.

There was a great deal for kings to do, apart from governing their kingdoms, and many of them in fact preferred other royal pursuits to onerous administrative tasks. In such cases the monarch was liable to devote his time to court entertainments, or simply to go off hunting. It was only in Berlin and Turin that these royal pastimes were less highly esteemed – in these capitals the monarchs worked for their living.

Three monarchs were spared such practical problems because of mental derangement – the two Spanish kings, Philip IV and Ferdinand VI, and Christian VII of Denmark. George III of Great Britain revealed symptoms of mental disorder at an early stage, but was not replaced until much later by the Prince Regent (1811), who subsequently succeeded his father as George IV.

The majority of monarchs spent their lives as official figureheads, remote from the business of government and far removed from the people they were supposed to be governing. Nevertheless, they were sustained by an unshakeable tradition of loyalty and devotion – appointed by God and answerable to God alone. All of them could look back with pride on their ancient pedigrees; and even if the succession within the royal Houses was bound to change from time to time in the absence of a male heir, the new line would, after all, also be very ancient, and suitable marriages would guarantee successors of equally noble descent. Whether it was the German Holstein-Gottorp family that ruled in Sweden, or the French Bourbons in Spain, the connection with the indigenous dynasty would be maintained via a

grandmother or great-grandmother. In this way the thrones of
Europe were dominated by an extended family of a generally
European character. Only Jonathan Swift was impertinent enough
in his *Gulliver* to conjure up a vision of a dozen kings with their
'true' forefathers. What he envisaged was not a long series of
crowned heads but, in one dynasty, a couple of fiddlers, three
flashy courtiers and an Italian prelate; in another he found a
barber, an abbot and a pair of cardinals. But Swift then dis-
continues his depressing catalogue, remarking that he has too
much respect for crowned heads to spend any more time on the
topic, fascinating as it may be . . .

But not even a Swift had any desire to shake the foundations
of established institutions. There were, in fact, very few people
who thought of calling the monarchs to account in some way or
other, as had happened in England in the middle of the seventeenth century with Charles I, who had been put to death by
Parliament. It was not until a century and a half later, in
1792/93, that two royal assassinations took place: Gustav III of
Sweden fell victim to an aristocratic plot, and revolutionary
France had its deposed King Louis XVI guillotined in public.

That happened, however, at the very end of the eighteenth
century. Until the outbreak of the French Revolution the
world of the monarchs was placid enough. Tsar Peter III, it is
true, had been strangled in 1762, but that was something out of
the ordinary, and it had happened in a remote and barbarous
country. The United States of America had indeed deposed King
George III in 1776, but that had happened in an overseas colony,
and the king had retained his European realm.

The monarchs' world was not represented, however, merely by
a dozen or so kings. In two countries, Germany and Italy, a host
of principalities had sprung up. In Germany especially their
number was legion. Italy was content with a fairly modest
number of sovereign domains: the grand duchy of Tuscany, the
duchies of Modena, Parma, Piacenza, Mantua, the kingdom of
the Two Sicilies, and the special case of the Papal State. The
Holy Roman Empire of the German Nation, on the other hand,
embraced some 250 princely dignitaries. Apart from the emperor and the king of Prussia, and the Electors of Saxony,

Hanover and Bavaria, all manner of marquises, counts palatinate, princes and common or garden counts might be found there – besides the prince-bishops and prince-priors – all of them claiming sovereign rights and hence having at their disposal a court establishment and a capital city with palaces, hunting-grounds, etc. These were the duodecimo princes of the Old Empire, midget princelings. Some of them nevertheless possessed the power and the means to furnish their miniature Versailles in grand style – even if they were of little account politically, or if one might say of them, as Goethe said in an epigram dedicated to his Duke of Sachsen-Weimar:[3]

> Of Germania's princes mine is far from the greatest,
> Small is his realm and modest are all its resources.
> Let each of us strain to the utmost our mental and physical
>   forces.
> What a feast of delight that would be, each of us German
> with Germans together.
> But why must you praise him whom works and good deeds
>   can proudly proclaim,
> And your praise, it may be, will seem to him venal,
> To me he has given what even the greatest have rarely
>   vouchsafed:
> Affection and leisure, his trust – and meadow and garden
>   and dwelling.
>
>   (Goethe, *Venezianische Epigramme*)

The Princely Court

The princely court was meant to reflect the power and fame of the prince. Its main manifestation was the prince's residence. The old castle in the principal city was abandoned, because the prince wanted to have greater freedom of movement than was afforded by the residence of his ancestors or a city that had grown too large for comfort. A rural setting was preferred to the confines of a town, but nature first had to be transformed through the medium of art. Thus, the French king turned his back on the Parisian Louvre during the seventeenth century and moved away to Versailles, the emperor and the empress left the Viennese Hofburg and moved to Schönbrunn, the Electors of Hanover moved from that city to Herrenhausen and the dukes of Württemberg from Stuttgart to Ludwigsburg – and there are numerous other examples that might be quoted. In the countryside plans could be made in accordance with the prince's own wishes and judgement, and there were fewer constraints on building development. Versailles was copied all over the continent, not only in terms of buildings and gardens. The new palace and its park called for a totally different complement of staff and servants. The whole complex was protected by the Palace Guard – in Versailles and elsewhere this was provided by the Swiss Guards in their scarlet tunics. In Ludwigsburg the guard was mounted by the Duke's *legionnaires*, whose uniforms were modelled on those of Frederick II's Life Guards; they were as tall and straight as poplars in their scarlet coats with black facings. On their powdered heads they sported stiff pigtails and pointed grenadier caps adorned with brass plates. Military parades as a demonstration of the might of the monarch were naturally an important part of life at court.

In the building itself with its lateral wings the most favourable locations were occupied by premises designed for official functions with all their associated ceremonial. But there were also a great many smaller rooms in which more intimate social intercourse was possible. In Versailles, for instance, the leading figures at court assembled each evening in Madame de Pompadour's room to spend long hours in gambling and conversation. The latest news of the day, especially events in Paris, were eagerly discussed. Rumours emanating from government offices were frequently the main topic of conversation. The intimate atmosphere had its own charm, etiquette was banished and the discussion was conducted 'without gloves', as people said at that time. To these meetings Louis XV brought 'a cheerful mind, free of worries, and a frank geniality, so that nothing reminded his companions of his rank'.[4]

Court balls were particularly brilliant occasions. In Schönbrunn, for instance, the imperial couple would open the dancing with a minuet by candlelight in the banqueting hall, which had been cleared to make room for the dancers. The highest ranking guests – foreign ambassadors, for example – then invited their partners to join the dance. The orchestra was placed at one end of the long, relatively narrow room, while at the other end stood armchairs for the princes and princesses. The other guests might sit on rows of benches or on low stools when they were not dancing. Priceless jewellery on their arms and bosoms and in their towering head-dresses glittered in the candlelight. They all wore elaborate formal costume, while their escorts had precious stones as buttons or mounted on their shoe-buckles. Those who preferred not to dance were at liberty to enjoy themselves at the gaming tables.

The ball was usually followed by a grand banquet, often with a strict order of precedence in the seating which inevitably gave rise to rivalries and jealousy. Their imperial majesties were joined at table by ambassadors and by ladies and gentlemen of princely rank. For ladies-in-waiting and other younger guests a table was laid downstairs, and the manners here were doubtless more informal. The arrangement of the table might vary; it might be in the shape of a horseshoe, or, if the prince's name happened to be Frederick, it might take the form of an F.

Society at court was fond of theatricals, and the palace normally incorporated a small court theatre. Here, ballets and plays were rehearsed and performed by members of the court.

Music occupied a specially important place and was to be heard everywhere. 'The Elector was wakened by music; music accompanied him to table, music played as he hunted, music inspired his devotions in church, music lulled him gently to sleep, and it is certain that music welcomed this truly benign prince into Heaven.' This is what Daniel Schubart said of the Elector of the Palatinate, Karl Theodor, who made his court in Mannheim into a musical centre that scarcely had its equal in all Europe.

The *Water Music* that George Frederick Handel composed for the English king still lives today. King George I and a large company of English noblemen boarded open barges on 17 July 1717 and sailed up the river Thames from Whitehall to Chelsea, where the whole company dined. One of the barges carried fifty musicians with their instruments – trumpets, horns, oboes, bassoons, flutes and recorders, as well as violins and double basses. The three suites were twice repeated on the way up the Thames, and the king liked them so much that he had them played a further three times on the return journey, which took place after midnight.

It was not only in the palace itself that the court found its entertainment. The park was an added attraction, with its fountains and waterfalls. At night it would all be illuminated, and the evening was rounded off with a grand firework display. Duke Karl Eugen of Württemberg celebrated his birthday during the winter, and in Ludwigsburg he would conjure up

> magic gardens like those we find in the tales of the *Arabian Nights*. In the autumn he had a huge glass-house, 1,000 feet long and 100 feet wide, erected over his truly superb orangeries, so as to protect the trees from the rigours of winter. Countless stoves diffused heat within the walls. The entire roof of the vast structure was hidden by the loveliest green foliage, and the whole edifice seemed to be floating in mid air, since there was not a single pillar to be seen. The orange trees were bowed down under the weight of their fruit. It was possible to stroll through vineyards laden with grapes, as though it were still autumn, and fruit trees offered an abundance of fruit. Other orange trees had been trained so as to form bowers, so that the whole garden constituted one mass of verdant foliage. More than thirty fountains sprayed cool water, while 100,000 lamps formed a starry firmament overhead, shedding their light on the most charming of flower-beds below.

Whenever there was enough snow, sleigh rides would be arranged. But the greatest of royal pastimes was hunting. This was where the Spanish King Charles III excelled:

> H[is] M[ajesty] . . . spends the best part of the morning and afternoon hunting and has made such a habit of it that neither inclement weather nor the total lack of any sort of

quarry can dissuade him from the practice even one day in the year. H.M. returns home late in the evening and is only then able to spend a brief half-hour with the rest of the royal family.[5]

Life at court was passed in a positive whirl of distractions. In the first place, due attention had to be paid to one's appearance, especially in the case of the ladies with their crinolines and elaborate hairstyles, which had to be tended to the previous evening by milady's personal maid and then finished off with the aid of curling-tongs. Her watch had to be cleaned, or else all manner of courtiers had to be received – officers, dignitaries, archbishops. Her ladyship had to be carried in her sedan-chair, complete with bonnet, muff and fan, to be present at mass, which would be attended by His Majesty. And the missal must not be forgotten. Then her ladyship might perhaps have a moment to write to friends, reporting the latest news from court. But then there were also replies to petitioners to be drafted . . . and already the drums of the Swiss Guard were announcing it was dinner-time. At table she might revel in 'brilliant conversation and join in the cheerful mood of the company, at the same time savouring all sorts of spiteful gossip'.[6] At least that was the style of Versailles in the age of Louis XV and Madame de Pompadour.

And besides all this, time must be found to govern the country. When Charles III returned from the chase late in the evening he would grant an audience to whichever of his ministers was due to report on his department's affairs. The situation was different in Schönbrunn, where Maria Theresa kept a watchful eye on the government of her vast realm.

What did a court do when it was not dealing with such matters of major or minor importance? There was a good deal of gambling, fortunes were won or lost, and occasionally a man might be ruined. There was less drinking in the eighteenth century than there had been in the seventeenth; entertainments were more refined and indulgence was less gross. People did not spend all their time gambling; they read and it was possible to lead a literary life. There were educated princes and, above all, educated princesses. After all, Leibniz enjoyed the patronage of a couple of princesses, while the Landgravine Karoline of Hessen corresponded with leading German men of letters. In the eighteenth century it was considered good form for a prince to found his own academy: every major monarch took pride in an establishment of that kind. And we ought not to overlook the court church or chapel with its preacher (who was not necessarily a fraud or a hypocrite). The model of the grand courts was passed on down to smaller courts, and from thence to the even humbler establishments of younger brothers or dowagers.

We might take as an example the court of the widowed Margravine Sophie Caroline Marie of Brandenburg-Bayreuth in Erlangen, a typical dowager's court from the period after 1750. The court was administered by a chamberlain, Baron von Künssberg. The Margravine was attended by two ladies-in-waiting, two pages of noble birth who were students at the university, and a court tutor, the Corsican Matheo Cella. There was a staff of twenty-one servants: chambermaids, valets, footmen, messengers, beadles, cooks, coachmen, and maids to look after the bedlinen and clean the silver. A total complement of some forty persons was subject in the case of minor misdemeanours to the personal jurisdiction of the Margravine. They were all paid from the proceeds of fourteen offices, which included a forestry department and the commercial guilds.

On a journey through Swabia, Franconia and Westphalia an Italian writer noted with astonishment

> The mania which persuades all these minor princes and petty squires in Germany that they have to keep their Grand Chamberlains, Grand Cellarmasters, Grand *Sommeliers*, Grand Stewards, Grand Masters of the Hunt, Grand Chefs and Captains of the Guard, as well as their own cavalry and foot – even if the entire force commanded by the petty count or baron numbers no more than three hussars, four grenadiers and half-a-dozen fusiliers.[7]

The courts, which did a great deal to foster architecture, gardening and arts of every kind – from the opera and the theatre in general to portrait painters – brought life and colour

into the humdrum existence of their capital cities, however large
or small they might be. Appointment at court was much sought
after as an education in worldly accomplishments. Even at that
time, however, the luxury and extravagance of the courts was
often severely criticized, particularly the indolence of those
courtiers who were mere parasites and who secured themselves
agreeable lives from the income of a principality without perform-
ing any real service in return.

Although courts might well have been centres of refined
culture – such as the Weimar of the Duchess Amalia and
Duke Karl August in Goethe's time – they might also be the
setting for embarrassing scandals and unedifying intrigues. Social climbers found it easy to make their way there, while
scheming women were able to rise from the lowest classes of
society to great power and influence – Madame de Pompadour
was not the only one! The *chronique scandaleuse* of the courts is
full of philandering princes and adulterous princesses. A great
many princely couples lived apart, for their purely diplomatic
unions were not conducive to sound married life. We are liable
to find a rococo idyll side by side with brutality and wretched-
ness.

It was, of course, usually the women who suffered. But men
might also be the victims, as was Count Königsmarck who was
stabbed to death on his way to an assignation with Princess
Sophia Dorothea of Brunswick-Lüneburg. This adultery on the
part of the wife of the future George I of England was punished
by banishment for the remaining thirty-two years of her life to
the castle of Ahlden. Later on there was a greater degree of
tolerance. Thus, Elisabeth of Brunswick, the adulterous spouse
of the equally adulterous King of Prussia, Frederick William II,
was indeed imprisoned for a time, but was then allowed a
measure of relative freedom.

An anecdote, at one time well known, combines a number of
typical features and may serve to conclude this chapter on the
courts. It is the story of Camila Perricholi, which was subsequently made the subject of literary works by Prosper Méri-
mée and Thornton Wilder. The setting was the remote viceregal
realm of Peru with its elegant capital, Lima. In about 1760

Mariquita Villegas caused a sensation as an actress in the theatre of Lima. The Regent, Don Antonio Amat, fell in love with the beautiful and passionate Chola, a member of the despised race of Indians and half-breeds. Mariquita Villegas became his mistress and subjected him to all sorts of artistic whims and tantrums, which on one occasion provoked the good Don Amat to let slip the expression, *'Perra Chola'* – 'bitch of a Chola'. From then on the Regent's favourite was known as 'Perricholi'. Eventually Mariquita expressed the wish to ride in the Viceroy's official coach in a state procession. The aristocratic society of Lima was shocked. The Regent was able to extricate himself from the affair only by presenting his mistress with her own gilded coach, so that the Chola woman was able to parade the streets of Lima in a status symbol of her own. On her way home in her gilded coach she encountered a parish priest bearing the sacraments to administer extreme unction to a dying man. The chance meeting brought about a remarkable change: the repentant sinner presented her gilded coach to the church, so that in future the sacrament might be transported in a fitting manner. From that moment on she devoted her life to good works.

Whether it happened precisely like that does not really matter; the point is that the story illustrates certain typical features of life at court – the possibility of social advancement, the informality of relationships between the different classes, the part played by social distinctions, the spiritual background to the mundane concerns of everyday life. In Lima, after all, the palace is next door to the cathedral.

2

The Aristocracy

The Old Landed Aristocracy

Kings and princes represented the summit of the first class of mankind, the aristocracy. We have already seen that the nobility in Germany, with its 250 sovereign monarchs, had plenty of scope to play its social role. To the social class of these petty German monarchies, however, we ought also to ascribe the higher aristocracy of other monarchical states: the English and Scottish lords with their vast estates and palaces and their permanent seats in the House of Lords, the *grands seigneurs* of France, the Rohans, the Condés, and the grandees of Spain. They felt themselves to be in a sense the equals of their kings, for in their family trees royal princes and princesses of the cadet line frequently figured. Great landed estates and lucrative appointments at court, as well as ecclesiastical appointments in the Catholic countries, secured their social standing.

Prince Eugen of Savoy – the 'noble cavalier' of the folk song – was descended from a collateral line of the Savoyan dynasty. He was unmatched in Austria as a general and statesman, the most brilliant paragon of the higher aristocracy in the whole of the eighteenth century.

From this eminence, however, a whole scale of titles led all the way down to the humbler minor nobility, the barons, counts and squires who peopled the European stage in their untold thousands. They were the last surviving knights of medieval times and still lived in their ancient little castles with an adjoining village. In their own sphere they were like biblical patriarchs, wielding judicial and police powers as their birthright. Within their own counties they had their traditional share in the antiquated administrative system; they sat in provincial parliaments and regional assemblies, in so far as these institutions still existed. From the local farmers they extracted taxes that had been laid down centuries earlier, they filled church livings, or else made nominations for the bishop's approval. They managed their estates and held commissions in their prince's army. In their peasant settings they hob-nobbed with other local landlords, went riding with them, escorted their daughters to balls, practised fencing with their social equals and rode out together to the local hunt.

It was in fact the hunt that was the emblem of their status. In his *Georgica curiosa* or *Noble and Field Life* of 1682, Wolf Hermhard von Hohberg pointed to the deeper significance of the hunt. What he wrote remained true until the end of the era:

> Hunting is a courageous and chivalrous pursuit and, as far as our nobility is concerned, a kind of prelude to warfare in which they learn to attack a wild beast with alacrity and cunning, fight it and slay it, on foot or on horseback, handling their weapons and firearms with due dexterity, suffering and defying cold, heat, rain and tempest as well as the fierce rays of the sun and ridding the countryside and their neighbours of fierce and predatory beasts. For these reasons hunting has ever been the love of great potentates and practised by them, for it is a stimulus to the mind, banishing melancholy, countering indolence and all those vices to which it gives birth, sustaining a sound constitution, training the body, a prelude and mirror of warfare and a good and openhanded victualler furnishing our tables with superb and wholesome dishes.

In these circles, too, as at court, people liked to organize entertainments, often in association with their tenant farmers. The squires were given to gambling and drinking and were liable to render the neighbourhood unsafe for peasant wenches and noble maidens alike. But they had been brought up in the spirit of chivalry and were not necessarily lacking in education. If they read, it was in the manner of the *Gentilhomme* – genealogies, histories of their estates and the privileges of their families, biographies and military histories. It was for this readership that the heirs of the humanistic tradition, the learned authors of universal or national histories, went on compiling their massive tomes right down to the beginning of the eighteenth century. Many castles and manor-houses boasted carefully selected libraries, and had paintings adorning their walls. The nobleman might well be on friendly terms with the local vicar, and a theological student was often retained as private tutor to the sons and daughters of the family.

It is true that the financial means for all this, drawn exclusively from agricultural sources, were relatively meagre. There were distinctly impoverished noblemen. Heinrich Heine speaks of 'lean and hungry knights'. A divided patrimony often did not suffice to keep all the children in the style to which they were accustomed and alternative sources of income were limited. People of their class and breeding after all were not in a position to practise a profession, only service at court or in the army was in keeping with their social status. In Catholic countries supernumerary sons and daughters might be settled in monasteries or convents, where they had a chance of becoming priors or abbesses. As far as the daughters of the German Protestant aristocracy were concerned, there were secularized foundations, former convents which were willing to take in ladies of noble birth. One of the most promising and honourable careers was offered by the army, which provided numerous commissions, and here it was possible to advance to positions of high command.

The type of minor nobility varied of course from country to country. In England the gentry, the minor nobility who owned land, were a powerful agricultural lobby – squires in commodious manor-houses that were no longer fortified, drinking and conversing with the local Anglican parson. In parliament the House of Commons was thronged with this class. In France, on the other hand, because of the concentration of power in Paris, the minor nobility were able to exercise a political function only in the parliaments of the marginal provinces, so that they lost a good deal of their former influence. Particularly powerful was the political and economic situation of the so-called *Krautjunker*, the rural squires and great landowners of the Prussian crown east of the river Elbe. In the kingdom of Poland every nobleman, however impoverished, had his seat in parliament and hence a voice in deciding the weal or woe of this aristocratic republic. The landowning Swiss patricians, especially in Berne and Freiburg, with their local judicial authority, represented a republican type of gentry or *Junker*.

A strong sense of their social prestige still prevailed among the knights and squires. To be a squire meant to be independent of those higher up or lower down the social scale. A man who went to court was no more than a courtier who might make his way in the world, but who had lost his freedom of action.

The Revolution was destined to some extent to cut the ground from under the feet of the nobility, to place them politically on an equal footing with commoners. Nevertheless, the aristocracy did not become totally extinct, even in France. In the eastern provinces of Germany, in Austro-Hungary and in England the landed gentry were to survive still for many years as an agrarian conservative party. Fontane's *Stechlin*, the Cherrels of Condaford Grange in Galsworthy's trilogy, *End of the Chapter*, and d'Ormesson's *Au plaisir de Dieu* bear witness to the nobility's tenacious survival into the nineteenth and even into the twentieth century.

The New Bureaucratic Aristocracy

Since the sixteenth century the requirements of growing political centralism in many states had entailed the emergence of a new bureaucratic aristocracy. Lawyers from the middle class began to find their way into the civil service, for academic qualifications had become a necessity: a knowledge of Latin was needed, for instance, in order to understand the Roman law that was gradually beginning to replace inadequate systems of common law. Patents of nobility had to be conferred on these legal experts, for no one could imagine a person of lowly origin exercising a high function in the entourage of a prince. In this way a *noblesse de robe* came into being, newly elevated aristocrats who took their place as 'parvenus' alongside the *noblesse d'épée*, the ancient chivalrous orders. In many cases the older aristocracy took the hint and began sending their sons to university, where, with their carousing and duelling, they were reckoned to be the dregs of the faculty of law. Fritz Wagner says of the civil service during this transitional period:

> Even in Prussia the long and tortuous passage from an office of state as a benefice to the same office as a salaried official appointment did not entirely lose the character of patronage. The social class of salaried bureaucrats remained a relatively small group. The continent as a whole was characterized by innumerable forms of self-government, albeit of the most rudimentary kind. Hybrid forms of state and corporate bureaucracy persisted, with regional influence playing an important part in securing the appointment of indigenous candidates or local worthies.

It was in the France of Louis XIV that a bureaucracy of this kind first became established. An observer in the latter part of the eighteenth century speaks admiringly of the *parlements*, the French high courts, of the 'propriety, the dignity and elegance with which the Parisian lawyers deliver their pleas, the force of their arguments and the eloquence with which they expound them'.[8]

Bourbon Spain followed the example set by the French, as did Maria Theresa's Austria, albeit a good deal later. In Prussia the transition took place under King Frederick William I (1713–40). In the eighteenth century special schools were founded for the training of civil servants: in Germany they were called *Ritterakademien* or *Kameralschulen*. One of the most celebrated was the Hohe Karlsschule, the Charles Academy which the Duke of Württemberg set up in his Solitude Palace – the college from which Friedrich Schiller escaped when he fled from the duchy.

The career of a German bureaucrat of noble birth generally conformed to the following pattern. He would study law at the local university, and possibly at other universities as well, preferably at Göttingen. Then he would enter the service of a prince, possibly after spending some time in the imperial administration in Vienna. In his capacity as minister to some German prince or other, he would try to bring a semblance of order into the antiquated legal system, attempting at the same time to put the state's finances on a sounder footing and to introduce certain economic and social reforms. If he was lucky and managed to keep in his monarch's good graces, he might expect to complete his task; if he was unlucky, then his progressive master might die at an inopportune moment, so that he was at the mercy of a successor who was liable to be influenced by the court and its intrigues and dismiss his minister in disgrace.

The Württemberg lawyer Johann Jakob von Moser (1701–85) suffered vicissitudes of this kind. Descended from an old aristocratic family of lawyers in Württemberg, he was for a time Professor of Jurisprudence in the Universities of Tübingen and Frankfurt. In 1747 he entered the service of the Landgrave of Hessen-Homburg. He then became legal consultant to the Württemberg parliament in Stuttgart and in this capacity tried in vain to curb the high-handed behaviour of his sovereign, Karl Eugen. The resulting quarrel did not end until 1759, when the Duke had Moser imprisoned in the fortress of Hohentwiel, where he remained until 1764. He was eventually set free thanks to intervention by the imperial authorities and, undaunted, continued his efforts to reconcile the antiquated common law with a modern policy for the duchy. He published an uncommonly large number of books and articles on legal topics, and it is here that we may find a passage that is characteristic of this caste of noble lawyers:

> In all my offices and in all that I have written I have never
> been any kind of partisan, and throughout my life I have
> never accepted the principle: I dance to the tune of the man
> whose bread I eat. On the contrary, as far as I am concerned,

right is right and wrong is wrong, whether it affects my client or anyone else. Therefore, in my service to my monarch or to parliament I have never been induced by promises, constrained by orders or intimidated by threats to defend anything I believed to be unjust or unreasonable.

By an honest man I mean an individual who shows himself at all times and in all his actions to be invariably honourable, sincere and straightforward, and who hence acts without deceit, ulterior motives or interests, without fear or favour, and always to the best of his knowledge and belief.

The list of important representatives of the civil service aristocracy is a long one. They were to be found at almost all courts, large and small. One need only think of the arduous and thankless task of the enlightened ministers in Bourbon Spain under such monarchs as Charles III and Charles IV, who were in fact themselves relatively progressive. We might mention Pedro Aranda, or the great economic reformer Campomanes, the moving spirit behind the *Sociedades de los Amigos del País*, in which freemasonry, progressive aspirations and a faith in the mission of the aristocracy were combined. After a brief career in the fields of education and finance this great reformer was posted away as ambassador to Paris.

Among these aristocratic civil servants there was one who has retained his reputation down to the present day – Montesquieu, one-time president of the Supreme Court, the *parlement*, of Bordeaux, who presented the sum of his practical and theoretical reflections to an enthusiastic public in his *Esprit des Lois* (1748). Here he attempted to outline a legal and social system for France that would not be totally dependent on the personality of the monarch.

In this connection we might also call to mind another Frenchman, René-Louis d'Argenson (1694–1757), member of an old Parisian family of noble civil servants. His father was the chief of police in Paris, and his grandfather a state councillor under Colbert. He himself was also a councillor of state, for some time a member of the supreme financial council and minister for foreign affairs. As a civil servant, he tended to get the worst of the conflicts that arose between his intelligent suggestions and the intrigues of the court. His *Considérations sur le gouvernement ancien et présent de la France*, which was published posthumously in 1764, had the effect of a second *Esprit des Lois*. It is here that d'Argenson reflects on the relationship of the individual subject to his monarch:

> It may be that no one has ever thought about the degree of freedom the law ought to allow its subjects in order that they may retain their natural zest and their ambition to embark on great enterprises. However great this freedom may be, it should not be such as permits any excess liable to disrupt the general order.

This was not only the thinking of the Enlightenment, it was also an expression of the idea of freedom cherished by a member of the civil service nobility with a mind of his own – or possibly by the nobility as a whole.

3

The Clergy

The clergy were originally the highest class in the universally recognized social hierarchy. True, to some extent they fell outside that social scheme, since, in consequence of the institution of celibacy, they were perforce recruited from other classes. The aristocracy as well as the middle class, and even the peasantry, provided recruits for the clergy, so that the ecclesiastical hierarchy reflected the social structure overall. Moreover, following the Reformation, the clergy were divided into Catholic and Protestant factions; these differed in many respects, although they also had certain features in common.

The clergy had always been involved in politics, as was still evident in the eighteenth century from the fact that they had their allotted seats in parliaments wherever these existed. The German *Reichstag* had its clerical bench, occupied by bishops and priors, and the same was true of the constituent states in the Empire. The French estates included the clergy as the second estate, and they were also active in provincial assemblies. The Upper House of the British parliament consisted of lords spiritual and temporal, that is, the Anglican bishops had their seats there.

Every state, whether Catholic or Protestant, had an established church which was strictly organized. Even the Calvinist-Zwinglian reformed church had, in the office of *antistes* or dean a superior authority resembling a bishop.

Every village had its church and a vicarage offering the financial security of a 'living', which had survived the Reformation.

35

Even after the Reformation, priests were regarded as the shepherds of their flock and exercised control over believers and unbelievers alike. Attendance at church was taken for granted in both the main confessions. Education and social assistance were under the control of the local parson. At this lowest level it was he who stood for spiritual discipline and spiritual jurisdiction. In Protestant as well as Catholic communities the church was the centre of the village – even though it may often have had to compete with the village tavern or the squire's manor-house on the hill above the village. In cities this order of things was repeated in the congregations of the various urban parishes.

In rural areas as a rule the parson was the only individual with any kind of higher education. Since the study of theology took pride of place, clergymen had come to represent the real backbone of the educational system. Lawyers were relatively few and far between, and physicians even fewer and certainly not as well informed as they are nowadays. It was theologians in the main who did the teaching in intermediate and higher schools, making teachers an ecclesiastical class as well as a class of educators.

Even though the two confessions resembled each other structurally in many respects, the confessional division of Europe had brought about considerable differences between them. These differences were particularly marked in the seventeenth century, but even in the eighteenth century loyalty to a particular confession was deeply rooted in the population: 'papists' and 'heretics' still glared at each other with mutual contempt and hostility.

Where they were obliged to live together – in those areas of Germany where the two confessions were on an equal footing, in Switzerland and, until 1685, in France – there were countless occasions for disputes in which more or less Christian compromises had to be arrived at – for example, by the provision of a second baptismal font and a second pulpit in the village church, or the use of a curtain to screen the Catholic choir from the nave, where the Protestant sermons were delivered, or by regulating precisely the tolling of church bells, or dividing the cemetery.

Voltaire describes the situation in France during the seventeenth century:

The king's council was obliged to issue decrees concerning graveyards in dispute between the two confessions in the same village, concerning the building of a reformed church on a site originally belonging to Catholics, concerning schools, the rights of the local landowner, burials, the ringing of church bells – and the Protestants very rarely won these cases.[9]

Louis XIV put an end to this state of affairs in 1685 by revoking the Edict of Nantes, thus bringing about a spectacular emigration of French Protestants. In the same way the Waldensians were expelled by the Dukes of Savoy. The *émigrés* took refuge in neighbouring Protestant countries, especially in some of the German principalities, where, for instance, the Huguenot quarter of Erlangen or the commercial centre of Karlshafen in Hesse were built for them. In the vicinity of the latter the Landgrave established two Waldensian villages, *Gewissenruh* ('Clear Conscience') and *Gottstreu* ('Faith in God'). There were further Waldensian settlements in Württemberg.

In 1711 the Protestants were driven out of Poland. In 1732 a final large-scale expulsion from the Lutheran enclaves in the Pinzgau and Pongau areas of the archbishopric of Salzburg took place. Approximately 14,000 evangelical refugees from Salzburg were resettled by the king of Prussia, mostly in East Prussia. Others accepted a proposal by the Society for the Promotion of Christian Knowledge and crossed the Atlantic to settle in the English colony of Georgia. In spite of all this persecution, however, Protestants remained in France and Piedmont and reorganized secretly as the 'Church in the Wilderness' or the 'Alpine Israel'. Their clergy were trained in Lausanne, in the Canton of Berne. From the middle of the century onwards greater tolerance began to be practised in France, while in 1781 Joseph II issued his celebrated Edict of Toleration; all the surviving non-Catholic sects began to emerge from their hiding-places and a Lutheran and a Reformed church were immediately built in Vienna.

A counterpart to the wave of Catholic persecutions at the turn of the century was represented by the repression of Irish

Catholics under the English crown. Large areas of Ireland had successfully resisted the Reformation. In the seventeenth century the situation became more critical, for Ireland had become a base for attempts to force England back into the Catholic Church. The freedom of religion promised by William III in 1691 remained a dead letter: Catholic teaching, Catholic schools and the attendance of English subjects at schools abroad were all banned. It was only towards the end of the century that these regulations became somewhat less stringent: in 1778 hereditary leasehold was permitted to Catholics, and in 1783 Catholic religious services were sanctioned, while compulsory attendance at Anglican services was abolished. In the meantime, however, the north-eastern part of Ireland had been entirely won over to Protestantism, an onerous mortgage on the future of the whole island.

The Catholic Clergy

Spain and Portugal, together with their vast colonies in Latin America, all the Italian monarchies and republics, France, the Austrian heartland and the kingdom of Poland were solidly Catholic domains. In the German Empire the Electorate of Bavaria, the episcopal sees on the Main and the Rhine and many of the smaller states, especially in the south, belonged to the Catholic confession. The same kind of motley picture might be seen in Switzerland, where a majority of the cantons – albeit the smaller and economically weaker ones – were solidly Catholic.

This was Catholic Europe, where people were conscious of their place in an ancient tradition reaching back to the earliest days of Christian conversion. The saints were fervently worshipped, Benedictine monasteries bore witness to medieval culture, the castles of the chivalrous orders recalled the Crusades, while Franciscan and Dominican houses reminded people of the social function they had exercised in the late medieval towns. The Capuchins had indeed brought a breath of fresh air into the world of the peasantry, while the Jesuits had done the same thing among educated people. Many of the Romanesque and

Gothic churches had been replaced by new buildings in the baroque style. All this represented a new trend in Catholicism. The easy-going, relatively liberal and extraordinarily colourful world of the autumnal middle ages had given way to a more austere and bigoted era. The Nordic nations, large parts of Germany and Switzerland and the whole of England and Scotland had been lost to the faith, and hence a particular part of the church with a distinctive national mentality had gone too. The fact that France, in spite of its persecution of the Huguenots, was still infected by Protestantism, was revealed by the stubborn nature of the Enlightenment in that country.

All the kings, with the exception of the two Scandinavians, the British and the Prussian monarchs, belonged to the Catholic faith. But it was mainly the kings who created problems for a church that was still ruled from Rome. The monarchs had long been reluctant to take orders from the Vatican and in the course of time they had managed to acquire all kinds of privileges. An attempt had indeed been made at the Council of Trent (1563) to restore to the Pope or the curia the powers they had once possessed and to discipline the bishops; the would-be reformers had at their disposal a body of the clergy who were devotedly loyal to the curia. Already in the seventeenth century, however, there had been a growing tendency to scrutinize Roman edicts closely before they were communicated to the populace. In the eighteenth century even the Latin monarchs were becoming increasingly independent. Pretty well all of them passed through a phase of opposition to the curia. Certain ministers – first of all Pombal in Portugal, then Aranda in Spain and Tanucci in the Two Sicilies – tried to free the schools from the grasp of the church, to achieve supervision over the training of priests and to bring ecclesiastical property ultimately under state control. In the end, under Maria Theresa and Joseph II, Austria and its ramified dependencies were also affected by this trend. Not only did Joseph II issue his Edict of Toleration in 1781, he also tried, with the help of a number of enthusiastic and loyal bishops, to bring the Catholic Church under the control of the state. The aim was to achieve belatedly something that the Protestant princes had initiated 250 years earlier and that became outwardly apparent in the dissolution of 'useless' monasteries and convents.

Even though this move against the curia represented an attempt on the part of the state to tighten its control over the church, the traditional structure of the church remained largely unaffected, and the Catholic Church was able to retain throughout the century the image it had had in previous ages.

At the lowest level of the secular clergy there was the parish priest in his vicarage or chaplaincy. Often this so-called lower clergy was of peasant stock, and hence very close to the local population. The parish priest would have been trained in the seminary of the local bishopric. His primary function consisted in the celebration of divine service in the form it had always taken, i.e. in the reading of the mass, as well as in the pastoral care of his parishioners, in which confession played a major part. Proficiency in the Latin liturgy counted for more than intellectual training, a fact which educated churchmen and laity alike deplored. No less an authority than the French Catholic writer, Charles Péguy, remarked at the beginning of the twentieth century: 'The Jews have been literate for 3,000 years, the Protestants for 400; I have been literate since my grandmother's day.' This bitter truth applied to the peasantry and the lower classes of the urban population. It was quite a different matter in the case of the higher clergy.

The higher clergy – the bishops, the clergy at episcopal courts or in the cathedral chapters in the cities, priests at the major parish churches in towns, or even secular courts – needed to have a much higher standard of education. Indeed, the whole century teemed with learned and witty *abbés*, and a considerable part of French, Spanish and Italian literature was written by clergymen. Abbé Nollet, for instance, was reckoned to be the best teacher of physics in Paris. Abbé Mably was the author of works on politics and moral philosophy that were destined to play a significant part in the prelude to the French Revolution. This higher clergy was recruited from middle-class families in the towns as well as from the nobility. In Germany there was the additional factor that the episcopal dioceses still had the dual character of spiritual and secular estates. Within, and sometimes even beyond, the limits of their dioceses the archbishops had since time immemorial exercised a sway, which in the case of the electoral dioceses of Mainz, Cologne and Trier, as well as those of Liège, Münster, Würzburg, Bamberg and Salzburg, was equal to that of a moderately sized German principality, the Palatinate, say, or Württemberg. When, for example, the Archbishop of Salzburg set out on a journey to Vienna, he travelled with all the pomp and circumstance of a sovereign prince. 'He not only had his suite of personal servants, but also his chamberlains, the director of his court council, his adviser in spiritual matters, as well as his own kitchen staff, complete with confectioner. Apart from all this, his retinue would also include a small band of musicians.'[10]

The Papal Nuntius in Vienna – Domenico Passionei, who was of the sober Jansenist persuasion – once said, 'Episcopi Germaniae non sunt episcopi, sunt Domini' ('the German bishops are not just bishops, they are great lords'), such as Franz Konrad Kasimir von Rodt-Bussmannshausen, cardinal and prince-bishop of Constance, who was described in the following terms by one of his parish priests:

> This prelate owed his prestige more to his dignified bearing, his natural affability and imposing physique than to erudition or the sanctity of his life . . . like his predecessors he visited his diocese only in the person of his suffragans, whose visitations were not particularly edifying . . . He allowed himself to be advised and guided for the most part by Jesuits, for whom he harboured such blind esteem that, when the bull ordaining the dissolution of this Order was brought to him at table, he twice flung it into a corner, being severely rebuked by Rome on this account. He was uncommonly addicted to the chase, kept a considerable number of gamekeepers and hounds and often drove through the streets of Constance and a throng of hungry citizens with his quarry, a stag, lashed to the back of his coach, making his triumphant way to the episcopal residence in Meersburg . . . his memory would have been that much more illustrious had he shown himself to his

subordinates in the apostolic sweat of his brow and fed the
poor more with the superfluity of his income than with the
vanity of his princely pomp.[11]

Nevertheless, there were bishops who approximated more to
the apostolic ideal invoked here. A paragon in this respect was
Fénelon, the French bishop who defied Louis XIV and who stood
at the beginning of a Catholic reform movement. There were
bishops who devoted themselves eagerly to improving their
subjects' standard of living or who did much to raise the intellectual level of their dioceses – for example, Franz Friedrich
Wilhelm von Fürstenberg, Vicar General of Münster, or Emmerich Joseph von Breidbach-Dürresheim, Elector and Archbishop
of Mainz. The ecclesiastical principalities would not fare too
badly in any comparison with their temporal counterparts.

The judgement '. . . sunt domini' was apt to apply, however,
not only to German bishops. Their French colleagues did not,
indeed, have the same political autonomy, but they might still
be high and mighty lords, such as the vain Bishop of Strasbourg,
the Prince-Cardinal Louis René de Rohan, who was involved in
1785 in the so-called 'necklace affair', one of the most embarrassing court scandals of the day, which revolved round the
purchase of a famous item of jewellery and its proposed presen-
tation to Queen Marie Antoinette. The lifestyle of such wealthy
prelates provoked popular anger that was ultimately vented
during the French Revolution: in 1793/94 the church, together
with the Christian religion, was officially banned.

Such high dignitaries of the church were often simply
noblemen who happened to find themselves in clerical garb,
who meant to live in the same style as their brothers and cousins,
and who often did not care a jot for their spiritual obligations.
High offices in the church had often become mere sinecures set
aside for certain families as a means of providing for supernumerary offspring or of enhancing the political influence of the
family.

Cathedral chapters had originally been set up as bodies that
would administer the diocese, but membership had in many
cases become no more than a lucrative sinecure. Since the seven-

teenth century something more than an old-fashioned simple patent of nobility certifying four aristocratic ancestors had been required for admittance to a chapter; the requirement was ultimately enlarged to sixteen noble ancestors, i.e. to the generation of the candidate's great-grandparents, and in one instance it called for thirty-two ancestors of noble birth. It was a good thing, it seemed, to be able to boast a few prince-bishops in one's family tree.

Besides the secular clergy there were monastic orders comprising monks and nuns of the most diverse origins in monasteries and convents with equally diverse observances, traditions and reputation. They frequently had very blue-blooded priors and abbesses or mothers superior; in Germany they might even be of imperial rank. In the course of the Counter-Reformation a network of Capuchin monasteries and Jesuit colleges had been superimposed on the original monastic system. Apart from them, there were more recent orders, such as the Salesians, the Eudists and others who practised the strict discipline of baroque Catholicism. The devotional exercises of the lay Tertiary Order, the instruments of castigation to be found in many aristocratic castles and manor-houses, bear witness to the persistence of a devout piety, especially in the case of women, that had by no means died out in the eighteenth century. The Ursuline Order provided a rudimentary education for women. The peasant coarseness of the Capuchins, who were active in rural areas or among the lower classes in towns, proved as effective as ever, and they provided welcome assistance to the parish clergy. It was the elegant and well-educated Jesuits, however, who still ran intermediate and higher education. In the course of the century they began to lose ground they had once held so confidently, and in 1773 the pope ordered the dissolution of the Order, which had already been banned in a number of countries. This implied the triumph of the Enlightenment in Catholic countries, but it was to be no more than a temporary victory. The fact that a pope could be induced by Catholic monarchs to abandon this mainstay of the curia – however reluctantly – shows how weak the papacy had grown in this century. Eight representatives of noble Italian families had vainly tried in turn to stem opposition to

the curia. The monarchs treated them courteously, but did what
ministers hostile to the curia advised. With the sole exception of
Benedict XIV (1740–58) the popes were hardly taken seriously
in the literary and learned world. After all, the pope was little
more than an Italian prince in a poorly governed and antiquated
principality that called itself the Papal State and boasted a ruler
with the supreme ecclesiastical title. The nadir of papal prestige
had been reached when Napoleon was able with impunity to
depose the aged Pope Pius VI and his successor, Pius VII, drive
them from Rome and treat them as prisoners in exile.

The Protestant Clergy

Catholicism, integrated in outward appearance and structure,
confronted a Protestant world that was divided within itself
into three confessional groups. The Lutheran group embraced
many of the German principalities and imperial cities, with the
kingdom of Prussia, the electorates of Saxony and Hanover and
the duchy of Württemberg numbered among its larger territories. It also comprised the two Nordic kingdoms – Denmark
(including Norway) and Sweden (including Finland) – and the
Baltic provinces of Estonia, Latvia and Courland, which were
under Russian suzerainty. To these territories might be added
Lutheran minorities in French Alsace and in the kingdom of
Hungary.

To the Reformed group, i.e. the Calvinist-Zwinglian confession, belonged the greater part of Switzerland, the Republic of
Geneva and the Republic of The Netherlands, including its
colonies, especially South Africa. Also belonging to the Reformed group were a number of West German principalities,
such as the Palatinate and Hessen-Nassau, as well as the Presbyterians – a majority in Scotland and a minority in England.
There were still remnants of Huguenot congregations in France,
particularly in the southern provinces. Those Waldensians who
had survived in some of the Alpine valleys in Piedmont were
tolerated by the authorities in the course of the eighteenth
century. In that part of Hungary once occupied by the Turks the

majority of the population was Calvinist. In this confessional group, states with the Reformed Church as the established religion were more or less matched by states in which Reformed believers represented a minority. As a consequence of emigration most of the North American provinces were Calvinist, but there were few places – apart from Massachusetts – where the Calvinists alone were in control.

The third group constituting an established church was the Anglicans – otherwise in a somewhat precarious position in Ireland, and a minority confession in Scotland. There were, of course, Anglican communities in the English colonies.

As we know, the Reformation had led to the splitting off of more radical sects which were unable to find a place within the state churches established by the Reformation. In a number of countries – in Switzerland, for instance – there were still Anabaptists, although they were subject to occasional persecution. It was only in England and Holland that such sects gradually began to be tolerated. Toleration was also practised in the English colonies, where the free churches began to put their stamp on American life and the American character. However important such sects may be in social history and in the history of religion, in Europe during the eighteenth century they remained no more than fringe groups. Until well into the nineteenth century it was only the established churches that counted, and there were no more than three of these: the Lutheran, the Reformed and the Anglican Churches.

In the period of the actual Reformation, and even more during the orthodox seventeenth century, the dogmatic differences between the three groups were heavily emphasized; they detested each other almost as much as they hated their common Catholic adversary. Structurally, however, they resembled each other in a number of respects.

They were all organized on a national basis. It did not much matter whether the state in question was a republic or a monarchy: the chief political authority, as a Christian authority, also governed the church. The formal freedom from the state which the Roman Catholic Church enjoyed, the independence of the Papacy, did not apply here. The clergy were more or less a part of the civil service, an extended arm of the political authorities. Governmental decrees were read out from the pulpit. On the other hand, the clergy enjoyed a special status, they bore much responsibility and exercised a good deal of influence in the state.

The priesthood constituted a class with distinctive features. They were organized and had their own administration. In the Anglican Church the Catholic episcopal organization had remained, in the Lutheran Church there were superintendents and consistories, while in the Reformed Church there were elders and an assembly of parish clergy. In many cases there was also a synod comprising all the parish clergy as a corporate body, as for instance in the Republic of Grisons or the principality of Neuchâtel.

Since the monasteries and convents had been dissolved and various other institutions abolished, the individual priest had to assume a much greater burden of responsibility. One of his principal duties was the preaching of sermons, i.e. the proclamation of the word of God through interpretation of the Scriptures. Compulsory instruction in the catechism improved the standard of education in the schools and may be seen as a feature of the fight against illiteracy that had been conducted for the previous two hundred years. A reform of the poor law system by which only the *deserving* poor were to benefit led towards the adoption of a new work ethic. In Reformed congregations the former ecclesiastical courts were turned into moral tribunals in each parish. Here the lay element played a major part, since the courts consisted of the elders of the congregation, with the parish priest acting largely in a consultative capacity. The whole system was based on intellectual discipline and training to specific ends. In the eighteenth century with its enthusiasm for education such a system could easily be developed and made more effective.

As with the Catholics, the teaching profession was in the hands of the clergy, but with the Protestants it was much more closely integrated with state educational systems than was the case with the internationally organized Jesuits.

In the curriculum the main emphasis was placed on Greek, Latin and Hebrew philology, i.e. on the biblical languages. Since the liturgy had been drastically reduced, more effort could be devoted to academic study. The Protestants had in common with the Catholics a general humanistic foundation in their educational system.

The social antecedents of the clergy, which had still been partly rural in the sixteenth century, had become increasingly urban and middle class. The clerical vocation turned out to be a path to social improvement for the artisan class, and soon there were regular dynasties of parsons. The evangelical clergy constituted the educated class in their own particular area; their theologians were respected not only as ministers of religion but also as intellectuals. The livings which had sensibly been retained from the Catholic past provided a more or less adequate income and sufficient leisure for intellectual endeavour.

The Protestant churches had deliberately abolished clerical celibacy (the Counter-Reformation had made this rule even stricter) and had in this way created a new social institution, the 'Protestant parsonage', i.e. the parson's family, complete with wife and children, a model family on a middle-class pattern which had been a novelty in the sixteenth century but which had become firmly established in the seventeenth and had reached its prime in the eighteenth century. The parson's wife in particular acquired a new and enhanced status: she was called upon to act as a paragon of the secular virtues within the parish. The parson's wife – often herself coming from a parsonage – was in a position to be an invaluable helpmate to her husband. For every hundred or so parishioners there would be a parson's family with a host of children. As a rule at least one of the sons would choose the clerical vocation, while the daughters might well marry parsons. In this way a distinct intellectual legacy was handed down from one generation to another. Clerical dynasties of this kind were typical of all the Protestant territories, although their lifestyle might vary from country to country. In England the Anglican clergy were often clearly intermingled with the gentry. In France the Protestant clergy, abolished as a body in 1695, had been drawn largely from the prosperous upper-middle class. In Switzerland the Protestant clergy were distinctly urban in character and associated with the middle-class authorities in the towns, even occasionally with local patrician families. The same was true of Germany and Scandinavia, where Lutheranism tended to emphasize even more the official status of the clergy. Here, too, the clergy had social contacts with the the aristocracy, although as a rule it was only court preachers or superintendents who sometimes married into noble families.

It should not be forgotten all the same that there were poverty-stricken parsonages in remote rural areas, and the path to a living was often long and thorny, leading through posts as tutor to noble families or teaching in grammar schools. It is not surprising that servility to the powers that be tended to alternate with a defiant independence based on the freedom allegedly conferred by the word of God.

Whether in some English county between Cornwall and Yorkshire, in Swedish Dalarne, in the march of Brandenburg or in the duchy of Württemberg, in the Jura of Vaud or the Engadine valley of Grisons, whether it was English, Swedish or Swabian, French or Rhaeto-Romance, the same type of parsonage was to be found, idealized in Voss's *Luise* or pictured with gentle irony in Goldsmith's *Vicar of Wakefield*.

4

The Urban Middle Class

The Middle Class in Republic and Monarchy

The 'third estate' as such was once understood to refer to the
remainder of the human race apart from the aristocracy and the
clergy, i.e. to the overwhelming majority of individuals. A more
specific third estate had, however, long been singled out and
identified. Initial distinctions might be drawn, for instance
between citizens living and working in the towns and a peasantry who cultivated the land.

In his book on eighteenth-century towns Jerzy Wojtowicz
writes:

—At the time of the Enlightenment European towns entered
a phase of rapid development following an era of wars,
epidemics and famines which still prevailed even in the
first half of the eighteenth century. The emergence of new
kinds of industry, the migration into towns and cities of
masses of people from the countryside, the evolution of
political life and trade — all this encouraged development
in the towns. It was English cities that grew most rapidly,
with the huge city of London and its 800,000 inhabitants
taking the lead. Before the Revolution France had 1,175
towns, sixty of them with more than 10,000 inhabitants.
The largest city was Paris, with more than 600,000 inhabitants. On the Iberian peninsula Madrid, with more than
160,000 inhabitants, and Lisbon were the major cities.

Otherwise, Warsaw at the time of the Great Diet, Berlin, Vienna and Amsterdam were among the largest municipalities.

As early as the twelfth and thirteenth centuries the urban middle class had become an economic and political factor with which the aristocracy and the clergy were forced to reckon. Permanent civic representation in the parliaments of the monarchies reached back to the late middle ages, e.g. the city bench in the German *Reichstag* or the members representing the boroughs in the English House of Commons.

It was in only relatively few parts of Europe that cities had managed to transform themselves into independent republics. The Swiss Confederation had emerged in the fifteenth century from a system of alliances that united urban and rural communities, while at the end of the sixteenth century the Republic of the United Netherlands had been established. In Italy, Venice, Genoa, Lucca and San Marino had survived from the municipal movement, and the ancient free city of Dubrovnik (Ragusa) had ceased to pay tribute to the Turks in 1718.

All the other cities of Europe were subject to monarchical rule. The greatest degree of independence was enjoyed by the German imperial cities, of which there were still about fifty in 1803. Frankfurt, Nuremberg, Augsburg and, above all, the Hanseatic towns Bremen, Hamburg and Lübeck were still important centres, but their significance then began to decline. They ranged from those that still possessed some territory of their own, such as Schwäbisch-Hall, to some that had become little more than villages, like Buchau am Federsee. As a typical example we might take the town of Lindau on Lake Constance, which was still in an intermediate and relatively flourishing condition. It is worth quoting the account of this city given by the Austrian statesman Count Karl von Zinzendorf in 1764:

> The free imperial city of Lindau possesses the best harbour on the Lake, being actually situated on two islands in the lake.
>
> The inhabitants are mostly Protestant, but there is also a home dedicated to Our Blessed Lady, a free and inde-

pendent Catholic secular foundation with its own Mother
Superior, who is a princess of the Holy Roman Empire, and
twelve noble canonesses who are permitted to leave the
home if they should marry.

The city comprises some 500 citizens and some thousands of inhabitants.

Among the imperial cities in the *Reichstag* it occupies
fifteenth place on the Swabian bench, while in the county
of Swabia it ranks twelfth.

The imperial city of Lindau has a fairly considerable
territory . . . Three villages, various hamlets and manors
are subject to the jurisdiction of its higher and petty
sessions; in the case of a fourth village and a number of
other places, however, the city holds no more than petty
sessions.

Looking back to his own childhood, Hermann Heimpel recalls
the petty majesty of these miniature republics:

Lindau was a little city, but there was nothing 'small-town'
about it – it was not dull and stagnant like its sister
imperial cities. The lake broadened its outlook, Mount
Säntis, its situation on the frontier, at the foot of the
mountain passes – all this had contributed to its history.
The grain trade made up for any lack of contact with
foreigners. However hostile to strangers the Lindau folk
might pretend to be, they still lived life to the full. There
were plenty of visitors and they were right royally treated.
The Lindau people devoted themselves to their guests,
dealt with their business in the early morning and enjoyed
themselves in the afternoon. They were well off and
cheerful, they went on family picnics to Mount Pfänder
and the Gebhardsberg and drank a fair measure of wine in
the *Weisses Kreuz* in Bregenz. They were more given to
living than to reading . . .

This description applies perfectly to the situation at a time when
Lindau was still an imperial city and not yet subject to the
Bavarian crown.

We may compare Lindau with the adjacent imperial city of Buchhorn, about twelve miles away, in order to get an idea of the more modest type of imperial municipality. Zinzendorf describes the place as follows:

> Buchhorn, a free imperial city on Lake Constance; its inhabitants are Roman Catholics and there are about sixty citizens. The local people are regarded as the most dimwitted in the whole of Swabia and stories of their antics are told which resemble those about Schilda in Meissen. The town itself is very poor, but a retail trade in Bavarian salt brings in a certain revenue.

It is little wonder that, following the abolition of the representation of the imperial cities in the *Reichstag* in 1803, this town was amalgamated with Friedrichshafen, which was subject to the kingdom of Württemberg.

The English boroughs had an independent status that resembled that of the imperial cities. Here, too, there were great discrepancies in their significance. London was a true metropolis and capable of setting the tone in parliament. The venerable cathedral cities, too, were after all still regional cultural centres. But there were other boroughs which had been totally reduced to the level of villages, or which simply no longer existed, where the right to return a member of parliament was attached to the former site of a borough, e.g. a meadow or a disused salt mine. It was not until the passing of the Reform Bill in 1832 that an end was put to these 'rotten boroughs' and the rapidly growing new towns – such as Birmingham – were at last granted seats in parliament.

Other cities were state capitals where the court set the tone, administrative centres with a royal civil service; some were garrison towns, trading centres, regional markets or just small, sleepy provincial towns whose citizens sunned themselves in a bygone glory. All of them, of course, still had their own municipal government. But in France, for example, since 1680, mayors had no longer been elected by the local councillors but appointed by the central government. Vital issues in such towns were no longer matters for the local citizenry to decide. No real civic pride could be engendered here and no pleasure in citizenship, since an historical awareness of former republican greatness was lacking and the citizens were hemmed in at every point by the world of the aristocracy.

Whether a town was a republic or subject to the suzerainty of some ruler or other, the pursuits of its population and their social structure were much the same. The citizens were for the most part still engaged in the traditional trade or craft that had once been characteristic of the town. According to circumstances, trade might assume greater importance, or else an industry on a commercial scale might evolve from some craft or other. A certain proportion of the citizenry would be employed in the municipal administration, mainly on a part-time basis. The clergy represented a considerable proportion of the citizenry – one-sixth in Zurich. Larger towns had more than one parish church, and Catholic cities would have the usual monasteries and convents: Franciscans, Capuchins, Dominicans, Poor Clares, Ursulines, as well as a Jesuit college. In Protestant towns a grammar school took the place of the latter. Certain towns were the seats of universities and other institutes of higher learning. In this case, apart from the clergy, there was an intellectual elite consisting of theologians, lawyers and various kinds of physician. Solicitors and apothecaries completed the academic profile of any of the larger towns. Thanks to a sound education, towndwellers possessed a certain degree of culture. They read a good deal, with a preference for books devoted to a religious interpretation of nature, morals or strange and remarkable phenomena from all over the world. Being politically aware, they also took a relatively lively interest in historical studies.

As a rule the town or city owned a certain amount of the adjacent land, for the administration of which it assumed responsibility. Venice was the city with the most extensive extramural territory – the mainland of Italy from Lake Como to Friuli, the Adriatic coast and the Ionian islands off the west coast of Greece. Genoa ruled the Ligurian coast, Lucca a moderately sized hinterland. Hall, Nuremberg, Rothenburg, Ulm and Rottweil each had an area corresponding to a medium-sized Swiss canton. Berne was the most sizeable city-state north of the

Alps, extending from the gates of Geneva to the very heart of the Swiss Confederation. Berne's territory was roughly the same as that of the duchy of Württemberg, the Republic bore on its coat of arms a prince's crown above the Berne bear, and it provided its mayor with a throne.

The first signs of democracy, dating back to the fourteenth and fifteenth centuries, had appeared with the guild movement, but the guilds were now only a pale shadow of what they had once been. Guild masters did indeed often have seats on the executive in one capacity or another, but the real power lay in the hands of an oligarchy, either of patrician landowners who affected a noble style of life and often possessed small estates, or of merchants who occupied key positions in the local economy. The history of the towns is turbulent, with the guilds and craftsmen opposing the merchants and the merchants feuding with the patrician oligarchy who dominated the town hall. Throughout the century the issue was most hotly contested in the Republic of Geneva, where the major entrepreneurs of this highly industrialized city rebelled against the old-established families who held seats in the city's government, and where even the working population was involved in the conflict. The ideological dispute over Rousseau, the 'Citizen of Geneva', imparted general significance to this local argument. After the insurgent party had scored a number of initial successes the patricians' rights were restored in 1782, with the aid of an armed intervention on the part of the combined monarchies and aristocracies of France, Savoy and Berne. As in the case of Holland, the unrest in Geneva was a prelude to the French Revolution, but it ended with a victory for the counter-revolutionaries.

It should be noted that the citizenry by no means included all the inhabitants of a town or city. Ever since the sixteenth century there had been moves to restrict citizenship and to admit as few newcomers as possible. In the eighteenth century Augsburg is reported to have numbered 6,000 citizens among its 30,000 inhabitants. Citizenship was more or less permanently barred to outsiders or newcomers, and citizens tended to assume an aristocratic or oligarchic character. Republican equality, then, applied only to those who possessed citizenship rights in a particular town, but it was enjoyed by rich and poor alike. The counterpart of the monarch's crown was still the cap of liberty, that symbolic headgear which a republican need not doff, even in the presence of a king. But both the crown and the cap of liberty had in the meantime become rather antiquated symbols . . .

The Merchant Class

From the very beginning the progressive element in the towns had been the merchants. The eighteenth century opened up new possibilities for trade and encouraged the expansion of industry. Mankind's needs were becoming more and more ambitious. To quote Wojtowicz again:

Important changes were also taking place in trade and industry. Following the Seven Years War, England became pre-eminent as a maritime and colonial power, since her ships were capable of reaching almost any point on the globe. In European trade France still played a major part, followed by Holland. Along with sea-borne and colonial trade, inland trade also flourished; international trade fairs acquired great importance, among them the celebrated Leipzig Fair. The capitalist system went on developing, most vigorously in England. In other countries, too, highly developed industrial zones began to emerge, e.g. the Verviers district in Belgium, a number of Swiss cantons, the linen-weaving industry in Silesia. In Germany, where a state policy of protective tariffs following the Seven Years War had produced significant results, industry had developed on a grand scale, particularly in Prussia, where the authorities sponsored the development of new branches of production.

The European merchant forced his way ever more eagerly into overseas territories. In Europe the seventeenth-century canal system and an improving network of arterial highways ensured more efficient transport. Industrialization had begun on a contracting-out basis, i.e. as a kind of cottage industry, in which spinning and weaving were carried on in the countryside for an urban employer, but this system was beginning to give way to factory production. The first industry to be affected was the textile industry, but gradually the manufacture of machines, other than in the ancient craft of watch-making, grew more important. Steam power had been discovered, and towards the end of the eighteenth century it was already being harnessed for manufacturing purposes.

We might once more take Lindau as an example of a town with a significant turnover from the exchange of goods. Heimpel sums up as follows:

> Lindau's trade routes extend as far as the Mediterranean, and did so long before the German Empire existed. In Lindau it was possible to learn about Leghorn and Trieste, Corfu and Athens without delving into ancient documents. The world and our home town belonged together. Like a miniature Zurich the town glittered on its Lake Constance, colourful and gay, like a modest Genoa on its Swabian Sea.

Lindau is an example of a town that was mainly engaged in commerce, but in the case of linen it combined manufacture and trade. In many towns, in fact, craftsmanship and commerce combined and turned into complex industrial enterprises: purchase of raw material, manufacture in cottage industries in the countryside, finishing processes in the town, sale abroad.

Commercial activity still centred in the urban home of the merchant, where warehouse, counting-house and residence were all housed under the same roof. A single merchant – often with the support of his wife – guided and supervised the whole business with a minimum of staff. To these responsibilities was added – especially in the case of republics – some involvement in municipal politics. Given the inextricable entanglement of republican responsibilities and commercial interests, it was taken for granted that a greater or lesser share of a man's time had to be devoted to municipal duties.

Admittedly, Friedrich Carl von Moser draws a grim picture of the merchant class. Of his stay in Holland he reports:

It is no easier to breathe in this heavy sea air than in the never-ending, daily, pervasive and revolting talk of having and giving, of profit and loss, saving and hoarding, not only among the trading fraternity, but even among those with whom one might hope more readily to find satisfaction, nobility of sentiment, taste and a more refined way of thinking . . . The public spirit is the spirit of the merchants. I would not indeed go so far as to say of the gentlemen of the government, as a certain lady said of them: this isn't any longer a republic, but a limited liability company controlled by the Prince of Orange; but in thirty or forty years it might very well look like that. The old Republicans are dying out, and with them their love of liberty, their ancient and authentic principles. The power of princes to appoint the leading officers of state and allot lucrative posts has already induced many families to bow and scrape, and their descendants will learn to do so even more effectively.

To this German aristocrat of the civil service the merchant Republicans no longer seemed to be the same men as their predecessors, the Dutch merchants who had resisted not only Catholic Spain since the start of the struggle for an independent Netherlands, but also the governors appointed by the House of Orange and their aristocratic hangers-on. Nevertheless, those old Republicans turned out to be modern patriots when they rose in rebellion against the Prince of Orange once more in 1785. Two years later, however, they succumbed to a Prussian Counter-Revolutionary intervention, just as the tradesmen of Geneva had done in 1782.

In spite of these setbacks in a couple of aristocratic states, the fact remained that the mercantile class was everywhere growing increasingly wealthy. It was their wealth that broke through the confines of the middle-class towns. The merchant's house in its narrow alley now often turned out to be too cramped. At a pinch it might be renovated to make a braver show, but it was more likely to be pulled down to make way for a kind of commercial mansion. The merchant class, like the nobility, aspired to a country estate, where they might enjoy more privacy and freedom in more elegant social surroundings. In the republics, merchants were able to acquire growing authority and infiltrate the guilds, where they were highly respected. In the eyes of the aristocracy, however, they were still upstarts, 'parvenus'. They had no time for aristocratic pursuits, for hunting, gambling and women; they worked hard and were wont to live somewhat puritanical lives.

The monarchies had once been able to absorb the nobility into the higher ranks of the civil service, but this could not be done to the same extent with merchants: the 'pepper sacks' were even more despised than lawyers. The battle against the old patrician families and the landed gentry might have been lost in Geneva and in The Netherlands, but from the time of the French Revolution onward the class of commercial industrialists, as the most prosperous middle class, was destined to start its triumphant advance all over the world — with or without the institution of monarchy.

The Craftsmen

It was merchants and craftsmen who had once made the town what it had now become. As we have seen, however, the time was past when the guilds had set the tone and represented the progressive element. It is true that their organization was still intact, especially in the republics, but they now often served merely as social clubs whose members were anxious to preserve their ancient privileges. Attempts were made to maintain the standing of the town *vis-à-vis* the countryside round it and to stifle the growth of independent craftsmen in neighbouring villages. On the other hand, the guilds were jealous of the growing prosperity of the business community, who were threatening to replace their workshops by factories. As far as their part in running municipal affairs was concerned, the guilds had finally been infiltrated by the merchant class.

The craftsmen were as a rule backward-looking and reluctant to accept innovations. It was easier to introduce reforms in

monarchies than in republics, where the guilds were in a better
position to block progress.

Crafts were still subject to regulation by the guilds as they had
evolved in the late middle ages. The artisan lived in a house of
his own in which he also had his workshop. The master craftsman would have a number of journeymen but, since he was
forbidden by law to take on unskilled workers, the business
could not be expanded. The change-over to a large-scale enterprise could be effected only by transferring work to the countryside, which was in fact done by major wholesale traders. It was
not until the guild regulations were abolished in the nineteenth
century that, for instance, a blacksmith's forge could be turned
into a metal-working factory.

In his memoirs, Ludwig Meyer von Knonau, a Zurich squire,
vividly and accurately describes the situation of this class in the
city of Zurich:

> The high-handedness of the so-called gentry was justly
> resented by members, both young and old, of what might
> be called the middle class of citizens. Expressions such as 'a
> gentleman and citizen' and 'I am a gentleman and citizen'
> were bold claims such as might be heard in alterca-
> tions with those who deemed themselves superior, or with
> country folk or foreigners. The meanest of the citizens of
> Zurich, proud of his entitlement to play a part in the city's
> government, was profoundly aware of being more than a
> peasant or a denizen of Winterthur and Stein, more or less
> as the most minor of Polish noblemen would look arro-
> gantly down on a merchant or other respectable citizen of
> Warsaw or Cracow. The baker from whom my parents
> bought their bread, Irminger, was a shrewd and experi-
> enced businessman; at the time when I myself became a
> citizen he was highly regarded as a master of his guild and
> was treated with great respect as a member of the Council.
> This was the case, too, with several others, and a good
> many craftsmen were entitled to an equal degree of respect
> as members of the Grand Council. The highly elitist man-
> ner of electing members to the Grand Council – they were

chosen by existing Council members and the aldermen of
the guilds – would inevitably have led to total domination
by a patrician clique, had not the guild masters, the two
principal officers, been elected by the guild as a whole, so
that they depended on the support of the citizens. It was
mainly the butchers who upheld the guild system, and
until 1798 one of the guild masters and six of the other
dozen members were butchers. They were followed by the
bakers and the millers, while the shoemakers and tailors
had only one member apiece on the Grand Council. A kind
of patrician class existed most obviously in certain social
circles and among women. Unseen powers dictated ad-
missibility to the higher ranks of society. No one who was
not a member of the upper class was ever admitted, and
certainly no woman from the tradesmen class was ever
admitted. It was a major step forward when, at the end of
the eighties, the family was sent the circular advertising
the concert programmes . . . and twenty years later they
were in the first rank of society. Women retained their
prerogatives for many years to come, however. It was in
military circles that the so-called middle class most clearly
came into its own. In the regiment in which I served, three
tanners, a book-binder and a cooper had the rank of captain, and in the company to which I was first posted, my
captain was a farmer and inn-keeper who also acted as
beadle to the local justice, a smart man who did his job
well.

To this example from Zurich we might add an example from
the German imperial city of Lindau, to which we have already
referred, a town that flourished mainly on revenue from the
passage of commodities through it. Zinzendorf makes a brief
reference to its craftsmen:

In the town there are many tanners of coarse and fine
leather, goldsmiths and silversmiths, clock and watch
makers, some eight weavers, a number of hatters, sack-
makers, dyers etc. In Lindau they manufacture fine green
tiles for stoves. There is a silk weaver with four looms who

produces cloth for export to Augsburg. There is a bell foundry which recently cast fifty cannon for Zurich. There is a powder mill and a paper mill; the latter can scarcely keep pace with the number of orders it receives.

This gives us a brief glimpse of the busy little world of the craftsmen. Hermann Heimpel tells us something of the mentality of the Lindau craftsmen when he records a conversation with his Uncle Ernst:

> When we go to the museum tomorrow, I'll show you the combs your ancestors used to make. They were comb-makers and their combs went all the way down to Italy in the days when the rococo ladies used to wear their hair piled high on their heads. The workshop was down by the lake where the Bayrischer Hof now stands. The last comb-maker was the brother of Johann Jakob Cadixer, your grandfather's godfather. But his father was a comb-maker, too, and his ancestors before him were probably comb-makers as well. Why is that? Because crafts were handed down from father to son in those days. You should know that our forebears were simple folk, craftsmen, comb-makers and fishermen like the Oberreits, and bakers like the Häberlins: your grandmother was the first of your relatives to come from a patrician family, but your grandfather had to become a respectable doctor before he was in a position to marry her. He was the first graduate in our family, so we are still fresh, not an intellectual elite of parsons and schoolmasters. So, let's get on with it!

At the end of this passage Heimpel refers to the function of the artisan class as a pool of talent for recruitment to other professions. While there were artisans who took a stubborn pride in their traditions and were content to remain in the narrow limits of the family business with their handful of journeymen, there were also competent and ambitious individuals who managed to climb out of their class, mostly becoming clergymen in the Protestant towns. As academics, lawyers, like doctors, were not particularly respected in the eighteenth century. They belonged to the middle class, to which their forefathers, the artisans, also belonged. Here, too, it was the nineteenth century that opened up unsuspected opportunities, so that it turned out to be a century of lawyers, far beyond the immediate needs of the law.

The small craftsman was to see his privileges dwindle with the revolutions of the nineteenth century, but he nevertheless held on with astonishing tenacity until well into the twentieth century.

5

The Farming Community

Ever since the rise of the towns, the third estate had been
divided into citizens in the towns and farmers or peasants in the
countryside. The latter's job was to provide food, not only for
themselves, but also for the towns, which in turn were supposed
to protect the population in the countryside and provide services
through the military caste, the clergy and other town-dwellers.
In the course of time we may detect considerable differences in
the agricultural population – depending partly on the type of
husbandry. A hill farmer was not subject to the same economic
laws as a farmer on the plains, a peasant in Tuscany could not
easily be compared with his Tyrolean counterpart, even though
both of them came under Austrian jurisdiction. And a wide gulf
separated the planter in Virginia from the farmer in Massachusetts, although both of them may have been actively involved in
the break away from the English crown.

Even the definition of *Bauer* as 'farmer' or 'peasant' is fraught
with difficulties. Modern scholars try to take as their starting
point the idea that 'farmer' applies only to those workers on the
land who are able to regard their land in some sense, directly or
indirectly, as their own property, and who consider themselves
relatively independent in their own locality.

It is true that it was only in certain areas in and around the
Alps, i.e. in five cantons of the Swiss Confederation and the
allied republics of Grisons and Valais, that farmers still enjoyed
a measure of political freedom. In these areas a homesteader with

his own land might still possess elementary democratic rights. He had the right to appoint the authorities in his own village community and on the territory of the republic as a whole, he was eligible for election to governing bodies, and was at liberty to take a hand in running the affairs of his local parish and the country at large. The supreme political expression of this freedom was the *Landsgemeinde*, a popular assembly of all those with a title to land. At the beginning of the eighteenth century the canton of Schwyz had laid down as the twenty-first of its twenty-six Constitutional Articles:

> That the annual May assembly of the *Landsgemeinde* shall be the supreme and sovereign authority with unlimited power to appoint and dismiss. And whosoever gainsays this, or in any way denies that the *Landsgemeinde* be supreme and sovereign with unconditional power to appoint and dismiss, he shall be proscribed outlaw and a price of 100 ducats set on his head; those in due authority, however, the criminal court and other courts, shall retain the right to adjudicate who owns what, and to confirm the people of the canton in their titles of ownership.

This meant that, apart from God Almighty, all authority in the canton of Schwyz, which comprised fourteen villages or valley communities, was exercised by the sovereign people in their *Landsgemeinde*. Every farmer, in so far as he had a title to land, had a share in that sovereignty and hence 'governed himself'. Article 21 was a declaration of independence from the encroaching power of the country's councils and a reaction against the aristocratic pretensions of the patrician social class of large landowners and salaried municipal officials that had in the meantime grown up. The small crofter and cattle breeder in the mountainous districts, even if he was proudly settled on his own land, was nevertheless dependent on these 'big Jocks', whom he would from time to time dismiss, or even send to prison, following rowdy meetings of the *Landsgemeinde*, which helped to reinforce his sense of being a free subject.

No one else in the whole world possessed anything resembling these Swiss democratic liberties − except, at a pinch, farmers in the rural provinces of The Netherlands. Those in scattered imperial villages were subject to the emperor: all other farmers were subject in some way or other to an overlord. Ever since the middle ages the principle had obtained: *Nulle terre sans seigneur*, 'no land without a lord'. Land belonged to the nobility, to the church, later to commoners from the towns and, above all, to the state or the king. A land tax in kind had to be paid to the owner in each case. In the matter of ownership uncommonly fine distinctions were liable to be drawn.

The situation of free farmers, such as the Alpine Swiss, was most nearly approached by farmers in the Austrian county of Tyrol, in the Dithmarschen district of Holstein, and in Sweden, Norway and Iceland. The English yeomen freeholders might also be included in this class, as well as those who were subject to the jurisdiction of Swiss towns. But the number of these more or less independent farmers in Europe was negligible, although we ought to bear in mind that in Western Europe generally, in France, England and Germany, the peasants were in no sense serfs – as they had become in the countries of Eastern Europe, east of the river Elbe, where peasants had become the landlord's property, just like his cattle and horses. The peasant was tied to the land and might not leave it without his landlord's permission, nor might he marry without his master's approval – although conditions varied greatly from one area to another.

As far as the economic structure of agriculture is concerned, distinctions might be drawn in central and northern Europe between large farms from which farmers derived an adequate income, average-sized farms which produced just enough to allow the farmer a fair living, and crofters who needed a supplementary source of income, although they were in fact settled on their own land. They all belonged to the local village community. The more prosperous farmers and those from old-established farming families virtually constituted a rural patrician class.

In fact many farmers were simply tenant farmers. Tenant farmers might still be well-to-do gentry, such as the grandfather of the well-known German American, Carl Schurz, of whom the latter wrote in his memoirs. This Heribert Jüssen was a tenant of the manor of Gracht in Liblar, near Cologne:

My grandfather was aged about sixty when I first remember him. He was well-built, over six feet tall and broad in the chest and shoulders. He had not had the advantage of a genteel education. He could certainly read and write, but reading and writing were not included among his favourite pursuits. He could make very little of books; on the other hand, he was a man of great authority among his own folk. People came from the village and from the country round about . . . to ask for his advice, or to submit their disputes to him for settlement.

But he was also a very capable farmer – sensible, energetic and tireless. He was out in the fields with his labourers at the crack of dawn, not only instructing and directing them, but setting them a good example in the most arduous of jobs. I can see him still as, in keeping with custom, he himself, whip in hand, drove in the first harvest wain, riding on one of the horses that were harnessed to it in couples. I often heard it said, too, that his advice in farming matters was sought by his fellow farmers and that it was highly prized. Of course, in his own home he was regarded as a king – not just a king whom people obeyed, but a king people were fond of, and a king whose failings were looked on as a natural necessity that could not be changed.

Alongside him my grandmother offered a remarkable contrast. She was a small, slender woman with a thin face that had once been pretty; her health was delicate, she was devout, gentle, domesticated, always busy and full of cares. The household she had to look after was indeed so large as to leave her little leisure time. She was on her feet from daybreak in summer and by lamplight in winter to see that the numerous farmhands, male and female, went about their work and that they were provided with breakfast. There were almost two dozen farm labourers and maids, not counting the day labourers who were taken on from time to time.

The farmer's world was a stable, long-term world, governed by the weather and the whims of nature. But this seemingly stable world now began to lose its stability, because it was proposed to interfere with the traditional course of nature. The soil had to be made to yield more. The God-given cycle of good and poor harvests, the seven lean and fat years of the Old Testament, were to be reduced to a more rational pattern.

The eighteenth century was a relatively peaceful age for the farmer. The great internal wars – in France, the Huguenot feuds; in Germany, the Thirty Years War; in England, the Civil War – were at an end. The epidemics were dying out and major famines were now less common. People began to recuperate, and the handsome farms in many areas still offer evidence of that to this day.

True, when war did pass through a rural area, then the old horrors were revived, for there were no fortifications to protect the villages. Even at the very end of the century a soldier noted of a campaign in France:

> Finally orders were given to look for forage for the horses and to fetch wood and straw from the nearby villages. The corn was for the most part still standing in the fields because the harvest had been later that year on account of the persistent rain. Foraging was conducted as if we were the enemy: crops were cut down or torn up, the grain trampled underfoot far and wide, so that a stretch of countryside which might have fed eight or ten villages for a whole year was turned into a wilderness in the space of less than an hour.
>
> In the villages the troops' conduct was even more horrific. [The soldiers had orders to fetch wood and straw.] But before taking these commodities most of them ransacked the houses and took away anything that was worth the taking, like linen, clothes, food and other articles a soldier could either use himself or sell to the sutler. Anything that was not suitable for this purpose was smashed or otherwise spoiled.

And if there was not actually a war, hunting by the gentry constituted a major nuisance. In this connection Baron von Hohberg strikes a critical note:

These days game reserves are often sadly abused in that game is unreasonably protected and allowed to multiply, so that our wretched tenants' fields, plots and meadows are ruined and reduced, the tenants pestered day and night and plunged into poverty and ruin by their fruitless vigilance and the grave damage to their crops. It would seem to be highly desirable, then, for our Christian gentry to abate somewhat this otherwise noble and legitimate pursuit, lest it be gravely discredited through its excessive practice and it appear that they prefer their game to a hard-working neighbour and fellow-Christian.

The original function of the nobility had been to provide military protection for the farming population, but this they often no longer did. It is Hohberg again who exhorts land-owners:

Those estates and domains are indeed fortunate that are settled by numerous, good, loyal and prosperous tenants, especially if they are good husbandmen. But they should be treated in a fair and Christian manner and well provided for and their privileges respected; they should be protected when they are in peril, their just rights should be granted when they seek them, and they should not be subjected to impositions that run counter to ancient usage. That much a landlord owes to God and the world.

That was written at the end of the seventeenth century. In the eighteenth century it meant that the state should, in its own interest, seek to promote and improve agriculture, that the village parson and the local justice of the peace should look after the material and spiritual welfare of the peasantry and intervene in the existing antiquated system with advice and instructions based on more modern practice. The nineteenth century was to continue on these lines, and here and there the farming community had become sufficiently mature to take its fate into its own hands.

6

The Common People

The Lower Classes and Fringe Groups

In the old hierarchy, 'below' the farmer and 'below' the citizen there was a motley collection of social groups which had in common their situation in the service of the middle class or on the fringes of society, or even totally outside it. They were the 'common people' in the social sense, although not yet the 'people' in a national sense, as they were to be glorified by the Romantics. If we bear in mind that, as a rule, no more than half of the inhabitants of a town were citizens, and that in the villages no more than a third were numbered among the actual farmers, then it is clear that this group included by far the largest proportion of the human race – although regional differences would have to be taken into account here. Most of them were dispossessed, certainly as far as land was concerned, and most of them could neither read nor write.

Every upper class actually had a lower class at its disposal to act as its servants. The citizenry in the towns had their maids and labourers, often from a rural background. Master craftsmen worked with journeymen who themselves subsequently became masters of their trade; manufacturers had their factory hands and outworkers. In the countryside a prosperous farmer had at his disposal not only his farm-hands and maids but the entire rural lower class – the day-labourers, cottars and crofters. They lived in humble dwellings, often with more than one family under the same roof, at best with a small plot of land on inferior sites subject to flooding or on the edge of woodland, where the soil was poor. To this class belonged also the charcoal-burners and the hucksters. This is where the farmer found part-time labour at harvest-time or for wood-cutting. The crafts were not highly regarded in the country and the finer crafts were carried on only in the towns.

The nobility had their own 'lower class' – those who were in military service. In principle the officers were of noble birth, the other ranks were recruited from the lower classes. The eighteenth century had become increasingly an age of professional soldiers and standing armies. The militia had long been in decline. Not so in Switzerland, which tended to export its poorer population into military service abroad. In the eighteenth century people used to speak of the wretched lives led by soldiers: service was arduous, garrison life tedious, punishments – such as running the gauntlet – degrading and harsh. There were indeed elite regiments where conditions were better. The Swiss, for instance, enjoyed a disciplinary code of their own and formed their own units. The outer appearance of the armies was dazzling and a joy for the watching citizens and nobility. The elegant, brightly coloured uniforms were an irresistible lure for all young females. In garrison towns and capital cities soldiering could be a form of service like any other. It was in campaigns that any craving for adventure might best be satisfied. 'In camp the soldier is usually cheerful and brisk, singing and playing all sorts of pranks, simply in order to kill time and forget his troubles.' Wars in the eighteenth century were still being fought with a certain air of chivalry: 'Permit the English gentlemen to fire first!' French officers are reputed to have shouted to their English opposite numbers at the Battle of Fontenoy. This opening salvo may well have mown down the ordered ranks of men in French uniform – who might not have been Frenchmen, but Germans, Scotsmen or Swiss mercenaries. Apart from episodes of this kind, we have various accounts of the wretched lives of common soldiers, e.g. from the retreat of 1792:

Up till then our underwear had remained fairly clean, but now that it could no longer be laundered and even the

linen in our knapsacks began to grow mouldy, those beast-
ly little creatures, the scourge of the soldier in the field,
began to torment us beyond endurance. Even the officers
couldn't escape them and now experienced for the first
time the full misery of war. But nothing affected our
people worse than the diarrhoea, the fearful diarrhoea and
the dysentery that followed it.

Another account describes the fate of the German mercenaries
who had been shipped off to North America: 'Life in camp
during the autumn was bad enough; no decent food and cold
enough to make your teeth chatter. Our battalion was a motley
bunch that rather resembled a harlequin's costume, since it was
made up of the uniforms of any number of different regiments.
We had neither banners nor cannon . . .'

For the common soldier the situation was hopeless in the sense
that promotion to commissioned rank was out of the question in
the case of most troops:

And so we did not exactly welcome the news of peace
when it came at last, for ambitious young people do not
care to see their progress brought to an abrupt halt. I had
been flattered by the suggestion that I might become an
officer and embark on a career. The peace had put paid to
these hopes, for, in keeping with our venerable and allegedly sound social order, no commoner could expect as a
rule to advance beyond the rank of sergeant-major, an
honourable rank indeed, but not one in which I had any
desire to spend the rest of my life. With us, a man had to
be of noble birth, or else have a great deal of money in
order to count for something in society. These are two
merits the philosophical validity of which is instantly
obvious to any reasonable person. Sometimes connections
and recommendation might help; even more infrequently
genuine talent might attract favourable notice. In war-
time, when men are sought for commissions, and not commissions for little men, exceptions are commoner and,
much to the disgust of our caste-ridden society, that crude

old, impertinent principle comes into its own and a man is taken for what he is really worth.

This was written at the close of the century and illustrates one possible response to this so-called 'sound social order' – not just on the part of soldiers, but on the part of the lower orders in general. Most individuals, however, were reconciled to their fate as underdogs, as though it had been ordained by the Almighty.

We have looked in some detail at the soldier as a representative of the lower class who may be taken as typical of others. Another profession – which nowadays enjoys a very different degree of esteem – was that of schoolmaster; not the professor at a grammar school with his theological training, but the village dominie. Johann Gottfried Seume, the soldier whom we have just quoted, a man from an impoverished rural family, dreamed of becoming a schoolmaster: a friend, advising him, exclaimed: '. . . become a linen weaver, a village schoolmaster is a wretched creature . . . and he proceeded to draw a frightening picture of the poor village schoolmasters in Thuringia and Meissen. I would not be dissuaded however, and said that any profession properly pursued might offer satisfaction.'

The German writer Jean Paul Richter describes the life of his grandfather, who was a schoolmaster, in his own ironic fashion:

My father was the son of the rector Johann Richter in Neustadt am Kulm, and of him we know nothing except that he was extremely poor and God-fearing . . . His schoolhouse was a prison, not indeed with bread and water, but with bread and beer, for the post of rector afforded little more – apart from a sense of pious satisfaction – although it was coupled with appointments as organist and cantor. In spite of this lion's share of no less than three appointments, his income never exceeded 150 gulden annually. And there the fellow stayed for 35 years, subsisting on the meagre starvation rations provided for schoolmasters in the province of Bayreuth. True, he might have advanced to become a country parson, i.e. by exchanging his dominie's gown for a cassock, so ensuring himself a more ample diet, like silkworms that are fed more each time they shed their

skins. Such an individual might improve his income by
multiplying his appointments, so that he might ultimately
vie with a civil servant with all the latter's perquisites and
gratuities, or indeed with a handsome salary, an instrumentalist sustaining his part in the symphonic score rendered
by the chamber ensemble of the treasury by no more than
a couple of entries and otherwise observing innumerable
bars of silence.

The art world was to some extent outside the common run,
even if it was not outside 'society'. Painters and sculptors were
in fact particularly talented artisans, and in this century, with its
elegant designs and decorations for manor-house or patrician
town residence, they had quite enough employment. Anyone of
any standing would insist on having his portrait painted.

Musicians could make a living in the service of the church and
the aristocracy, although it would be frugal, and they might
have to double as footman and instrumentalist. Prospects were
gradually improving, however, as middle-class circles began to
take an interest in concerts. In London, for instance, music
publishers and instrument makers flourished. Concerts were
open to everyone, and the audiences that streamed into the
grand concert-halls in the cities included a relatively broad
social cross-section. Franz Joseph Haydn, who was popular and
famous in London during the 1790s, noted in his diary in
reference to his latest concert: 'This evening I made 5,000
gulden. That sort of thing is possible only in London.'

In capital cities actors, too, might achieve great fame and
fortune: we have already come across the case of 'Perricholi'.
Minor German princes liked to engage Parisian actresses at their
courts, where they were well provided for as the prince's mistress
and could go on playing the part on and off the stage. One
example was Madame Clairon, from the 1750s one of the greatest actresses in Paris, who later played a leading part at the
Ansbach court as the 'motherly friend' of the Margrave Carl
Alexander – much to the benefit of his realm, incidentally. But
there were also strolling players with their chequered careers,
immortalized in Goethe's *Wilhelm Meister*. And they went all the

way down the social scale to include jugglers, mountebanks, street musicians and acrobats, all of whom played their part in this century in bringing fun, entertainment and a spice of variety to every class of society. A thankless world, however, banished them to the fringes of society, and the zealots of the Enlightenment even banned the clown from the stage, thus bringing about a schism in the world of art.

It was not by choice or by any fault of their own that various ethnic and religious groups found themselves on the fringes of society. In many Protestant countries descendants of the Baptists and some other more recent sects were able to survive only in secret; in Catholic France and the Catholic provinces of Austria they were also obliged to live clandestine lives. Towards the end of the century even stricter policies against them were adopted. The only places where such sects had freedom of movement were The Netherlands, England and the latter's colonies. There were any number of religious refugees – Huguenots, Waldensians, Protestants from Salzburg, Bohemian Brethren – all of whom had lived normal lives before their expulsion and who now suffered the fate of refugees.

There was, of course, still ethnic and religious discrimination against Jews, even where they were more or less tolerated and living in ghettoes. The Enlightenment took their eventual emancipation for granted and made it possible in the end.

A further ethnic group might be mentioned here – the gypsies, who added an uncommonly picturesque note to the century with their nomadic mode of life, their huckstering and thieving.

The thefts committed by gypsies were fairly minor, but the century also had to cope with outlaws and footpads, the highwayman in England, the brigand in the Abruzzi region of Italy. Spain was also reckoned to be unsafe: 'There is not much to be said of public order in this kingdom. . . . The security of the inhabitants . . . is everywhere signally curtailed, and there are more than enough highwaymen at large in the countryside.' The overturned and plundered coach is a favourite theme in novels of the day, and robbers enjoyed great popularity as literary heroes down to the time of Tommaso Rinaldini, whose fame has persisted to the present day, thanks to Vulpius' novel, *Rinaldo*

Rinaldini. People sang of him: 'In the darkest depths of the wilderness, hidden safe in caverns deep . . . between the lofty, gloomy cliffs', there Rinaldini had his lair, from whence he terrorized the Papal State.

Those who did not care to join the thieves and cut-throats, joined the horde of beggars. There had always been beggars: poverty was, so to speak, sanctioned by Holy Scripture. Up to this point the problem had been dealt with by Christian charity: St Martin had torn his cloak and shared it with a beggar. If God had endowed a man with an adequate living, then that man had an obligation to share it fairly with the poor; a 'fair share' implied the giving of alms, and that applied to king and peasant alike. Apart from this, the church had its mendicant Orders, who, themselves begging, catered for the needs of the poor, particularly in the towns. This tradition of the Franciscans and Dominicans was carried on from the sixteenth century by the Capuchins or by new Orders such as the Lazarists and the Sisters of St Vincent, who combined popular evangelism with social service.

The Reformation had tried to get rid of the crude notion of alms-giving. Certainly, the wealthy were still expected to give alms, but it was also expected that charity would be rationally organized. In Reformed communities a distinction now began to be drawn between the 'deserving' poor and the 'undeserving'. Alms should not be distributed at random but directed to specific ends. Congregations had to institute a 'poor box', and taxes were actually to be levied for the benefit of the destitute. Moreover, the ultimate aim was to eliminate poverty, which had hitherto been taken as a fact of life, by training the poor to work. He who did not work, should not eat either, as it said in the Old Testament. Poverty had ceased to be one of the Christian ideals.

The eighteenth century was faced with the problem that poverty was on the increase, since the population was growing. There was no inclination to regard the problem as an ineluctable fact of life: a parson in Berne replied to a question on begging proposed as a topic in a competition launched by the local Economic Association as follows:

For wherever mendicancy and the practice of begging flourish there is poverty, for any industrious impulse and any inclination to work and earn an honest living is suppressed and discouraged, while indolence and sloth are implanted and flourish. What happens with the proceeds of begging is similar to what happens to gains from gambling – what is so effortlessly come by, is easily spent, and the inevitable result is bound to be poverty.

This is a Zwinglian, Calvinistic way of thinking. Begging discourages industrious habits and any inclination for hard work. It was no longer good enough simply to dispense alms and certify that the poor recipient was 'deserving'. Nor was it any longer a satisfactory solution to hound out the poor and push them over the boundary into the next parish.

The Working Class

As industrialization advanced a new social class began to emerge, especially in England, France, The Netherlands, Germany and Switzerland – the workers in cottage industries and in factories. Since, as we have seen, craftsmen alone were no longer able to meet the demands of society, recourse was had to the labour reserves represented by the poorer classes who were unable to make a living either in the towns or in the countryside, and were only too eager to take any employment that would improve their lot. Individuals with capital to invest, textile manufacturers, say, found that they could have the rudimentary processes in the production of their wares carried out cheaply in this way. Landlords, for their part, sometimes required their tenants to engage in manufacturing, i.e. taking in work for factories: clockmakers often had components made in the countryside. Frequently, too, cottage industry was introduced on humanitarian grounds, as when Dean Heidegger in the canton of Glarus, or Pastor Oberlin in Steintal (Alsace) collaborated with local industrialists to provide the impoverished inhabitants of remote areas with a means of augmenting their income. Before then, the only escape from the dreary life of cottars and crofters had been emigration or enlistment in the army.

Workers in cottage industries were mostly recruited from these lower classes of the rural population, the cottars and crofters. They did their weaving or spinning in addition to any modest contribution they made to the farming economy, or else lived exclusively from the earnings from their industrial labours.

In the third book of *Wilhelm Meister's Journeyman Years* Johann Wolfgang von Goethe has occasion to describe this kind of work when his hero visits a country district where cottage industry flourished.

> Going into various homes, I had a chance to revert to my old hobby-horse and take a lesson in the art of spinning. I noticed the children were kept busy carefully teasing the tufts of cotton and plucking out seeds, fragments of nutshells and other impurities: this they call 'picking'. I asked if this was a job for children only, but I was told that it was also done by men and by their elder brothers on winter evenings.

From this task, which was performed as a matter of course by children, the processing passed to adult workers.

> As was only to be expected, it was the buxom spinners who then attracted my attention . . . The girl doing the spinning sits in front of her wheel, not too high up; some of them held the wheel with their legs crossed, others used only their right foot, keeping the left foot drawn back. The girl spins the wheel with her right hand, stretching her left hand out as far and as high as she can and taking up all manner of pleasing postures, so that a slender figure makes a very fetching sight, what with the graceful evolutions of the body and the comely plumpness of the arms. The movements entailed in this latter mode of spinning especially offer very picturesque effects, so that our finest ladies need not fear to lose anything of their true grace or charm, were they now and then to lay aside their guitars and take up a spinning-wheel instead.

In this setting strange new feelings came over me; the
whirring of the wheels has a kind of hypnotic effect, the
girls sing psalms and also, though rarely, other songs as
well. Finches and siskins in their cages twitter now and
then, and it would be hard to imagine a busier life than in
a room where a number of women are busy spinning.

Goethe is mainly interested in the technical aspect of this
cottage industry and views the whole process with a pleasure
derived from aesthetic sources, or possibly his interest in folk-
lore. But he does not fail to note a social aspect as well, which
might assume a religious connotation: it was in these circles that
pietistic congregations and sects tended to gather, since the
clergy of the established churches felt more affinity with the
farmers and peasants, who corresponded more closely to their
biblical prototypes. The weavers had plenty of time to ruminate
and reflect, to read and tell stories. They were livelier characters
than the local farmers. But they were by their origins poor
folk and their earnings were often squandered on modest
luxuries that had hitherto been the prerogative of the sons and
daughters of well-to-do farmers. As a rule they were regarded as
feckless because the strict customs and standards of the farming
community meant little to them. What our Weimar courtier
does not describe is the distress of cottage workers, who were
liable to be affected by periodic slumps, if a world market
collapsed, so that they were once more reduced to the bare
subsistence level of the rural lower class, indeed to poverty and
begging.

By way of introduction Goethe quotes an elderly weaver, speaking of another impending threat: 'For there was no denying
that mechanization was spreading throughout the country and
gradually threatening busy hands with idleness.' Factories developed more and more rapidly towards the close of the century,
with a corresponding concentration of workers in their buildings under harsher conditions of social discipline. Soon factories
were to be wrecked in England, and desperate workers in cottage
industries would rise in impotent revolt against those novel and
more efficient forms of industrialization.

In conclusion, Rudolf Vierhaus says of 'rural craftsmen and manufacturing processes':

> Governments and the enlightened authors of the eighteenth century saw in manufactories an effective vehicle of economic progress, a way of reducing poverty and unemployment in the populace and preventing their demoralization. This expectation was fulfilled only up to a point, and only after a long period of acclimatization, a learning process that entailed high social costs. The poverty of the lowest classes of the population in the eighteenth century was not eliminated by cottage industry and the development of factories, but without these factors it would have been even more dire.[12]

With the emergence of cottage and factory workers in the eighteenth century a new class had come into being which was distinct from the peasantry. Given the rigid social order, which was maintained in spite of everything, they had no chance of advancement, except as middlemen – go-betweens serving the merchant in the town by conveying his wares to and fro. In the nineteenth century, when the barriers of class and those of the guilds fell – at least officially – it then became possible for this class to become manufacturers themselves. Possible, too, was a move into other professions and also the growth of the nineteenth-century working class with its mighty and explosive political and social potential.

Part III

Europe and its States

1

The Way of the World

\The eighteenth century started with a great war. It was fought over the succession to the Spanish throne, which the French king, Louis XIV, and the Austrian emperor both claimed, in order to maintain or install in that country collateral lines of their own Houses. They had been forced to wait for decades for the death of the ailing King Charles II. Then the war broke out, with almost everyone pitted against the might of France. Thanks to their excellent generals, the Duke of Marlborough and Prince Eugen, Britain and Austria at last won the day. At the same time the Nordic War waged by the insane Swedish King Charles XII against his neighbours was raging. The peace treaties led to the establishment of a balance of power which was to set its seal on the century, even though the continent still had to suffer a whole series of wars of succession.

For the average contemporary looking back over the years the situation appeared to be more or less as follows. The miraculous deliverance of Vienna from the besieging Turks in 1683 no doubt seemed to him to herald better times. The War of the Spanish Succession passed and Louis XIV died following the defeat of his glorious armies. The escapade of the crazy Swedish king came to an end when he was struck by a cannon-ball fired from the fortress of Frederikshald. After that the powers quarrelled over the Polish and the Austrian succession, and the rise of Prussia began under its 'great' King Frederick II.

A calendar from south Germany from the beginning of the nineteenth century describes the way of the world as it was to continue:

> In the meantime the city of Lisbon in Portugal was destroyed by an earthquake, and the Seven Years War passed, and the Emperor Francis I died, and the Jesuits were dissolved, and Poland was partitioned, and the Empress Maria Theresa died, and Struensee was executed. America was liberated, and the combined forces of France and Spain failed to take Gibraltar. The Turks besieged General Stein in the Veterans' Cavern in Hungary, and the Emperor Joseph died. King Gustavus of Sweden conquered Russian Finland, and the French Revolution and the long war began, and the Emperor Leopold II was also borne to his grave. Napoleon conquered Prussia, and the English bombarded Copenhagen . . .[1]

This narrative strikes us like the old regime's dance of death, beginning with the Lisbon earthquake, an event which touched a vital nerve of this optimistic century that had so much faith in the future.

The calendar quoted here gives a highly condensed account of the eighteenth century: a jumble of squabbles over succession that were fought out in international wars waged on land with the well-drilled ranks of professional armies with their drum and bugle signals, their timely orders to retreat and their clearly ordered field formations; or else at sea with frigates armed with cannon, tacking precisely to and fro with the aid of sail or rudder, as we learn from a French sailors' song, *Au trente et un du mois d'août* telling of a naval engagement on 31 August in one of those years of naval battles. On that day an English frigate was sighted making for Bordeaux under full sail. A French vessel of the *corsaire* class, armed with no more than half a dozen cannon, was able, by a skilfully executed manoeuvre, to put on board the 'clumsy, rotten English ship', that had no less than thirty-six guns, a boarding party armed with axes, grenades, pikes, cutlasses and muskets. The impudent chorus that rounds off the various verses with their account of each tack of sail or rudder, goes like this:

> *Buvons un coup, la-la, buvons en deux*
> *A la santé des amoureux,*
> *A la santé du roi de France*
> *Et merde pour le roi d'Angleterre,*
> *Qui nous a déclaré la guerre.*[2]

Let's drink a glass, let's drink a couple
To the health of our sweethearts,
To the health of the king of France
And . . . . . to the king of England,
Who declared war on us.

In these wars on sea and land there were victories and defeats on both sides, but in the end a solemn peace was concluded with an exchange of delegations in accordance with time-honoured tradition. Since everyone believed in the balance of power, certain countries tended to be shunted backwards and forwards on the political map. For instance, following the War of the Polish Succession, which was fought out in Italy and on the Rhine from 1733 to 1735, the king of Poland was 'shifted' to the duchy of Lorraine, while the erstwhile Duke of Lorraine was moved to the grand duchy of Tuscany, since it so happened that the ancient Medici dynasty had just died out. A game was played with masterly skill according to tried and tested feudal monarchical rules, and after the Seven Years War Europe was blessed with a peace that lasted for almost thirty years.

The succession of events was complicated and bewildering, with ministers committing their armies or their money as they thought fit in the interests of their royal masters, or their country's commercial or military power.

The calendar from south Germany just quoted ends its tour through the history of events with the words: '. . . and the farmers sowed and reaped. The miller ground and the blacksmith hammered, and the miners delved for veins of precious metal in their underground workshops.' This is what French historians call *histoire de longue durée*, long-term history – that history in which politics, wars, the moving of frontiers hither and thither are merely momentary incidents – although they may be as traumatic as an earthquake – while economic and social developments proceed on their way soundlessly and without any obvious upheaval.

2

Venerable Monarchies and Republics

Was Europe a single entity, or was it hopelessly divided? An answer to this question was offered in the 1770s by an Italian author of the Enlightenment, Carlantonio Pilati, after he had visited a number of countries:

> Those who simply rush from one country to another find it hard to detect differences between the different regions of Europe. They imagine they can find a great measure of uniformity everywhere and they think they can convince their readers of this. They are gravely mistaken, however. There are indeed features that bring the various European countries closer together, such as the same moral code, the same basic religious assumptions, the same legislative principles − but character, lifestyle and customs produce marked differences, even within one and the same nation: climate, food and drink, the nature of the terrain, certain maxims adopted by the powers that be, and, last but not least, a more or less intricate legislative system, more or less well adapted to one nation, less suited to another.[3]

A similar balance was struck in a leaflet entitled *Political Barometer* that was circulated in 1785:

Portugal begs for everything,
Spain provides everything,

Naples puts up with everything,
Parma comes to terms with everything,
Venice keeps mum about everything,
Genoa laughs at everything,
Sardinia keeps an eye on everything,
England helps with everything,
France meddles in everything,
Switzerland passes comment on everything,
Russia frightens everyone,
Germany apes everything,
Sweden harks back to everything,
Denmark puts up with everything,
Poland loses everything,
Prussia stirs up everything,
The Turk is amazed at everything,
The Holy Empire believes everything,
The emperor is ready for anything,
The pope permits everything,
Everything is higgledy-piggledy,
Everything has gone to pot,
And may God help us,
Or else the Devil, he will grab the lot.[4]

This political barometer appeared two years after the Peace of Versailles had ended the long war that had been waged for the independence of the English colonies in North America. At that point no one knew that only four years later, revolutionary events would be set in motion in France, culminating in 1792 in a world war in which the 'Devil', as the kings and nobles liked to call Napoleon, would grab more or less everything.

Portugal begs for everything: This probably refers to the close ties that had bound Portugal to Britain ever since 1703 and that were meant to save the country from the grasp of Bourbon Spain. Both countries had an interest in defending the Portuguese colonial empire in Africa from seizure by France and Spain. Similar considerations applied to Brazil and settlements on the coasts of Africa and India. The situation in Portugal itself was uneventful, until the country attracted general interest, because power had devolved on the prime minister, the Marquis de Pombal, who introduced a vigorously radical policy of modernization that abolished the Jesuit Order as well as slavery. It was only after a rule of some twenty years that he was dismissed by a new king, Pedro III. The country remained poor, however, because the gold from its colonies went to the court, or else into the pockets of foreign traders: Portugal remained dependent on the goodwill of Great Britain and Spain.

Spain provides everything: This probably refers to the situation in 1785, the year the leaflet was printed. Spain had regained a number of its lost possessions, thanks to its involvement in the war of American independence. Disputes with Portugal had been settled, and a trade agreement concluded between the two countries. In the Mediterranean, an understanding had been reached with Turkey. The ruling Bourbons aligned their policy more or less with that of France, which implied Enlightenment, or at least political centralization on the French pattern. Enlightenment could come only from above in a country so utterly imbued with the spirit of the Counter-Reformation, where, at the beginning of the century, the baroque style of church architecture, already at its zenith, had slithered into the bizarre excesses of Churriguera. It was not until the end of the century that a savagely realistic style was to be introduced into Spanish art by Goya. The greater part of South America was still subject to Spain, with Spanish viceroys and archbishops from Mexico to Peru, and governed by a Council of the Indies in Madrid. However, it was still the great mercantile companies that mainly profited from the wealth of the colonies, an anomaly that was becoming increasingly obvious. The domestication of the indigenous Indians was presenting problems for the Creoles, those inhabitants of Spanish descent, who were already dreaming of an end to Spanish rule.

In the *Barometer*'s list the two Iberian monarchies are followed by Italian states. Italy was a cultural and geographical, rather than a political, designation. Memories of Roman antiquity as well as recollections of Renaissance genius encouraged a certain sense of unity and a certain pride – the excavations in Pompeii were just beginning. A high degree of cultural diversity was a consequence of its political fragmentation. An intelligent Italian noted at the time:

> This region has advantages over other countries that have
> only one capital. In such countries it is the capital that
> dictates the line taken by science and scholarship. It obliges its subjects, of whatever class they may be, to undergo
> a single type of education and to adopt its own mode of
> thought. But Italy is divided into many states and has
> many different capitals. Accordingly, modes of thought,
> the choice of topics for study, and tastes in the arts and
> sciences are much more diverse.[5]

Politically, Italian states were repeatedly the victims of dynastic machinations and suffered in wars into which they were drawn by their Cabinets. Austrian or French troops were liable to claim the right to march through their territory. Along with Flanders, northern Italy was the cockpit of Europe. Our leaflet is certainly right about that.

Naples puts up with everything: This probably means in the sense that the Spanish Bourbon monarchy of the Two Sicilies, like other Catholic monarchies, endured both enlightened reform and the reaction that was liable to follow it.

Parma comes to terms with everything: Wedged in between Sardinia, Piedmont, the Republic of Genoa and Austrian Milan, Parma had little choice; a fief of a collateral line of the Spanish Bourbons since 1749, it experienced both reform and reaction under Napoleon.

Sardinia keeps an eye on everything: With a popular but philistine monarchy, Sardinia-Piedmont kept a watchful eye on its weaker neighbours. Since 1748 it had been pushing its frontiers closer to Milan, and in 1782 it had helped to humiliate its ancestral foe, the Republic of Geneva, and it still had command of French-speaking Savoy. Its western frontier was on the Rhone.

The leaflet omits the grand duchy of Tuscany, to which we might apply the motto, 'tries out everything', bearing in mind the impressive enlightened reforms under the Grand Duke Peter Leopold and his minister, Rosenberg-Orsini. Tuscany had been ruled by the House of Lorraine since 1735 – when the Medici had died out – and was ultimately subject to the Austrian Habsburgs.

Two other minor Italian states are also missing from the list: the duchy of Modena, for one, to which we might apply, as to Parma, the motto, 'comes to terms with everything', since, still patriarchally ruled by the indigenous dynasty of d'Este, it was forced, like Parma, to tack to and fro between the great powers, Austria and France. The second, the Republic of Lucca, could share the Venetian motto, 'keeps mum about everything', for this little republic had been able to widen the aristocratic basis of its government discreetly by raising commoners to the peerage.

Another republic, Genoa, *laughs at everything*. Here, people were indifferent to the church, enlightened in the Masonic sense, but they could barely hold on to the Ligurian seaboard after surrendering Corsica to France – Corsica, where father and son, Giacinto and Pasquale Paoli, had fought in vain for the island's independence.

The third republic was Venice, which *keeps mum about everything*. This was the silence of a state that could still pride itself on its greatness. Even though it had lost Crete and the Peloponnese in the seventeenth century, it still controlled the Adriatic coast down as far as the Ionian islands and possessed the mainland from Friuli to Lake Como. At the beginning of the century, when Crete had been temporarily regained, this triumph was celebrated by the commissioning of Vivaldi's *Juditha triumphans*. Subsequently Venice was able to steer clear of wars through a shrewd policy of neutrality and promoted moderate reforms. Canaletto and Guardi immortalized in their pictures the grandiose culture of the republic's close-knit aristocracy.

The Papal State could not be overlooked, stretching as it did right across Central Italy between the Mediterranean and the Adriatic. *The pope permits everything* applies not only to the ecclesiastical policy of enlightened Catholic monarchies, but also to the pope's own state, 'where agriculture is neglected, one vast stretch of land lies fallow and another is no better than a swamp that no one thinks of draining.'[6]

The leaflet then goes on to record the barometer readings north of the Alps, leaping straight from Sardinia to England.

England helps with everything: Even though the nation had just lost thirteen of its colonies, it was still rising steadily in power and influence. At home, industrialization was in full swing, and British merchants made sure that Britannia ruled the waves. It was a proud nation, which had revealed through Newton hitherto unknown laws of nature. In a bloodless 'glorious revolution' it had created the first constitutional monarchy, making civic rights the law of the land through its Bill of Rights. Through a Toleration Act it had sought to put an end to religious persecution, and the Duke of Marlborough's troops had halted the advance of Louis XIV's super-power. The nation was credited with a monopoly of common sense, and it was from Great Britain that the most ingenious technical devices found their way on to the Continent. Nor should Scotland be forgotten, although it had been absorbed into the United Kingdom: it had produced its own school of philosophy. It was only Ireland that was reactionary for there Hanoverian Protestants proved to be intolerant, from fear of a Catholic Stuart insurrection.

France meddles in everything: whether in Europe or in overseas colonies, although it had little success under the sway of Louis XV and his various mistresses. It had better luck with its involvement in the Enlightenment, initially more of an English movement. In speech and writing Paris was the undisputed capital of the 'republic of letters'. 'French has virtually become a universal language,' wrote Voltaire, amongst other reasons, 'because it is more suitable than English for the expression of ideas'.

Switzerland passes comment on everything: because it was the source of a copious literature of a moderately enlightened nature in German, French and, occasionally, Italian. Switzerland was in a position to comment on and gloss events, because it found itself in a relatively comfortable state of neutrality between the great powers France and Austria, was not obliged to take sides and had not suffered a European war on its territory since 1536. It was regarded as an interesting country of free republics, it was prosperous and no longer exported only cheese, but also textiles, clocks and watches.

Apart from Switzerland, the only independent republic north of the Alps was the Republic of the United Netherlands, which is ignored in our leaflet. 'Harks back to everything' or 'puts up with everything' might apply here, as well as to Sweden or Denmark. The mighty economic, political and intellectual upsurge of the seventeenth century lay back in the past, and soon this system of republics was to fall victim to Prussian intervention in support of the Governor General at the cost of the country's ancient patriotic liberties. But the proverbial phrase about 'the wealthy man in Amsterdam' still applied and was backed by a colonial empire in every part of the globe.

Germany apes everything, because in the life of the courts as well as in literature there was still a predilection for French or English models, and talk of a 'German national spirit' was still distinctly tentative. Germany was still the 'Holy Roman Empire of the German Nation', not a state in the sense of a modern, much less a national, monarchy; it was no more than a kind of medieval matrix. The 'Empire' consisted of no more than a multitude of small, even miniature, states wedged in between France, Prussia and Austria – secular and ecclesiastical principalities, counties and imperial cities. When the leaflet goes on, *The Holy Empire believes everything*, this is no more than a repetition of 'Germany apes everything'. The empire was still suffering the aftermath of the Thirty Years War and the French aggression that had followed it. It was a patchwork of religious confessions: Lutheran for the most part, Calvinists in a minority, a great many Roman Catholics. The leaflet makes no reference, however, to the flourishing economic and cultural condition of many of the principalities – not only Goethe's Weimar, but many cities besides Lessing's Hamburg. Germany in all its cultural diversity was full of slumbering talents that were about to awake. What they had in common was a language that had at last been standardized, the literature written in that language, and a memory of the empire's erstwhile power and glory. Towards the end of the century Germany was to make its way into the first rank, putting many other countries in the shade. A view expressed in the eighteenth century was to prove prophetic: 'It is true that the Germans are extremely hard-working.'[7]

When we think of the German capacity for hard work, then it is Prussia that first springs to mind. Prussia gets a line to itself in our leaflet: *Prussia stirs up everything*. This is no doubt an allusion to its restless King Frederick II, who 'stirred up' the Seven Years War and the partition of Poland, and who was consequently in possession of Austrian Silesia and Polish West Prussia. But Frederick II also meant 'Frederick the Great', who had made his Berlin and Potsdam focal points of the Enlightenment.

Austria is mentioned only in the person of its ruler: *The emperor is ready for anything*. The German nation also included the old Austrian state, which had become a high-handed great power. The particular emperor who was 'ready for anything' was Joseph II, a monarch who was only too eager to unify his vast motley collection of states and to extend his power in opposition to Turkey and Poland. Austria was a pluralistic state with a cosmopolitan capital, Vienna. It had its far-flung frontier in Flanders, on the Upper Rhine, while the ancient, more or less German-speaking, land of Austria proper extended from the Tyrol to Burgenland and Carinthia. The crowns of Bohemia and Hungary were also held by the Habsburgs, but Prague and Budapest were major capitals in their own right, with their own cultural identity. Hungary, multilingual and multi-confessional, prided itself on its independence. The duchy of Milan and a collateral line in Tuscany imparted an Italian accent to the empire. Over a dozen languages were spoken – and written – within the Austrian frontiers, while any number of foreign influences were reflected in Vienna: Italian and Spanish from the pre-Bourbon era of Spain, more recent French influence via the House of Lorraine, for the Austrian dynasty was linked through Maria Theresa's consort with this former marginal territory of the empire. However irreproachably Catholic the Austrian empire may have claimed to be, there were still Protestant minorities here, there and everywhere, and in Hungary they even had some kind of official standing.

We also find a couple of Nordic states in the *Political Barometer*. *Denmark puts up with everything*: because the country is well-nigh indefensible and subject to the territorial and maritime interests of England, Russia and Sweden. Long gone were the days of the royal naval hero, King Christian IV, who had taken his stance 'by the tall mast' in the seventeenth century, and the country was forced to pursue a slippery policy of neutrality. The Danish royal House still held sway over the kingdom of Norway, Iceland and the duchies of Schleswig and Holstein. A prosperous middle class was emerging on the strength of the Norwegian timber and agricultural trade, and Copenhagen was turning into an elegant metropolis of the north. A kind of genial absolutism had led to growing equality among its citizens and this led in turn to widespread emancipation of the peasantry. Norway had always been a land of yeoman farmers remote from the centre of political power. Here, the Enlightenment was in full flood: a golden age of Danish literature had dawned. There had been no censorship since 1770 and the Danes had made prudent use of this freedom.

Sweden harks back to everything: back to the previous century, when it had been a great power, intervening spectacularly in the Thirty Years War with its formidable army of Finnish cavalry under King Gustavus Adolphus and aiming to found a Swedish Lutheran Kingdom of God all round the Baltic. But half a century later the mad King Charles XII, who kept the whole of the north on tenterhooks for a good eighteen years, had forfeited nearly all the Swedish gains, in spite of his heroic campaigns in successive wars. One by one, Swedish dependencies in Lower Pomerania and on the Baltic were lost – and ultimately the whole of Finland, which became a Russian grand duchy in 1808, albeit with a fair degree of autonomy. The not inconsiderable export of timber and iron ore brought in a good deal of money, but the ill-starred wars proved to be very costly. At home, royal absolutism alternated with parliamentary regimes under an aristocratic assembly. The peasantry had long enjoyed local self-government, which was gradually extended. Gustavus III behaved like an enlightened monarch in the manner of Frederick II of Prussia. Academic and literary life flourished, and Stockholm figured as a brilliant court.

Poland loses everything: Poland, once a proud medieval kingdom extending from the Black Sea to the Baltic, had not progressed beyond its medieval constitution, so that the Polish government under its weak kings failed to benefit from the discipline inherent in absolutism. Poland fell victim to the concerted onslaught of Prussia, Russia and Austria: a first partition took place in 1772, a second in 1793 and the ultimate partition in 1795. The country had once been powerful, it had initially adopted a liberal attitude to the various religious confessions, then taken the side of the Counter-Reformation, and ultimately adopted enlightened reforms. Now it had simply vanished from the map. But the Poles themselves survived, along with their language and their Roman Catholic faith, between Protestant Prussia and Orthodox Russia. They had to wait 130 years before they could see the resurrection of their own state.

Russia frightens everyone: With the accession of Tsar Peter the Great at the beginning of the century this land-locked empire on the far side of Poland, the Baltic and Swedish Finland became politically active and underwent a process of modernization. The capital was moved from the remote city of Moscow to St Petersburg on the Baltic coast. An academy was founded and the finest brains from the West were elected to it, the army was brought up to date, and the style of government became even more authoritarian than it had been hitherto. Ultimately the enlightened Empress Catherine II adopted an aggressive foreign policy on all fronts – against Sweden, Denmark and Poland. With its formidable Cossack cavalry, Russia now presented a broad united front extending from Riga to the Crimea.

The leaflet concludes its readings of the political barometer with Turkey: *The Turk is amazed at everything*, because the outposts of his empire were starting to crumble (Hungary, Siebenbürgen, the Crimea had already been lost; Moldau, Walachei, Tunis and Tripoli were aspiring to autonomy), and because he felt excluded from the exciting and ambitious world of the European Enlightenment. Turkey is the only non-European state to be mentioned in the leaflet, because it still ruled the Balkans that were mainly Christian, along with a subjugated Greece, where the first stirrings of a liberation movement might just be detected.

That the newly founded federal state of the United States of

America is not mentioned in the *Barometer* is hardly surprising, since the world is virtually limited to Europe in the minds of Europeans. Not that the other continents were totally unknown to Europeans – not only Spanish and Portuguese America, but also the English, French, Portuguese and Dutch coasts of Africa and India (at this time mainly an English possession) and Dutch Indonesia had all been heard of. People were interested in even more exotic countries: they admired the wise government of China, and loved to adorn their homes with genuine or fake exotic *objets d'art*, and to lay out their gardens in the Chinese style.

Nevertheless, vital decisions were still being taken by agreement between London, Paris and Vienna, including at best St Petersburg, Berlin and Madrid. But *Everything is higgledy-piggledy* is the final reading on the *Political Barometer*.

3

Cosmopolitanism versus the Nation States

'I am a citizen of the world, I am not in the service of the emperor or the king of France, I am in the service of the truth,' wrote Pierre Bayle, the Huguenot author of the first encyclopedia of the Enlightenment in 1700. And at the close of the century Friedrich Schiller was to state: 'I write as a citizen of the world who serves no prince. I lost my fatherland at an early age and exchanged it for the wide world.'[8]

The states that constituted the world of the eighteenth century were not yet nationalistic, even though nationalism was latent everywhere and was due to be noisily aroused. The century of the Enlightenment thought of itself as one cosmos, the whole world as a single entity.

The monarchs were a kind of international association bound together by family ties. Only the Brandenburg dynasty in Prussia, the Estes in Parma and the Savoys in Turin were truly indigenous rulers. The monarch's ministers were frequently not natives of the country they served, while among the field marshals and generals – in the Russian army, say – we might find a motley assortment of Frenchmen, Swiss and Germans from the Baltic and elsewhere. The royal courts also reflected this international complexion – Germans in Copenhagen and a world of many races in Vienna. In Sweden, for instance, the higher ranks of the aristocracy included the de la Granges from France, the Irish Hamiltons and the Baltic German Wrangels. The nobility were in fact cosmopolitan, their rules of precedence were in force everywhere, as was the officer's code of honour, his principles of duty and loyalty, and the convention that sanctioned marriages only between partners of equal rank. At their feet were the 'plebs', who, from an aristocratic point of view, might well include the middle class.

Although it used to be said that God and the king could speak any language they had a mind to, French nevertheless became the standard language of the courts and the aristocracy, who, in so far as they knew the local language at all, reserved it or its dialects for use with their servants. French took over from Italian, which had previously been widely spoken, and also tended to displace Latin as the language of learning. The courts were modelled on French prototypes, and people there wrote to each other in that language, which was also the first foreign language that middle-class intellectuals and businessmen had to learn. The French theatre was popular everywhere, even among the common people. The presence of Huguenot refugees in many Protestant countries also represented an important factor in the dissemination of French: the French church of these enclaves often advanced to become the favourite place of worship of the better class of citizen. The Huguenots retained their mother tongue right down to the beginning of the nineteenth century. By and large, French was the written and spoken means of communication of cosmopolitanism.

The middle class actually had a less pronouncedly cosmopolitan profile. Its members tended to live together in the confines of a town and to marry among themselves. However broadminded they might be in enlightened circles, marriage into another town was generally out of the question. 'They did not mean to dilute the noble blood of Basel with foreign elements',[9] as one of the city's mayors put it during a debate in the Grand Council on a proposal to make citizen's rights available to non-citizens. Thus, cosmopolitanism remained little more than an intellectual and purely theoretical possibility, although the merchant class was socially more mobile, as were craftsmen, who customarily moved from one country to another.

Since the world of nation states was traditionally taken for granted, it could not very well serve as a model for the Enlightenment movement. Moreover, the cosmopolitanism of the nobility was at odds with the aristocratic belief in the inequality of men. It was possibly only in England that certain ideals of the Enlightenment came close to realization. It was there that avenues of advancement were opened up, thanks to a time-honoured tradition of liberty, now revived through parliamentary government, thanks to the intermingling of gentry and the middle class, and thanks to a free press and a tolerant approach to religious issues. It was, therefore, England that was elevated to the status of an ideal country through the very influential *Letters on the French and the English* by Béat-Louis de Muralt, and Voltaire's account of England (which was actually published in French). France was too deeply compromised by its legacy of intolerant absolutism to serve as a political model.

Models might be found elsewhere as well – among the 'noble savages' of North America or the islands of the South Seas or, if one preferred to stay in Europe, among the shepherds in the Swiss Alps. Until the beginning of the eighteenth century Switzerland had been regarded as an inhospitable country with uncouth manners and a backward population, but now scientists began to discover for the first time this highly intriguing geological specimen. The mountains and lakes first attracted itinerant British lords who feasted their eyes on the Lake of Geneva with its romantic Castle of Chillon and the magnificent scenery of the Alps in the canton of Valais. They were followed by travellers from many countries who wrote enthusiastic accounts of their journeys. It was in this superb natural setting that the people of the Alps were also first discovered. The didactic poem, *The Alps*, by the scientist and physician Albrecht von Haller read like a travel diary, as did the *Idylls* of Salomon Gessner, which were subsequently translated into many major languages. Rousseau made political capital out of these landscapes: Alpine democracy, hitherto so despised, suddenly became the ideal political system.

Enthusiasm for all things Helvetic was boosted by the fact that the country had in its cities an enlightened elite of international standing who were capable of expressing themselves in

French as well as German. Together with the 'free Swiss' of the Alpine valleys the historic myth of this republican land was also unearthed: the wondrous heroic legend of the oath sworn by the three forest cantons on the Rütli meadow, and the story of Wilhem Tell, who slew the tyrant, Gessler. In this way the Alpine and the historic myth were fused, became a model and were ultimately given their classic form in Friedrich Schiller's drama, which gained universal and cosmopolitan currency.

That the reality did not quite match the ideal was not clearly realized by the Swiss themselves, nor by outsiders, until the outbreak of the French Revolution, when the slogan *Liberté et Egalité* put all other political ideas in the shade.

An unsolved problem of cosmopolitanism was that of peaceful collaboration between the nations: should it be limited, as it always had been, to peace conferences following the conclusion of a war – conferences at which territorial adjustments containing the seeds of future conflicts would be made?

Ever since Erasmus in his *Querela pacis* (1517) had exhorted men to realize at last the futility of war, lawyers and theologians had been trying to patch up some kind of worldwide scheme for keeping the peace. In his *Law of War and Peace* (1625), Grotius had suggested a congress of princes based on internationally recognized laws. Charles-Irénée, Abbé de Saint-Pierre, a critic of Louis XIV's regime, went even further in his *Projet de Paix Perpétuelle* (1713), proposing a European union with a rotating chairmanship, a court appointed to adjudicate and to keep the peace. In the course of the succeeding centuries the project proposed by the Abbé de Saint-Pierre has been frequently discussed; one of the major writers who tackled the problem was Immanuel Kant in his essay, *On an Everlasting Peace*, published in 1795, at the very time when yet another peace conference was in session. In the years that followed, however, cosmopolitanism was doomed to be overshadowed by the nationalistic mentality.

Part IV

The Champions of Enlightenment

1

The 'Association' Movement

Enlightenment, the new spirit of freedom, of movement, of enquiry involved not only thinkers, philosophers, writers and others trying to come to terms with their age and taking part in contemporary events, it also involved more or less highly organized associations.[1]

As a rule, such social alliances resulted from discussions among friends. Friendship was of great importance for the men of the Enlightenment, a topic that was discussed and written about over and over again. Already in the *Spectator*, the most influential of English journals, one might read of the great 'benefit of friendship, that vital elixir'.[2] 'An association of friends has been formed': the founding of a society in the eighteenth century was frequently announced in some such terms. Wherever an 'association of friends' came together in this way, their aim was to contribute to the reform of existing cultural, social or economic conditions. They were concerned with *émulation*, with 'encouragement', with improvement of the world. They were not content to remain within the old social matrix, in the guilds, say, or in the fraternities, whose aims were circumscribed by creed or calling, or by their own traditional customs and usages. There were in any case new tasks to be tackled in the developing sciences, in the widening field of cultural education and in the provision of social benefits called for by the grand utopia of the Enlightenment.

It is remarkable how in the eighteenth century Europe and

both the Americas were spanned by an increasingly dense network of associations which commonly went by the name of 'society' (*societas, société, Sozietät, società, sociedad*). At the beginning of the eighteenth century, for instance, Germany boasted no more than two learned academies; by the end of the century there were at least a dozen. In 1723 the first public society of this kind was founded in Edinburgh; by the time of the French Revolution about 150 such associations might be counted in Europe and overseas.

These associations began as a rule when a group of like-minded friends began to extend their activities. In many cases the need for more efficient organization very soon made itself felt. Such organization was often rudimentary and, in principle, republican. Members were recruited who pledged themselves to finance the society and to help realize some specific aim that was stated in the association's constitution. The governing body would be a meeting of all the members empowered to take final decisions, in which all the members would have equal rights. The day-to-day running of the society would be entrusted to a committee consisting of a chairman, a secretary, a treasurer and a number of elected committee members. Subcommittees would be set up for various specific projects. Often proceedings were published in the form of a journal or a series of papers reporting the society's activities; these publications would sometimes be available to a wider readership.

2

The Academy

Quite early on, a number of different types of association were developed. The oldest was the learned society or academy, which took as its model Plato's Academy in Athens, or its successors in the Italian Renaissance, some of which were still active in the eighteenth century. In September 1786, during his Italian journey, Goethe was present at a public session of an academy in the Venetian town of Vicenza:

This evening I was present at a meeting held by the Academy of Olympians. It is not much more than a game, but it is a useful game that helps to preserve a modicum of wit and vivacity in the populace. It took place in a commodious, handsomely illuminated chamber next door to Palladio's theatre. The 'Captain' and a number of noblemen were present, as well as an audience of educated people, a good many clerics, about five hundred in all.

The topic proposed by the president for today's session was: 'Whether the fine arts have been fostered more by invention or by imitation?' It was a well-chosen topic, for if the alternative implied in the question were to be closely examined then the argument might be bandied back and forth for a century or more. The gentlemen of the Academy took full advantage of the occasion and made all manner of contributions to the debate in prose and in verse, some of them very good stuff indeed.

Then it was the turn of the lively audience. The listeners shouted 'Bravo!', applauded and laughed. If only we could stand up in front of our own people and hope to be so entertained . . .

The academies had for the most part scientific aims. What could not be done in the universities was to be accomplished through the voluntary labours of the academies. The topics were mostly taken from the natural sciences, but academies also concerned themselves with language, literature and history – subjects which were otherwise pushed into the background by the all-powerful faculties of theology and law.

As far as Europe north of the Alps was concerned, it was the Parisian academies that provided the model: the Académie française, founded in 1635, which was concerned with the cultivation of the French language, and the Académie des inscriptions et des belles-lettres, founded in 1663, which was devoted to historical studies. The French academies were originally private foundations but they were soon taken over by the state, financed and provided with an effective organization. A good many academies were then founded in the provinces.

In the course of the eighteenth century practically all the European monarchies set up academies, which became an integral part of the court like the court theatre, the court ball and the palace guard. States which lacked a central court made do with 'learned societies' that pursued the same aims as the academies in a somewhat less formally organized manner.

In England research into the natural sciences was carried on in a rather different manner. The Royal Society of London for Improving Natural Knowledge, founded in 1660, did indeed enjoy royal patronage but was rather more loosely constituted than the French Academy. The Royal Society for its part did in fact have considerable influence on the Continent.

Societies seeking to promote the arts might also enjoy royal patronage – in Spain, for instance, where one report states:

In this country the arts and sciences are still in their infancy. At the instigation of the Marquis de Grimaldi an Academy for Architecture, Sculpture and Painting has been founded. A number of eminent and wealthy gentlemen are members and it must be said to their credit that they spare no effort to promote these excellent liberal arts. Last summer the king purchased a large mansion for the greater convenience of the society, and it will also house a section devoted to natural history under the direction of a certain Don Pedro Dávila.[3]

Two examples may serve to illustrate the typical academy of the eighteenth century. First, the Royal Academy of Berlin.[4]

The determined wish of the Elector of Brandenburg to make something greater of his outlying principality was bound to be expressed in the field of learning as well as politically and militarily. However, the founding in 1701 of a Brandenburg Society, i.e. the Berlin Academy, was not just a gesture intended to adorn a newly conceived state, the kingdom of Prussia – it was based on a genuine interest in learning. No less a personage than Gottfried Wilhelm Leibniz was commissioned to inaugurate the society; the choice of Leibniz was due to the keen intellectual interests of the new queen, Sophie Charlotte, and her mother, the Electress Sophie of Hanover, in whose service Leibniz was then engaged.

At long last the philosopher had been given the chance to realize the idea of an academy that he had so often propounded with the threefold aim of propagating a liberal Christian view of life through the sciences, fostering learning and promoting the welfare and reputation of the German nation, its learning and language. Leibniz was particularly concerned with *utilitas*, the practical application of the sciences. The academy got off to a promising start. From 1710 onward it published *Miscellanea Berolinensia* and hence reached a relatively wide public. The situation soon changed, however, with the beginning of the authoritarian rule of Frederick William I, who had very different interests and who deliberately neglected the academy; government of the country and the army seemed to him a great deal more important. The academy had to confine itself to publications on military subjects. It was only Frederick William's successor, King Frederick II, with his philosophical interests, who once again showed a proper appreciation of the part that ought to be played by a royal academy. After 1741 the Academy flourished once more and endeavoured successfully to find a place among the leading institutions in the world of learning. It invited the mathematician Leonhard Euler to become a member, and the physicist Maupertuis held the post of director until his death, when the directorship was assumed by the king himself.

The Academy was divided into four classes: The experimental philosophy section included chemistry, anatomy, botany and other experimental sciences. The mathematical class included geometry, algebra, mechanics, astronomy, and all the theoretical sciences. Speculative philosophy embraced logic, metaphysics, moral philosophy and ethics. A fine arts section covered classical philology, history and languages.

The Academy was thus competent to deal with practically every branch of learning. It was run by its president and a secretary; for decades the latter was the descendant of a Berlin Huguenot family, Johann Heinrich Samuel Formey. Each section had its director and a 'curator', who was responsible for managing its finances. A certain amount of cash was raised from the sale of calendars. The membership comprised sixteen ordinary members, who lived in Berlin and who were paid a stipend. Another group of members were external, or so-called 'corresponding', members – they included scholars scattered all over the continent who were thus loosely attached to the academy. Honorary members might also be nominated. Acceptance into the academy was a matter for its president or the king. The majority of members were French or Swiss, often of the Protestant faith, since the king preferred scholars who were versed in world languages.

Ordinary members were required to submit two papers annually. These were read at meetings of the academy and subsequently published in its *Mémoires*. There were also other occasional publications. Very important was the network of correspondence with corresponding members or with other academies. This spanned the whole of Europe.

The Academy addressed itself annually to a wider audience through its competitions. The topics set included the concept of infinity in mathematics, the metabolism of the human organism, examination of the principle 'Everything is for the best' and the problems of settling eastern Germany.

Frederick's academy was to be the typical institution of the Enlightenment between 1740 and 1770. Its influence was widespread precisely because its proceedings were published in French: this was German Enlightenment, but in the French language. The academy played its part in blazing a trail for relatively liberal views such as the king liked to affect. In 1745 the academy's secretary, Formey, said: 'It was only natural for us to do everything we could to polish and refine the keys that would open up to us everything that could be opened up to human intelligence.' The German philosopher Wilhelm Dilthey praises these approaches which went beyond the 'older philosophy', i.e. the purely psychological and historical view of phenomena. The philosophical task that the academy set itself was 'The defence by rational argument of the divine personality and the moral responsibility of man.'

The academy grew old as the king grew old. After 1770 other intellectual forces took the lead in Germany, although the academy continued. Following the founding of the University of Berlin it formed a close partnership with this new humanistic model university of the nineteenth century.

In the course of the eighteenth century the academies tended to devote their energies more and more to utilitarian ends. An example of this trend might be found in the French provincial academy of Châlons sur Marne. Already during the seventeenth, but particularly during the eighteenth century, a considerable number of provincial academies had sprung up in France; they included that of Châlons sur Marne, about which we are particularly well informed, thanks to a study by Daniel Roche. Châlons was the administrative centre of the Champagne district, it was also an episcopal see and the seat of a provincial governor, various law courts and administrative departments, and a garrison. In 1775 a literary society which had existed since 1750 was elevated by royal patent to the status of an academy. Its organization conformed to the customary pattern: twenty titular academicians, and ordinary, associate and corresponding members –

as well as honorary members. The presidency was held jointly by the provincial governor representing the royal administration and the senior prelate of the diocese. The society's activities involved regular meetings, of which one meeting annually was public and conducted in the presence of the governor and the bishop on St Louis' Day. At the meetings papers were read: a quarter of them dealt with empirical scientific topics, one-fifth with literary or rhetorical subjects and one-fifth with historical themes, with the rest being devoted to ethical or economic topics. The academy had its own library and organized competitions for essays, with the emphasis on social topics.

Thanks to Daniel Roche's researches, the sociological profile of this academy is known, as is the case with all the provincial academies. Of the honorary members 24 per cent were clergy and 76 per cent nobles, without a single representative of the third estate. Of the ordinary members, the clergy constituted 21 per cent, the aristocracy 33 per cent and the middle class 45 per cent; of the associate members the clergy accounted for 30 per cent, aristocrats for 20 per cent and the middle class 50 per cent of the membership.

In 1775 the academy chose as its motto *L'Utilité*, indicating that it belongs to a late phase of the Enlightenment. It was trying to find in science the means of improving the province's economy, and this applied even to its historical research. In Châlons the academy represented one way in which provincial life might be stimulated: ideas of the Enlightenment were now to be popularized in a regional context, and what had hitherto taken place mainly in Paris was now meant to happen in the provinces.

3

The Salon

Informal conversation in a group of individuals without any particular organization may be observed even in classical times, as in the circle round Socrates, for instance. This form of social conversation was revived in the Italian Renaissance – an early example may be found in a characteristic form in Boccaccio's *Decamerone*, with its informal group of men and women who met to discuss subjects of common interest. This kind of social intercourse continued into the seventeenth century, when it often evolved into more or less organized sessions – in language societies at court or in the towns, for example. By the eighteenth century, then, the ground for this relatively informal mode of cultured conversation had been well and truly prepared.[5]

In 1710, in his *Brief Outline of Political Wisdom*, Thomasius examined mankind's sociability, his propensity for social intercourse:

> For Thomasius, man was a domesticated and social animal rather than a wild creature destined for a solitary existence. The basis of any society is conversation, and Thomasius distinguished between two kinds of conversation – the daily exchanges we have with those we happen to meet, and the special kind of conversation we have with close friends. But Thomasius not only distinguished between *conversatio privata* and *conversatio publica*, he also drew distinctions within the category of private conversation.

113

Conversatio publica he confined to intercourse with hostile
partners or strangers, while in his chapter on conversation
with close friends he offered a clear contrast which went
beyond the limits of the prevailing theory of conversation.
. . . Intimacy was a prime condition of communication
between individuals. Thomasius's manifest criticism of the
traditional idea of conversation, and hence of the society
that sustained it, had its sociological roots in the emerging
enlightened class and the social institution of friendship on
which this class was based.[6]

It was not in Germany, however, that this new mode of conversation flourished, but in France, in its brilliant capital, Paris. Already
at the end of the seventeenth century, ladies of the aristocracy or the
upper-middle class had begun to invite private persons, friends and
acquaintances, into their drawing rooms on a particular day, in
order to converse and chat with them – not just the usual social
chit-chat, but discussions on serious subjects of some moment.
These informal coteries of individuals with intellectual interests
came from the nobility and the middle class. Members of these
circles would bring with them friends who were visiting Paris in
the course of their travels. In this way little informal academies
were formed which did a great deal to improve cultural standards
in general and to foster friendships between educated people. The
main topic of conversation was literature, *belles-lettres* and poetry,
but discussions on philosophical subjects and the approach to them
became increasingly frequent.

In the age of Louis XIV cultured aristocrats used to meet in
the home of Madame de Sévigné. At the house of Ninon de
Lenclos sceptics and free-thinkers met to discuss Epicurus and
Montaigne, while Madame de Sablé's *salon* was the meeting-
place for moralists, i.e. critics such as La Rochefoucauld. He
himself said: 'The conversation of educated people is one of my
special delights. I love to see how earnestly it is conducted,
especially when it concerns ethical issues.' But people were not
only concerned with moral and psychological questions: they
were also interested in physics. At the London home of the
Duchess de Mazarin the natural sciences were discussed along

with philosophical and literary topics. 'There you may find the greatest freedom in the world, and people who behave with the utmost propriety. True, there are often arguments, but they are conducted with more good sense than passion. The aim is not simply to contradict one's adversary, but to clarify the issues being discussed.'

Following the death of Louis XIV the prevailing tone in the *salons* became more liberal, the topics discussed more philosophical. Fundamental issues in politics, economics and society in general were debated. Around the middle of the century, when the number of *salons* was already legion, Fontenelle, Montesquieu, Mably, Helvétius and others used to meet at the home of Madame de Tencin. 'In her house there was no question of rank or precedence . . . It was only the better argument that carried the day . . . So people came to agree among themselves in her company and under the influence of her philosophical mentality: by virtue of Madame de Tencin's magic wand, as it were, everyone turned into a philosopher.' From 1764 on, the contributors to the encyclopedia – d'Alembert, Marmontel, Condillac, Condorcet, Turgot and others – used to meet at the home of Mademoiselle de Lespinasse:

> She contrived to gather together a very numerous, diverse and enthusiastic company of individuals. A constantly changing circle of friends met at her home every day from five o'clock until nine in the evening. There one could be sure of meeting distinguished men from every rank of society – from the government, the church, the court and the army – besides foreigners and eminent authors. She guided the talk by her shrewd comments, enlivened it and varied it according to her own taste. Politics, religion, philosophy, fiction, the latest news – nothing was excluded from the conversation.

Gradually the *salons* began to make their mark in public, whether through elections to the academy, or even in the political field during the initial stages of the French Revolution, and they continued to play a part until the time when the whole world was turned upside down.

Salons were not confined to Paris, they could be found in the provinces, too, and also outside France. When, for example, Rousseau was a fugitive seeking asylum in the principality of Neuchâtel he was welcomed into the circle of Isabelle Guyenet-D'Ivernois. In the same principality there was Isabelle de Charriere, Dutch by birth, who gathered together a circle of friends whose influence extended far beyond this little state. In Geneva there was the *salon* of Suzanne Necker-Curchod, wife of the Geneva banker and later finance minister to Louis XVI, so that this group had an alternative meeting place in Paris. Suzanne's daughter, Germaine de Staël-Necker, was subsequently to extend the link to Germany.

Towards the close of the century there were also a number of *salons* in Germany, especially in Berlin, some of them presided over by Jewish ladies. Henriette Herz was able to boast that she could 'attract, as if by magic, all the outstanding young men who were either living in Berlin or else visiting the city'.

Vienna, too, had a number of *salons*, for example that of the Countess Maria Wilhelmine von Thun, where Mozart felt so much at home. An English visitor to her home wrote of this *salon* and of the Countess Thun:

> The Countess has the gift of keeping round her a company of friends and of inducing them to entertain each other, and she has this gift to a greater degree than anyone I have ever known. Although she is quick-witted and has a perfect knowledge of the world, she still has the kindest of hearts. She is the first to discover her friends' virtues and the last to recognize their failings. One of her greatest pleasures is to demolish the prejudices of her acquaintances and to form and foster friendships. She has an inexhaustible fund of cheerfulness and good spirits, which she dispenses so prudently that she pleases the cheerful without offending those who grieve. I have never known anyone who has such a host of friends and who expends on them such a wealth of generous friendship. She has created in her own home a little system of happiness, of which she herself is the centre that attracts and unites the whole.[7]

The *salon* had become an international phenomenon that was destined to exert its influence, even into the following century. Such gatherings were feasible wherever the necessary degree of sociability and intellectual interest were to be found.

In England it was the exclusively male clubs which were in the best position to fulfil the function of the *salons* and to rise above the level of mere social intercourse, as was the case for instance with the Scriblerus Club (1714) of Jonathan Swift, Bolingbroke and Alexander Pope. Some of these clubs had a distinctly political complexion.

The Club d'Entresol in Paris (1724–31) also had a political character, so that it could be said that 'it was a kind of club in the English style, a loose association of individuals who argued about everything that was happening and wanted to voice their views on events without compromising themselves'. The Club d'Entresol was presided over by a clergyman, the Abbé Alary, and its members included d'Argenson, the Abbé de Saint-Pierre and Bolingbroke. It was also known as the *café des honnêtes gens*, for the coffee-house, the literary café, was now beginning to play a major part everywhere as the meeting-place of philosophical minds; it was more public and less exclusive than the *salons*. It was the literary coffee-house that provided the setting for the 'reading societies'.

4

The Reading Societies

The *salon* was not an organized society, although it shared the aims of the organized literary societies. The latter had their model in the older cultural societies of the seventeenth century which had concerned themselves with the cultivation of language and literature. Linguistic societies were especially important in The Netherlands at the height of the republican era, for this was when attempts were being made to develop a standard language from a host of dialects. Denmark, Sweden and Germany were faced with the same problem. Once the aim of a standard language had been achieved in the course of the seventeenth century and the beginning of the eighteenth century, attention could be focused on literature, and this is where literary societies came into play. Reading societies were founded from the middle of the eighteenth century onwards to improve general knowledge in a public that was no longer interested simply in scholarship and literature. To this end the societies acquired libraries and organized discussions, which ultimately led to the emergence of the literary coffee-house. Reading societies were particularly common in Germany, but they were also to be found in France, where they went by the name of *musée* or *cabinet de lecture*. In the reading societies which were to be found in every large German town, and even in some of the villages, the aim was to indoctrinate a broad readership with the ideas of the Enlightenment.[8]

We might quote the example of a reading society in an eccle-

118

siastical principality: the Learned Reading Society of Mainz. Mainz was the ancient seat of the three electoral archiepiscopal dioceses in the Holy Roman Empire, and an administrative centre of a mainly ecclesiastical character. It was something of a backwater, calm and uneventfully Tridentine, Catholic and baroque, until 1770, when wide-reaching reforms, particularly in education, were begun by Archbishop Emmerich Joseph and his chief minister, Baron Anselm Franz von Bentzel-Sternau. The death of Emmerich Joseph in 1774 led to the abrupt discontinuation of his innovations. The new archbishop, Friedrich Karl von Erthal, soon broke away from his reactionary advisers, however; Bentzel was recalled in 1780, making it possible to continue the task begun by Emmerich Joseph. Mainz thus became a typical case of a belated but vigorous Catholic reform movement.

One symptom of that reform was the founding – with the archbishop's approval – of a reading society.

In 1782 the society concluded an agreement with the Frankfurt bookseller Hermann for the regular supply of books and periodicals. The members did not attend simply in order to read: the society called itself a learned society, and there are accounts of historical researches carried out by its members. The society had premises at its disposal, but it was concerned with problems of social behaviour, for it was determined not to degenerate into a coffee-house. Innocuous refreshments such as tea, chocolate, coffee, almond milk, lemonade and punch were permitted and even available on the premises, but gambling and smoking – those two besetting vices of the century – were strictly prohibited. Prohibitions went even further: talk detrimental to religion, the state and the moral order was not permitted either!

According to a register compiled in 1782 half of the members were of noble birth and a quarter belonged to the clergy. Nearly all the members were in the service of the Elector; the few who did not belong to the civil service were foreign diplomats, doctors and lawyers, with no more than a couple of businessmen. But a teacher of singing, Heideloff, who had rendered notable services to the arts, an indubitable member of the middle class, exerted considerable influence in the society. Ladies and students were not admitted, and this latter restriction was frequently criticized. The Mainz society followed a distinctive political line: it was anti-Jesuit and supported enlightened reforms. Fifteen of the members were also members of the Order of Illuminati. This society was to become the model for reading societies in Aschaffenburg (1783), Trier (1783) and Coblence (1783) – all three of them cities in the electorate of Mainz – as well as in Bonn (1787) – which was in the electoral archdiocese of Cologne.

The Learned Reading Society of Mainz, like many other similar societies, did not survive for very long: it was dissolved in 1790. However, in that same year another reading society was founded in association with the bookbinder Sartorius, and nine years later a 'corresponding reading circle' was started.

For our second example we may turn to a society that brought together the upper classes of a rural district that lacked a capital city, the Reformed Moral Society of Toggenburg.[9]

In the eighteenth century Toggenburg was a flourishing centre of rural industries in the foothills of the eastern Swiss Alps. It was under the rule of the Prince Abbot of St Gallen, but in fact enjoyed a fair measure of autonomy under the protection of Zurich and Berne. In the summer of 1767 the county clerk, Andreas Giezendanner, proposed the founding of a society to raise funds for the acquisition of a selection of works on moral and historical subjects; the society would foster 'the intercourse of close friends, to the benefit of the whole community'. Fifteen members responded to his appeal – nine of them were clergymen – and on 24 August 1767 they formed the Reformed Moral Society of Toggenburg. The society, which never numbered more than forty members, embraced the intellectual elite of the Protestant and Reformed majority in this confessionally mixed county. The members were parsons, senior bureaucrats, businessmen, manufacturers and doctors. They were joined at the very beginning by a crofter, trader and part-time man of letters called Ulrich Bräker, the 'poor man in Toggenburg'. His candidature was accepted only after a certain amount of debate, for he could scarcely be regarded as ranking with the rural gentry. However, Bräker proved to be a very active member, and his growing literary reputation – fostered by literary circles in Zurich – soon gave him the necessary status.

The society, whose motto was *Ordine et Concordia* ('By order and harmony'), required its members to donate books, which were then lent out. An annual general meeting was held in Lichtensteig, the chief town of the county. Two chairmen and a secretary conducted the business and an address was delivered on a topic of moral or utilitarian interest; in 1790, for instance, Bräker spoke about the poor law. The society's main function, however, was the expansion of its library and the selecting of suitable purchases for it. The works it bought dealt mainly with theology, history, the natural sciences and Switzerland; *belles-lettres* were not represented to a large degree, although the society did possess the works of William Shakespeare.

The society remained somewhat elitist and self-satisfied until 1787, when the county clerk, Josef Meyer, sharply criticized the way in which it had been run hitherto:

We bow deeply to one another, and amid a wondrous bustling to and fro and an equally wondrous babble of voices, we exchange the most courteous and amiable expressions of pleasure, each of us asserting how cordially delighted he is to see the other looking so well and cheerful. Observing all manner of ceremonial of this kind, which we must not neglect any more than we neglect various other trivialities, we duly seek out our appointed places, having regard to proper precedence, and sit down. Then our duly appointed treasurer submits his annual report as apprehensively as he had assumed his responsibilities a year previously, and we congratulate him on his auspicious delivery. We approve our chairman's accounts with well-merited applause and thanks and confirm him and his fellow-chairmen in their appointments, or request them kindly to bear us in mind in future. And so we come to the discussion as to which masterpieces of reason, wit and imagination we should acquire from our annual fees and contributions, and with which new German or French titles we might enlarge and enhance our library stock.

Finally we pay out our reading dues and take leave of each
other as fondly and courteously as we greeted each other at
the beginning. Obviously, this may be all well and good,
but if we are to be quite frank, we would have to admit that
it benefits no one other than the members present at the
meeting. For we are the only people who enjoy once a year
the pleasure of a well-turned discourse, often couched in
witty and ironic terms. We are the only people to benefit
from our library, which we augment as we add to our
wardrobe, in keeping with the latest fashion. And finally,
only such topics as seem suitable to our little society and
in keeping with the views of its honourable members are
ever proposed for debate – only to be promptly forgotten
once they have been briefly aired. In short, our social
gatherings are concerned only with our good selves, as
though each of us had resolved to become wiser, cleverer,
and hence happier, to the benefit of no one but ourselves.

These remarks precipitated a crisis which was up to a point
political: the clerical members especially wanted nothing to do
with any enlargement of the society's aims, such as was implied
by Josef Meyer. On the occasion of the annual general meeting
in 1791, when fifteen members had partaken of a communal
lunch at the 'Pike' inn – in the best of spirits – the society's
activities were suspended until 1797, when it was proposed that
they be resumed in what were undoubtedly stirring times. The
general upheaval in 1798 made this impossible, however, and it
was not until the years between 1820 and 1824 that attempts
were made to resurrect the old society. These culminated ultimately in the founding of a new, and less select, literary society,
which took over the function of its predecessor.

The Toggenburg Moral Society was essentially a reading society, although it acquired something of a literary character, by
virtue of the lectures and discussions it promoted. The reference
to morality in its title suggested certain utilitarian or charitable
purposes which were not effectively realized: these purposes
were left to other 'moral', i.e. voluntary charitable, societies that
were dedicated to improving actual living standards.

5

Voluntary Charitable and 'Economic' Societies

Scientific academies and reading societies were not as a rule primarily intended to engage in practical social activities; they served the mutual edification of their members or the study and cultivation of *belles-lettres*. Public welfare in a much wider sense – from poor law administration to agrarian reform – was the business of societies specifically founded to promote economic advances and improve social services. They were commonly known as 'utilitarian' or 'economic' societies. The earliest of these societies to make a name for itself was the Society for the Improvement of Husbandry, Agriculture and other Useful Arts, founded in 1731 in the Anglo-Irish city of Dublin. A similar society was founded in London in 1754, and these two societies served as models for the continent of Europe. Soon, such societies sprang up everywhere – for example, in the French provinces, the Sociétés royales d'agriculture; in the Habsburg Empire, the Imperial and Royal Agricultural Societies; in Spain and its overseas dependencies, the Sociedades de los Amigos del País. Depending on their location, the societies concerned themselves either with reform of the urban infrastructure or with the improvement of living conditions in the countryside.[10]

Let us take the earliest and most successful of these bodies, the Dublin Society, as an example. It was founded as a consequence of the Irish famine of 1724. It was the English gentry in Ireland who best understood the catastrophic consequences of English

123

policy in Ireland, which entailed the destruction of the indigenous Roman Catholic economic system and confiscation of the land. It was these English landowners who had settled in Ireland who were determined to make something of the country.[11]

In 1731 a philanthropist with an interest in economic matters, Thomas Prior, and an extraordinarily energetic Anglican clergyman, Samuel Madden, together with a dozen other individuals of like mind founded the society. From the outset its aims were eminently practical:

> The members of the society do not mean to entertain the public with ingenious and elaborate speculations nor to enrich the academic world with novel and remarkable observations; their aim is to encourage the ordinary, hardworking craftsman, they wish to bring practical and useful knowledge out of libraries into the light of day. In short, their sole intent is to be of benefit to the public, whether this aim is achieved by new discoveries, or by the publication of discoveries already made, or by the dissemination of knowledge to a wider public.

We might detect in these remarks an implied criticism of the academies – the Royal Society, for instance, which was 'merely' concerned with the pure sciences. As far as the Dublin Society was concerned, what mattered was not theory but practice. Every member was expected to choose a particular subject and to specialize in natural history, agriculture, horticulture, trade or manufacture. The results would be communicated through the society's journal, the *Dublin Society's Weekly Observations*: 'The Dublin Society sees its principal task as the advancement of the spirit of industry (i.e. of trades and crafts) in our country and it will continue to pursue this aim by publishing instructions regarding husbandry and other useful occupations.' The society's proceedings were also published in the *Observations*, along with statistics and accounts of new inventions. The intention was to bring research in Britain and elsewhere to the notice of the Irish public and in this way to overcome the country's isolation.

Awards and distinctions played an important part: competitions related to specific subjects were one means of stimulating general interest. Awards were given for the best imitations of foreign lace, for textiles in general, for the draining of water-logged land, for the brewing of cider, beer and gooseberry wine, for the best bread and for new methods of catching fish.

A model farm was developed and model industrial plant erected. The society was also concerned to promote Irish art and an Academy of Art was even founded in Dublin. From the very start, efforts had been made to build up a library, and it eventually became one of the most important libraries in Ireland.

The society derived its income initially from voluntary contributions by the Irish gentry, but in the 1750s the Irish parliament began to vote substantial subsidies for the society and it was soon granted a royal charter. Its continued existence was thus secured, and in 1981 it was able to celebrate its 250th anniversary.

Its success was so notable that in 1754 a similar society for England was founded in London – the Society for the Encouragement of Arts, Manufactures and Commerce. The Dublin Society had succeeded in enlisting the support of the leading classes of society, and its general character, commitment to the common good in the broadest sense – from industry to agriculture – provided the model for the whole movement involving what were often called 'patriotic societies', i.e. public charities and associations devoted to social and economic progress.

An example of a society specifically concerned with crafts and industrial development was the Lunar Society in Birmingham.[12] It came into being more or less in association with the London Society of Arts, which had been founded in 1754 to encourage the arts, industry and trade. In 1700, Birmingham in Warwickshire was still a small market town in the English Midlands. Then rapid industrial expansion began, largely led by Dissenters, non-Anglican Puritans with outstanding business acumen. By 1760 Birmingham, with its 30,000 inhabitants, was already a considerable urban centre. In its Boulton-Soho Works it possessed a machine factory of international reputation, a business that drew its customers from far and wide. From about 1765 a group of friends – manufacturers, inventors and designers – began to meet at the home of Matthew Boulton, an eminent businessman. This gathering took place once a month at the time of the full moon.

It was not until 1775 that the group formed itself into the Lunar Society. It subsequently drew up statutes, but otherwise its organization was relatively loose. It took care in selecting its members, for it wished to remain a circle of personal friends, and its members were in fact often related to each other. The scientific standard was notably high.

The members of the Lunar Society belonged to the class of businessmen during the early phase of the Industrial Revolution, i.e. they came from the English middle class. Apart from Boulton himself, the prominent members included the Scottish scientist, William Small, who had earlier been a professor in William and Mary College, Virginia, and, notably, James Watt, also of Scottish origin. Watt had first come to Birmingham as an instrument-maker and had formed a business partnership with Boulton. He was an indefatigable researcher and experimenter who was able to apply his discovery of steam power to industrial processes. The Lunar Society also counted among its members – as it could not fail to do in this century – a leading progressive physician, William Withing.

The society went on meeting monthly, but it also held an annual general meeting, and its members conducted a widespread correspondence. Its activity consisted in an exchange of information about scientific findings, mainly in technology, optics, astronomy, chemistry, mineralogy and botany. The members conducted their experiments in their own works, and the founding members virtually constituted a research team, whose collaboration was facilitated by their business connections. They could indeed boast of considerable scientific achievements, although fluctuations in the economy were liable to have an adverse effect on their efforts.

The members were also concerned with the development of the rapidly growing city of Birmingham. They took the lead in building hospitals and roads, in lighting the streets and in the provision of sewerage. They also held discussions on the supply of commodities, including problems of the workers' diet.

Towards the end of the century the society's activity began to dwindle. In the disorders of 1791, distant tremors from the earthquake of the French Revolution, the homes and laboratories of some of the members were wrecked. That brought the society to an end, but its fame long survived the relatively brief period of its activity.

As our third example we might take the organization of the Sociedades de los Amigos del País, which co-ordinated the progressive public activities of an enlightened Spanish monarchy.[13]

The movement was initiated by the chief minister of King Carlos III, Pedro Rodriguez, Count of Campomanes, who held office from 1762 until 1791. The first such society made its appearance in the Basque region in 1764. The proximity of a French agricultural society in Auch in Gascony, with branches in Dax and St Gaudens, may have played some part here: it had been founded only two years earlier. The Real Sociedad Bascongada de los Amigos del País was promptly granted a royal charter.

Some ten years later the Council of Castille, of which Campomanes was treasurer, recommended the local nobility to set up similar societies. Here, again, it was a question of the state seeking to encourage local initiative on the part of the upper classes. Such societies would aim to encourage and promote education, social services, agriculture (including appropriate training establishments), industrialization and commerce. Their models were the Académie des Sciences in Paris, the Royal Society, the Dublin Society and the Berne Society. Between 1770 and 1811 about seventy *sociedades* were founded in the mother country, and between 1780 and 1822 a good dozen in the viceregencies. They were extremely active until the French Revolution and its aftermath – war and a French occupation. They were in part revived in the nineteenth century, but never again achieved the significance they had had as a driving force in the two or three decades preceding the Revolution.

In the case of Spain the movement naturally affected the colonies as well as the mother country: Campomanes's appeal led to the founding of *sociedades* in all the viceregal territories in the years after 1780, both in Latin America (in Lima and Quito) and in the Philippines. The Lima Society also had a literary section and acted as a publisher. 'Patriotic' or 'economic' societies were founded in Buenos Aires, Caracas, Puerto Rico and in the Mexican city of Chiapas as late as the period between 1812 and 1819. These societies must be seen, of course, against the background of an anti-colonial revolution.

We might at this point usefully single out an example of the *sociedad* movement from Latin America. When Don Francisco de Viedma, Governor of Santa Cruz de la Sierra in the viceregency of Peru, set about compiling a geographical and statistical account of his province, the present-day Bolivian district of Cochabamba, he had occasion to mention the Spanish Sociedades de los Amigos del País. He referred specifically to the first of them, the Basque Society: it was common knowledge, he goes on, that it was modelled on the academies of natural science in London and Paris; it was also a matter of common knowledge how much these societies had benefited their respective provinces, their cities and even local villages. The society in Quito had devoted its efforts especially to the care of the poor in that city, thanks to the patriotic zeal (*del patriótico celo*) of a priest, José Pérez Calama. Viedma further refers to an article in the *Mercurio Peruan* of 19 January 1792. The establishment of this society had led to a general increase in activity under the leadership of the local officials, who were collaborating to the best of their ability. Finally, a similar society had been started in 1788 not far from Cochabamba, in Charcas (now Sucre) on the initiative of the archbishop and the Governor. It was now high time for the city of Cochabamba, Don Viedma's administrative headquarters, to undertake something on the same lines.

These observations from the remote and isolated highlands of the Andes and the viceregency of Peru indicate just how widely the idea of the *sociedad* had spread its influence.

6

Agricultural Economic Societies

A particular type of voluntary utilitarian society was the so-called economic society, which dealt mainly or exclusively with problems of the agrarian economy. That part of the population that did not live in towns was for the most part engaged in farming and in fact represented a majority of a country's inhabitants. During the course of the eighteenth century, agriculture – particularly arable farming in Central Europe – found itself in a crisis which was more acutely felt than any previous crisis. People were accustomed to the fact that poor harvests due to adverse weather conditions, or sometimes for political or military reasons, might lead occasionally to privation, shortages and even famine. The eighteenth century tried to cope with such cycles of poor harvests and the problems of uneconomic farming by reforms based on scientific knowledge. It turned out that the agrarian structure which had become established in the period since the fourteenth century was no longer capable of meeting contemporary demands. The three-field farming system meant that every year a third of the arable land was left fallow. The cycle – winter wheat, summer wheat, fallow land – could be dispensed with, if the soil was better prepared. A change in the rotatory system, however, would entail political intervention in the traditional village structure, and changes in the system of tolls and levies. Were tithes to be levied, for example, on land newly brought into production, or on new-fangled crops, such as potatoes?

Landowners would have to seek changes in land use, e.g. by turning unprofitable grazing into arable land, or by cutting down the area of common land, even by confiscating it. As things were, no one had any interest in improving common land, so that its yield was correspondingly meagre. The conservation of woodland had also become a vital issue. Such measures as were actually taken tended to deprive the poorer population of their common rights to graze a cow or a goat, or to gather firewood, so that fresh social problems arose which were left for the nineteenth century to solve.

A further problem was the need to increase output to satisfy a growing market: an expanding population now had more diverse requirements than previously. Improvement of the soil might help, grazing might be improved by growing more fodder crops, the yield of arable crops might be increased by improving fertilizers and irrigation. Potatoes might be planted to augment cereal crops; vegetables, fruit and wine, cattle and dairy produce might all be improved in quality. Pests could be eliminated by modern methods and new land gained by draining marshes. The regulation of water-courses, their tributaries and outfalls was another obvious necessity. There were problems of storing foodstuffs to be coped with, i.e. the effective use of drying methods to conserve produce. There was also the question of improved technical equipment – more modern ploughs and other agricultural machinery. Finally, there were problems of accessibility and communication which could be solved only by the construction and upgrading of roads.

The most pressing problem, however, was the current crisis. It was, in fact, often a poor harvest that set in motion the forces leading to the founding of an economic society. Short-term measures might be taken, but there was an increasing tendency to look for long-term solutions, and here a liberalization of trade designed to overcome the monopolistic isolation of each state authority seemed to offer the best hope of salvation. Attempts were also made, however, to cope with climatic problems, and this meant the start of regular meteorological observations. Finally, there were the problems of rural households, hygiene and schooling.

A highly controversial issue frequently discussed was that of cottage industries – the encroachment of manufacturing industry on to the rural scene. Some saw in this the doom of a world that, with all its attendant traditional values, was worth preserving and developing; others believed that real poverty could be alleviated only through this kind of industrialization.

The general situation – especially the reform movement in landowning circles of the aristocracy – was noted in a French economic encyclopedia that came out in a new edition in Paris in 1767:

The laudable desire to improve the soil and to improve the appearance of our rural properties by the cultivation of new crops has advanced by leaps and bounds. Formerly there were very few people in France who thought about the importance of our rural economy. Now, however, science is held in high esteem by our nobility, and many aristocrats may now be seen to devote all their time to managing their estates, having come to realize the difference between managing one's own property and a ruinous talent for squandering its revenue. The urge to cultivate one's own estate has become, if you like, something of a fashion, but it is a very felicitous fashion which produces a real profit, and we only wish that it may persist . . . We have followed the example of classical Greece and Rome, and of Holland and England. The rest of Europe, which is already strongly influenced by French manners, has hastened to copy us. The importance and the seriousness of our modern taste has been duly noted. We are the reason why agriculture has been reformed and much improved in this fair quarter of the universe.[14]

The author is at least partly right. The agrarian movement did indeed hark back to classical authors such as Cato and Columella. Holland in the seventeenth century, with its intensive methods of agriculture, had become a model, precisely through its celebrated landscape painters. England, or rather, Great Britain, had had a start of some decades over France in the development of modern agricultural methods. The gentlemen farmers of the day had long been preceded by the country gentry who occupied leading political positions in the land. It had been the Irish gentry who had created in the Dublin Society the first example of the way in which all the necessary conditions for agrarian improvement might most easily be achieved through collaboration in an economic society. Even before the founding of the London Society, the influence of the British agrarian movement had spread to the Continent: in 1753 the Accademia dell'agricoltura ossia degli Georgofili (the Society of Farmers' Friends) had been established in Florence; in 1754 the Academy of Useful Sciences was founded in Erfurt, a town in the electorate of Mainz; in 1757 there followed a Société d'agriculture in Rennes, the principal town of Brittany and, in 1759, the Bernese Economic Society. By then the barriers had all been broken down. In 1764 Spain joined the movement with its Real Sociedad Bascongada de los Amigos del País, and in 1765 Austria joined in with an Agricultural Society in Carinthia. In the wake of the founding of the Dublin Society we can count more than one hundred such foundations in Europe and the Americas.

The contribution to progress made by these 'economic' societies consisted largely in their realization of the distressed condition of agriculture and in their awareness that administrative practices and production methods were outdated. It was on the basis of this realization that they began to encourage and to emulate in an attempt to escape from stagnation. This is what the Enlightenment meant to the aristocrats and 'patriotic' landowners and the farming community at large. They were no longer satisfied with mere side issues, with household hints and advice on husbandry: they were intent on promoting agriculture as a whole by soundly reasoned measures and major suggestions for improvement.

Among the societies that were primarily concerned with the reform of agriculture on a large scale was the Société d'agriculture, de commerce et des arts, établie par les Etats de Bretagne.[15]

Brittany, once a duchy, and still with its own assembly, was situated on the outskirts of the centralized French state. Its agriculture was going through a major crisis: attempts to revive it undertaken during the first half of the century by local squires had remained few and far between, because they were not supported by the larger landowners and because the necessary theoretical and technical knowledge was lacking.

In 1757, however, after a long period of preparation, it proved possible to found a regional society for the advancement of agriculture, commerce and crafts in Rennes. It was created by an astonishingly united effort of the entire upper class of Brittany: the landed aristocracy of ancient or more recent lineage, aristocratic circles associated with the supreme court, the *parlement*, and businessmen of noble or middle-class origin. There were even a number of the clergy, including the Bishop of Rennes. Since these groups represented a majority in the provincial assembly, they had no difficulty in achieving official recognition for the Société d'Agriculture – and hence the necessary financial support. No doubt local pride and patriotism played a part in founding the society. This may have been the main motive for many members of the ancient Breton aristocracy who were not all that interested in agricultural innovation as such.

The society's programme envisaged the introduction of artificially fertilized and irrigated fields, the cultivation of new crops, the dissemination of new ways of increasing crop yield and increasing trade, and the improvement of marginal land. Finally, liberalization of the corn trade was also considered.

The programme corresponded to the ideas of the 'physiocrats', which were the subject of animated discussion at the time. In Brittany, Montaudoin and Abeille, the secretary of the society, were ardent supporters of the physiocrats.

The society published memoranda and promoted competitions and was particularly keen to contact the peasant population. *Bureaux secondaires* (branch offices) were opened in a number of regional centres: Dol, St-Malo, St-Brieux, Tréguier, St-Pol de Léon, Quimper and Vannes. Data considered necessary for a better knowledge of the province were gathered together in a *Corps d'observation*, the first volume of which appeared in 1757/58. It was produced by Abeille and a certain Védier, who represented the central government. The latter died in 1762 and this proved to be a serious setback for the society, which suffered a further blow only three years later when its secretary was suspected of having had a hand in the publication of an article on the royal revenues in Brittany, which had incurred the disapproval of the old aristocracy. As a result Abeille was obliged to leave Brittany, and the society was discredited in the eyes of the central government and the provincial assembly.

It did try to recover its lost prestige, although it now tended to concentrate on the encouragement of commerce, so that, from 1769, the society attracted more support from the towns. It was in a position to publish a second volume of its *Corps d'observation* in 1772, but its activities had to some extent been crippled – and not simply for political reasons.

As was so often the case in the French provinces, there were too few landlords (mainly the nobility) who farmed their estates themselves. Even if they took an interest in agriculture, they were frequently ignorant of the state of affairs in the industry generally. What interest the nobility had in their estates was mainly concerned with the breeding of horses. The main problem the society had, however, was its failure to get through to the actual farming community. Attempts were made to do so through publication, but this proved to be ineffective: it had to be admitted that the farmers and peasants simply laughed and took no further notice. The society's plans foundered, because the ignorance and poverty that prevailed in Brittany turned out to be an insuperable obstacle.

The sole concrete success of the Société d'Agriculture was scored in the matter of land reclamation. The attempt to lay down artificially fertilized and irrigated pasture produced a number of successful experiments. Only slow progress was made in propagating potatoes as a crop, even when, in collaboration with the royal Governor in Brittany, seed potatoes were imported from Belle-Ile in America in 1774 and distributed throughout the province. This was probably the last campaign mounted by the society.

Already in 1770 a section of the nobility in the provincial assembly had refused to vote the necessary credits, and the king's Governor noted at the time that this portended the demise of the society. Activity did in fact decline steadily, and fifteen years later it was observed that the society had long since ceased to exist. Attempts to revive it came to nothing. What remained, however, was the fact that a serious attempt at improvement had been made, and in the long run this did have an effect in encouraging agriculture.

The society in Brittany was in fact the model for the founding of a highly successful Economic Society in Berne.[16] Berne was the largest of the city states north of the Alps and constituted by far the largest cantonal territory in Switzerland. It was subject to the efficient, if somewhat patriarchal, government of the patrician families who lived in the capital. They were responsible for the upkeep of roads and the conservation of woodlands, but otherwise tended to leave things as they were and looked back on a policy of industrialization that had not proved to be successful. As a rule these patrician families owned more or less extensive estates which they generally still managed themselves. Most of the officials (*Landvögte*) in rural districts had an intimate knowledge of their own constituencies. A traditional work ethos that was associated with the Reformed Church had coincided with the Enlightenment idea of public obligation. Encouraged by news of the societies in Dublin and London, as well as by the tendency of the Natural Science Association of Zurich to deal with agricultural topics, a group of patricians, led by a former *Landvogt*, Samuel Engel, and a landowner, Johann Rudolf Tschiffeli, proceeded to found an economic society in 1759. It was initially planned for the canton of Berne, but was intended ultimately to apply to the whole of Switzerland.

Berne was just emerging from something of an agricultural crisis. The winter of 1756/57 had been prolonged and in July 1757 the cold and rainy weather still persisted. The grain had to be harvested and brought into the barn when it was still wet, so that it began to sprout. Tithes, on which the state depended for its revenue, had sunk to a record low level.

The society's aim was the same as it had been elsewhere: 'The society's aim is to encourage and improve the cultivation of the soil, to raise the standard of nutrition and stimulate commerce, i.e. to increase the yield from the land, to improve the processing of the produce and to facilitate the marketing of the same.' In so far as these aims applied to the agrarian economy, it was stated that 'the most economical approach is that which achieves a relatively abundant yield with a minimum of seed, land and labour'.

The society had a three-tiered organization. A 'Grand Society' was responsible for promulgating and judging the prize competitions in formal session once a year. A meeting of an 'Intermediate Society' once a month was responsible for the society's accounts and for drafting the terms of the competitions and assessing the entries. The 'Minor Society' met once a week (once a month in the summer) and actually conducted the business of the society, including its correspondence. By 1798 the total number of members was 184, of whom about half were active participants in the society's affairs. They were mostly land-owning patricians, together with parsons, physicians, professors and businessmen. No more than a couple of farmers were admitted to membership, and that was during the early years of the society's existence.

The society's journal, *Proceedings and Observations*, was published in two versions, French and German: the canton was bilingual, and the necessity of a French version was also dictated by the society's aim of reaching an international readership. This publication rapidly became known throughout Europe; it was widely consulted and gained as much influence as the English journals, if not more. A comprehensive correspondence was developed with other parts of Switzerland, and with England, France, Spain, Sweden, Denmark, Germany, The Netherlands, Poland and Italy. Entries submitted for the society's competitions were published in this journal.

In 1761 branches of the society were opened to serve various regions of the canton more effectively. There were about a dozen of these, and the upper classes throughout the canton, the clergy and local government officials were thus drawn into the scheme. At the same time independent economic societies were founded in the neighbouring federal cities of Freiburg, Solothurn and Biel; they all had close ties with the Berne society.

In the *Proceedings*, the agricultural, scientific and geographical sections predominated, accounting for about 70 per cent of the contents and dealing with such subjects as cereal farming, irrigation, viticulture, treatment of fertilizers, soil science, cattle breeding, the partition of common land, Alpine farming and land reclamation. No more than 8 per cent of items dealt with trade and industry, which did not bulk large in the economy of Berne. Topographical and statistical accounts of various areas of the canton and other parts of Switzerland were an important feature.

Then there were reports of various projects undertaken by individual members of the society: the development of an estate into a model farm, practical experiments in the surrounding countryside, meteorological observations, the propagation of novel farming methods. All this activity was carried on in close collaboration with the farming community itself. However, the society did not go as far in this respect as the Natural Science Research Society of Zurich, also founded in 1759, the economic section of which organized 'farmers' colloquia', at which members of the society were able to hold discussions with farmers themselves.

The high regard in which the Berne society was held is illustrated in a report written by Count Karl von Zinzendorf, who had visited this highly developed neighbouring country on behalf of the Austrian minister of state, Kaunitz: 'The Economic Society of Berne is the mother of all similar institutions that have since been founded in France, England, Germany and in Switzerland itself.' Even if this observation is not entirely accurate – especially as regards England – it indicates the degree to which the Berne society was regarded as leading the field. Zinzendorf goes on to speak of the activities of individual members of the society:

The society consists of very worthy and capable members, including the president, Herr Sinner, and both the Tscharner brothers. They themselves carry out experiments and award prizes. An extremely active and useful member is the vice-president, clerk to the cathedral chapter, Herr Tschiffeli. This worthy and admirable patriot has achieved very notable results in the irrigation of grazing land on a small farm which he has in Kilchberg. His principal aim is to see that the land is evenly watered, and some of his drainage ditches have a twofold function: they serve to drain the land, but they also conduct the water over fresh beds where it absorbs nutrients before being collected once more and used to water adjacent pastures to greater effect. He believes it is of vital importance not to allow grazing land to be irrigated with water that has not been thus treated.[17]

Zinzendorf strikes one critical note in his account of the society: 'It does the government little credit that the society has so far enjoyed very little support from that quarter.' Only two years later the society did in fact fall out with the Bernese administration. The conservatives in the government had never looked kindly on the society's economic activities, and an article in the society's journal on the population of Vaud gave them the pretext they had been looking for. Discussion of population statistics suggested an intrusion into the political and military sphere. A majority in the government, including its leader, now attempted in effect to cripple the society's activities. A trial of strength began between progressive forces and the entrenched element of the patrician class. It proved possible to save the society in Berne itself: the presidency was taken over by Albrecht von Haller, who was politically unassailable. The branch societies perished, however, since their activities were now made subject to supervision by the local *Landvögt*. The Society's work in Berne continued, but at a very low level: it was given government contracts for reports on the regulation of mountain streams, on pest control and on mulberry plantations. In 1771 harvest statistics were compiled in collaboration with the government, and in 1787 the society conducted a survey of livestock. Under Haller's presidency, however, it turned to the less contentious subject of the natural sciences. In the 1770s, under the chairmanship of Nikolaus Emanuel Tscharner, the society once again devoted its attention to economic topics. By the time of the French Revolution, however, it seemed generally more like a patriotic learned society without specific practical aims.

7

The Freemasons

The Freemasons occupied a leading place among the protagonists of the Enlightenment.[18] It was their association that provided a constitutional and organizational framework for the general aims and ideas of the movement. Masonry was international in structure and cosmopolitan in spirit. Freemasons were soon to be found everywhere in government and in reforming societies.

Freemasonry went back to the tradition of the 'free masons', who were employed in the building of cathedrals and who formed associations resembling guilds which survived in Anglican England through the Reformation and the Counter-Reformation. In the seventeenth century, these craftsmen began to admit into their ranks certain of their noble patrons and other interested individuals, particularly surveyors and scientists. These new members began to dominate the association, while the craft element receded more and more into the background. What remained and was further developed was the association's ethos, its customs and ritual. Italian heretics living abroad played some part in introducing certain ideas of the *Accademie*. The successes of the Royal Society and the powerful upsurge of the Enlightenment in England generally also helped to advance the movement. On 24 June 1717, Midsummer's Day, or St John's Day (St John is the Freemasons' patron), the London lodges combined to form the Grand Lodge of England, which adopted the firm organization embodied in Anderson's Constitutional Articles.

The Grand Master of the Grand Lodge of England was the supreme head of all the lodges which shared the same organization. The members were divided into apprentices, journeymen and masters, ranks through which they all had to pass in succession.

The meetings comprised a formal dinner, a lecture and discussion, followed by the collection of an offertory. St John's Day was a particularly solemn festival: 'Every quarter, or at least once a year, on the day of St John the Baptist or St John the Evangelist, as our Grand Master deems fit, we meet for a love-feast which is attended by the masters, journeymen and apprentices of all the lodges.' Equality between the brothers from all the lodges

> was observed, without regard to precedence or disputes relating thereto. Everyone takes his seat at the festive board as he happens to arrive, so that if a common workman sits down next to a duke, the latter will converse with him in as intimate, cordial and amicable a fashion as if it were his born brother. It is amazing that, in spite of the large number of guests (often 500 or so), the whole affair is carried off in such a calm, decorous and friendly fashion, and the meal concluded in good time . . . Grace is said by the Grand Master himself, or else he requests one of the brothers in holy orders, or the secretary, to lead a prayer service before and after the meal.

The lodge often maintained a library of its own – rather in the manner of the reading societies. Correspondence with other lodges was an important feature of a lodge's activity.

A strong sense of solidarity prevailed among the brothers of a lodge:

> If one of the brethren is arrested for debt, then his debts are paid as soon as a certificate of his honest character has been submitted.
> A brother who is sick and who has not the means to provide for his own needs receives from the lodge of which he is a member the sum of two guineas per week, provided that his indisposition has not been brought about by dissipa-

tion and loose living. The lodge's physician, surgeon and apothecary are prepared to minister to him free of charge and to provide him with such care, service and remedies as he needs. These three medical practitioners are paid a stipend by each lodge.

The Freemasons were conscious of standing at a turning-point where the middle ages, merging into the period of the baroque, were giving way to the dawn of a new light. They meant to invest the ancient symbols of the building of the Temple with fresh meaning. This entailed a new interpretation of Christian tradition in a humanitarian and enlightened sense. Here we may sense the background of the Glorious Revolution with its reduction of social and confessional differences and its emphasis on the rights of the individual citizen. Freemasonry was an expression of the need to inspire religious ties that had become outworn or fossilized with a new vital meaning through the spirit of brotherhood. The Constitutional Articles state that a Freemason should be an individual imbued with goodwill and humane feeling, a 'good human being', loyal, guided by honour and decency. He should be a friend to rich and poor alike, in so far as they are virtuous. This was later put in the following terms in a tract published in 1746 and designed to defend the Order: 'The Society of Freemasons has no aim other than to foster peace and harmony among men. Every civilized state should afford its members protection, if it is interested in its own welfare and happiness.' In the language of the Freemasons this is expressed as 'continuing to build the Temple of Solomon'. What they seek is the 'Kingdom of God on Earth'.

The movement saw itself as rooted in very ancient Christian ideas; on the other hand, it stood for a modern, enlightened version of Christianity – or simply for a religion of Nature. Differences between the confessions were glossed over, Anglicans, Dissenters, Roman Catholics (in 1772, a Catholic, Lord Robert Petre, had become Grand Master of the Grand Lodge of England) – they all joined, and even Jews were eligible for membership at a very early stage.

The Freemasons' lodges thus offered an object lesson in tolerance: it seems that the movement met a need in this age for the breaking down of narrow confessional barriers. At the same time the Freemasons upheld traditions to which each confession might subscribe.

The age-old Masonic rituals and their symbols were to be protected from public profanation by a strict pledge of secrecy:

> Soldiers have their ensigns by which their regiments are distinguished one from the other, their officers have watchwords by which they recognize each other in war and peace . . . And we, too, have certain words by which we recognize and acknowledge each other, e.g. Jachin, Boas, set-square, compasses, plumbline, Kütt, Hiram, Solomon, etc.

It was in fact the element of secrecy which exerted a powerful attraction in a world that seemed to many to be growing increasingly shallow and boring.

Freemasonry very rapidly achieved phenomenal success. In 1725, only eight years after its founding, there were as many as fifty-two lodges in Great Britain alone. By 1730, the idea had been spread – mainly by British aristocrats and officers, often by Jacobite refugees – first to France, then to Spain and to the French, Spanish and British colonies. At the same time it was also making its way through the whole of Italy – especially in Rome, Florence, Milan and Turin – then in The Netherlands, in western Switzerland (Geneva 1736), and from Hamburg (1737) through northern and central Germany, via Berlin and Breslau to Vienna, Prague and Dresden. From Dresden it reached Warsaw. St Petersburg was involved early on; in the 1740s Sweden and Denmark followed, and finally south Germany, Siebenbürgen and Hungary.

By the middle of the century the urban centres of Europe and their overseas dependencies had been gained for the Freemasons' cause, and the movement began to spread into the remoter provinces of the European states. It was mainly the upper classes who joined: Duke Franz Stephen of Lorraine, later to become emperor (1731) and the Prussian Crown Prince Frederick (1738), later king of Prussia, both joined the Freemasons. It was not only the higher and the minor nobility who became members: many scholars and clergymen – particularly the Anglican clergy – joined the Order. In the lodges the higher aristocracy, officials of the courts, advisers and friends of royalty, travelling foreigners, diplomats, bankers, businessmen and the military all met and mingled. New acquaintanceships were made, letters of recommendation were exchanged which opened the doors to the homes of important people. In the lodges vital conversations might be conducted with a degree of intimacy that could not be found elsewhere.

Admittedly there were two obstacles to the movement's progress – one internal, the other external. In 1738 the Roman Catholic Church issued a bull, *In eminenti*, imposing a ban on membership of the Masonic lodges, and it was renewed in 1751, clearly indicating the church's opposition to this aspect of the Enlightenment. The ban proved to be relatively ineffective, however. Even though virtual persecution of the Freemasons began in the grand duchy of Turin in 1743, and the Empress Maria Theresa dissolved the Viennese lodge that same year, while there was spasmodic action against the Order elsewhere, other Catholic states took little notice of the ban. Since the society was in any case a secret society, the lodges that had been disbanded simply continued to exist under other names. It was actually Catholic countries that became the most influential centres of Freemasonry, and Freemasons had considerable influence at certain courts. Even in Protestant states the movement was not entirely free from harassment. The republics of Hamburg, Geneva and Berne, The Netherlands and Sweden banned the lodges for longer or shorter periods – probably for political reasons rather than on theological or religious grounds. What mainly offended the authorities was the swearing of an oath of allegiance to an international organization beyond the jurisdiction of any one state. In the long run, however, all such attempts at intervention were doomed to failure.

What caused more confusion and disruption within Freemasonry was its division, from the 1740s onward, into a number of separate Orders resulting from the evolution of the Masonic ritual. This in turn was a regression of the age as a whole towards archaic or mystical ideas.

In spite of these schisms, the movement lost none of its popularity, and by the end of the century most of those who supported modern ideas were Freemasons.

What linked the Freemasons with other progressive societies, apart from their organizational structure, was a keen interest in the sciences: 'This is where we may find a veritable school of the sciences, the arts and morality, a learned academy, whose members, with their wide range of talents, constitute the most erudite society in the world.' In fact, a large number of scientists did belong to the Masonic Order.

The obligation to take part in charitable enterprises is also worth noting. In England especially, but in other countries as well, this was expressed in a great many moves for economic and social reform, either directly or indirectly (through collaboration with other societies). There were campaigns for the establishing of schools for the poor and almshouses, as well as for the organization of medical services such as vaccination against smallpox.

As was the case with many other societies, the Masonic Order fostered and maintained manifold international connections.

Freemasonry resembled these other societies in stressing the equality of its members within the Order: noblemen and commoners were on the same footing as 'brothers', united and dedicated to a single ideal – the building of the Temple.

The degree to which Masonic ideas might become popular far beyond the confines of the lodges is illustrated by the song, 'Brothers, all join hands to form one bond'. The melody is ascribed to Mozart, who composed in Vienna in 1791, as one of his last works, a 'Masons' Song' with words probably written by Schikaneder. Shortly afterwards, different words were substituted and, as 'The Masons' Song' or 'Song of the Society', it gained wide popularity. It sums up the basic ideas that inspired the reform movement as a whole:

Let us, then, all hand in hand be joined!
In this, our finest festive hour.

Lead us up to lustrous heights,
And banish all our earthly cares!
That union of our brothers may
For ever firm and splendid stay.

Praise and thanks to God our Master
Who our minds and all our hearts
Inspired to join in endless striving
To bring to earth His Justice, Light and Virtue
Through the truth, our hallowed weapon
May this be our godly task!

You, upon our planet here,
The best of men in East and West
And in North as well as South,
Speak the truth and practise virtue,
From the heart love God and man,
Let this be our watchword still![19]

8

The Societies Within the Enlightenment Movement

In the course of the century, society in general became positively riddled with all manner of associations, and where organization was otherwise lacking, the Freemasons tended to fill the gap, especially in eastern Europe. Scientific societies, educational associations and societies devoted to the improvement of trade and industry were the three main types of association during the latter half of the century. Around them were clustered many other societies with the most diverse combinations of enlightened objectives, occasionally of a religious, and sometimes – but rarely – of a political nature.

An Englishwoman, Jane Leade, gathered together adherents of a pietistic or mystical turn of mind in a loosely organized Philadelphian Society, which found a good many supporters in Germany, Holland, Sweden and Finland, as well as in Britain. The Society for the Promotion of Christian Knowledge was an official foundation of the established Anglican Church; it had a marked influence on the teaching of Christianity in England, on education generally and in the fight against illiteracy. Its work was soon complemented by a subsidiary society, the Society for the Propagation of the Gospel in Foreign Parts, the specific purpose of which was the teaching of the Bible among emigrants to North America. Sweden, with its established Lutheran Church followed suit in 1771 through the Societas Suecana pro Fide et Christianismo. This association, too, fought for the dissemination of the Christian faith and sought to promote piety among the masses in response to a progressive decline in moral standards. It was with the same object in view that a group of God-fearing Swabians in Basel founded a German Christian Society in 1780.[20]

Most societies, however, did not specifically profess religious aims: membership of a church, like nationality, was so much taken as a matter of course that it was implied in the spirit and constitution of most organizations. As a rule they did not profess specific political ideas either, but it was in fact the economic and utilitarian societies which had most political influence and effect. Politics in the narrower sense was regarded as a matter for the government, but the societies were indeed concerned with the welfare of their *polis*, their town, or their state in general. They assumed certain functions which the state was not prepared or not competent to fulfil, they filled gaps here and there. If, for example, an agricultural society was formed in Brittany, then it was concerned specifically with that duchy. If Hamburg had its Patriotic Society, then it was concerned with that one Hanseatic city – not in a narrow or nationalistic sense, but in the sense that Brittany and Hamburg were the places where these societies had to work to the benefit of all men, and where they could do so most effectively.

When a number of Swiss from various cantons founded a Helvetian Society in 1761, they were indeed concerned with Switzerland, and meant to promote the cause of the Enlightenment in that country. They wished to arrest the decline in national awareness, a political objective affecting the nation as a whole which at that time could be pursued only by organizing a circle of friends from all the cantons, the individual states that comprised the nation under its federal constitution. This group of friends were in the habit of meeting once a year for a session that lasted a few days, during which informal discussions were held. Since leading representatives from the various reform movements were numbered among its members, the Helvetian Society became a sort of umbrella organization for societies from the different cantons and was ultimately to turn into a kind of national assembly on a voluntary basis. It was unique among the societies of the eighteenth century.[21]

It is true of all societies that they owed a good measure of their support to a local or ecclesiastical elite, consisting of the nobility, the clergy, civil servants and businessmen. In the circle of friends that constituted these societies aristocratic court functionaries or country gentry might meet parsons and middle-class businessmen. Through their relatively liberal membership policy, which attracted individuals from different social classes – occasionally including even artisans and farmers – these numerous societies did a great deal to ease the transition from a society based on rank or guild membership to a middle-class democratic social order, such as was to dominate the nineteenth century. In the monarchies they advanced the emancipation of the middle class, while, in republican states, they helped to reunite the patrician class with the body of the citizenry.

The societies usually began simply as a circle of friends and thus initiated a new kind of social intercourse. However seriously they took their reforming function and pursued the duties that it imposed on them, there was still always time during the meetings for informal conversation and convivial gatherings with food and drink, with coffee, tea, tobacco or wine. There were even societies that admitted women. The latter rarely figured in the membership lists, but they were very much in evidence in the fringe activities of the societies, and not only in purely social contexts. In their social gatherings the societies contrived to strike a sensible balance between the folksy conviviality of the guilds with their carousing and the affected manners of the snobbish court culture.

It became the fashion to take part in the activities of some society or other – and even quite the thing to belong to a number of societies or academies. For example, the Count d'Albon, Prince d'Yvetot, who was closely connected with the physiocrats, wrote a general account of the states of England, Holland and Switzerland, published in 1779, on the title page of which he appears as a 'Member of the Academies of Lyon, Dijon, Rome or Nîmes, Member of the Academy of the Arcades and the Academy de la Crusca, the learned societies of Florence, Berne,

Zürich, Chambéry, Hessen-Homburg, etc., etc.' Who knows how many other academies are suggested by the couple of 'etc.s', but there is no doubt that the Prince was deeply involved in the Enlightenment.

9

Periodicals and Books

Any society that sought to extend its activities over a relatively wide area would publish its own periodical. Journals were, however, not just the prerogative of learned societies: they played an eminent part generally as a new medium of enlightened communication available to a wide readership. They contained not only reports of disasters and crimes from all over the world, but also comments designed to enlighten their readers.

An essential precondition for this form of communication was the existence of printers and publishers able to operate freely, i.e. freedom of the press. At first, this freedom existed only in The Netherlands, particularly in Holland, where freedom meant not only independence from Spain but also tolerance for confessions other than Calvinism. In the seventeenth century anyone wishing to evade censorship sought refuge in Holland. Even the mere fiction of Amsterdam or some other city in The Netherlands as the place of publication was enough to make a book attractive as probably containing critical or subversive matter. Then Great Britain followed the lead of Holland. At the time of the English Restoration the principle still held that 'the printing or publication of any manner of newspaper, pamphlet or other means of communication is forbidden by law'. Then came the Glorious Revolution: John Locke demanded freedom of the press, and when the old Licensing Act expired (licences had mitigated censorship up to a point), Parliament did not renew it and hence permitted complete freedom of the press.

The pattern for the periodicals that were to follow was set between 1710 and 1724 by the *Spectator*, edited by Addison and Steele. Vice and ignorance were to be banished from England and the ethical programme of the Enlightenment proclaimed in their place. The journal purported to be a collection of observations by an English country squire, Sir Roger de Coverly, who visited London as a 'spectator' and recorded his impressions. Along with him there appeared a soldier, Captain Sentry, a businessman, Sir Andrew Freeport, and Will Court, an elderly man-about-town and barrister of the High Court.

In brief essays published each week in the *Spectator* all manner of topics were discussed, e.g. between 24 November and 20 December 1714 the following appeared:

Division of Mankind into Classes
On Eternity
Improper Behaviour in Church
On Cleanliness
On Aiming at Perfection
Enlargement of the Power of the Mind in a Future State.[22]

These essays tended to be larded in each case with quotations from classical authors. Such weekly reports and essays, brief and succinct as they were, soon found favour with readers, and the way was opened for periodicals of every kind, for so-called 'moral weeklies' published in various places and sometimes specializing in particular subjects.

The Continent quickly followed the English example and soon periodicals with a great variety of titles appeared: *Journal, Giornale, Tagebuch, Diario, Zeitung, Gazette, Magazin, Memorias, Mercure* (a French, a German and a Swiss *Mercury*), *Anzeigen, Beiträge* and *Almanache*. A necessary precondition was a discreet censorship, for unlike England the Continent was not free. In 1778 it was reported from Paris, 'The censors of books in Paris are the most reasonable and fair in the whole world . . . Paris is the city where the largest number of newspapers and periodicals is printed: *Journal des Savants, Journal des Sciences et des Beaux Arts, Mercure de France*, etc.'[23] From Berne we hear in 1786: 'Our censorship laws, which were never very strict, are quietly falling into abeyance.'[24]

Every country, indeed practically every city, had its own periodicals, some of which exercised considerable influence on the Enlightenment. Germany, for instance, had *The Patriot* in Hamburg, which appeared from 1724 to 1726 and was edited by a group of five city councillors, two professors, two clergymen, a professional journalist and an academically educated businessman. From 1723 onwards the editors met for a weekly editorial conference. *The Patriot* was a descendant of the English *Spectator* and set out to be a guide for its readers in a bewildering age. It included satires, dialogues, fables, 'dreams', portraits, stories, readers' letters – both authentic and bogus. It aimed to demonstrate the superiority of sound common sense over ignorance, conformism and prejudice. A patriot in the sense in which the word is used by this periodical was an individual of cosmopolitan views, free from prejudice and engaged in practical activities for the benefit of the entire community. The true patriot would make his mark by the credibility of his example. Criticism in *The Patriot* is not directed at the existing social and political order, but at abuses within that order. The journal was to become one of the major publishing successes during the first half of the eighteenth century. In the first nine months the number of copies printed rose from 400 to 5,000, and by 1765 it had appeared as a book in four separate editions.

At about the same time, in another commercial centre, Zurich, a group of young people, half a dozen theologians and a couple of doctors had come together to form a society called The Painters, which met from July to October 1722. From 1721 to 1723 they edited the *Painters' Discussions*, which was also a successor to the *Spectator*. It followed the same patriotic political line, with rather more emphasis on art and literature. The fact that the censor intervened to restrain it suggests that this journal did have some political influence. The prime movers and main supporters of the society and the journal were Johann Jakob Bodmer and Johann Jakob Breitinger, both of them subsequently professors at the University of Zurich.

These examples from Germany and Switzerland may be

augmented by an example from Italy, the Accademia dei Pugni (the Academy of Fists), which was active in Milan from 1764 to 1766, at the very climax of the Enlightenment. It, too, began more or less as a coterie of friends who constituted themselves as a society and planned to approach the public in print with a periodical entitled *Il Caffé*. The titles of the society and its journal suggest an element of self-irony in this lively, indeed frivolous, undertaking. These were the years when the ideas of Rousseau and Helvétius and other daring innovators were in the air. The Accademia dei Pugni was a kind of debating society which included the most astute minds of the Enlightenment in northern Italy: Pietro Verri, Luigi Lambertinenghi, Alfonso Longo and Cesare Beccaria. They used to meet once a week, together with other friends round the white tiled stove in Pietro Verri's home. They discussed the needs of the day, condemned policies of purely pragmatic statesmanship, suggested reforms of a practical nature: *belle virtù, doveri – virtù senza noia*, 'comely virtues, duties – virtues without pedantry'. It was a kind of Italian *Sturm und Drang*, but with a dash of Lombard wit and Latin humanism. But they were not content just to discuss these matters among themselves, they hoped to appeal to the public through *Il Caffè*, and even to intervene and correct defects in the government of the northern Italian states. It was against this background that Marchese Beccaria wrote his epoch-making work, *Dei delitti e delle pene*, which criticized conditions in general and not just the criminal law.

The *Pugni* society ceased to be active after the publication of two volumes of *Il Caffè*, but it was in that society that the ground had been prepared for the Cisalpine Republic.

These are just three examples of periodicals that cherished certain political ambitions alongside their ostensible moral and aesthetic aims. They were also concerned with questions of taste: many journals contained reviews of new books. Indeed, it might well be said of this period in general, 'of making many books there is no end', to quote Solomon in the Old Testament (Ecclesiastes XII, 12), an authority much favoured in the eighteenth century. For this was after all a century much given to 'splattering ink', a time when the inkwell took pride of place on the desk and every quarto sheet was liable to be belaboured with a quill pen in true Enlightenment style.

Part V

Utopia and Reform

1

'Improvement and Dreams'

The terms 'reform' and 'utopia' used by Franco Venturi as the title of his book, *Utopia e Riforma nell'Illuminismo* would have been translated into German in the eighteenth century as 'improvement' and 'dreams'.

Whereas the German philosopher Christian Wolff published his ideas under rationalistic titles – for example *Rational Thoughts on God, the World and the Human Soul, Rational Thoughts on the Powers of Human Understanding*, and *Rational Thoughts on Human Conduct* – between 1713 and 1720, a generation later the Swiss writer Isaak Iselin published his views in 1755 under the title, *Philosophical and Patriotic Dreams of a Philanthropist*, while that solitary French stroller, Jean-Jacques Rousseau, recorded the dreams of his life and work in *Rêveries d'un promeneur solitaire*.

The eighteenth century did in fact dream of a better world – but it was not content with dreaming, it was determined to make the dream come true. This is why we find countless works dealing with the reform of some intolerable contemporary abuse or other. We might quote, almost at random, any number of works in the principal European languages that speak of the need for reform:

Di una riforma d'Italia, 1767, by Carlantonio Pilati – a work that comments critically on the backwardness of Italy and appeals to the princes to introduce reforms of an anti-clerical tendency.

Apuntes para una reforma de España, 1797, by Victorian de

157

Villava, a treasury official in the viceregency of Peru – a similar work dealing with Spain and its colonies.

De l'administration provinciale et de la réforme de l'impôt, 1779, by Guillaume François Le Trosne, a legal officer in Orleans – criticized the privileges embodied in the French economy and made suggestions for the reform of the provincial administration and the rationalization of taxes.

Address to the People of England on the Intended Reformation of Parliament, 1783 – an anonymous publication proposing the modernization of parliamentary representation.

On the Improvement of the Condition of the Jews in Civil Society, 1781, by a Prussian civil servant, Christian Wilhelm Dohm – an enquiry into discrimination against Jews, with suggestions for their emancipation.

Suggestions Regarding the State and the Improvement of Church and School in the Royal Electoral Province of Brunswick-Lüneburg, 1801, by the Hanoverian court preacher and consistorial councillor, Johann Christoph Salfeld – a critical account of the dogmatically fossilized church and the correspondingly backward school system, with suggestions for a more practical approach to pastoral care and preaching and the introduction of more advanced psychological methods in teaching.

On the Need to Improve Husbandry and the Best Means of So Doing, 1760, by Pastor Albrecht Stapfer – an examination of agriculture in Berne with relevant proposals for reform.

These seven works are merely a selection of the many books and pamphlets calling for reform, but they indicate the breadth of the reforming movement, which extends from overall political changes, through reforms in religion, to technical 'improvement'.

Hitherto, 'reform' had had a limited sense. In the military sphere it might mean cutbacks in the numbers of troops following a war, in the textile trade, the shortening of a length of material, or else the relaxation of an ecclesiastical code of discipline. In the form 'reformation' it was widely used, but it was a controversial term, since the Roman Catholic Church refused to recognize its application to certain events in the sixteenth century.

Until the 1770s terms such as *émulation*, *amélioration* or *éducation* had been used and translated into German as *Aufmunterung* (encouragement), *Beförderung* (advancement) and *Erziehung* (education). 'Reform' or 'improvement' had always been understood as referring to non-violent change, and even the term 'revolution' had that sense, retaining something of the original metaphor, 're-volutio', a reversion to an originally better condition. This had been the case with the English and their Glorious Revolution of 1688, which had, as far as possible, been conducted within the law.

The Enlightenment movement evolved in several stages. For the first phase Paul Hazard coined the expression *crise de la conscience européenne*, which may mean a crisis of consciousness as well as a crisis of conscience. This initial phase is marked by a rationalistic reassessment of all previous assumptions and by a comprehensive critical examination of the status quo. The *Dictionnaire historique et critique* (1696/97), edited by the Huguenot emigrant Pierre Bayle, had international influence as the epitome of this process. An intellectual elite then emerged which set about 'improving' the human race. Every member of this elite was inspired by faith in the feasibility of a world which – as Leibniz had said – was in any case the best of all possible worlds. The further the century proceeded, the more optimistic the mood became, since, to quote Jan Huizinga:

> . . . for the first time ever the summons rang out loud and clear – not back into the past, but forward into the future. This was an age that looked for its salvation, not in a supposed resurrection of the past, but in its confidence in its powers of reason and intellect. For the first time mankind was experiencing a vision of a future on this earth rather than a dream of the past! . . . The intrinsic goodness of human nature, its potential for perfection, the advancement of culture – these were now articles of faith. If only reason would follow the path of nature, which was now understood and loved with a purer love than ever before, then everything would turn out for the best.[1]

The ultimate aim may be summed up in Jeremy Bentham's

familiar phrase: 'the greatest happiness of the greatest number'
(1788), a maxim that had already been voiced by Cesare Beccaria
in the *Società dei Pugni* in 1764: *la maggiore felicità divisa sul
maggior numero possible*, or even six years earlier in Isaak Iselin:
'that [in the state] the greatest sum of human happiness ought
to be distributed in a just and proper proportion.' Bentham's
phrase crops up word for word, in fact, as early as 1726 in
Hutcheson![2]

2

Philosophy and Philosophers of the Philosophical Age

Eighteenth-century thinkers liked to refer to their century as a 'philosophical century', and liked to think of themselves as philosophers. During the period of the Enlightenment 'philosophizing' still meant, as it had done in ancient Greece, the pursuit of wisdom, or simply knowledge, an interest in scientific investigation, study, elucidation by a process of cogitation, the acquisition of a knowledge of nature and of man's duties. In an ironic sense a 'philosopher' was a man who was unfamiliar with the real world, or else someone who took life as it came, who stood apart from life's problems. In the eighteenth century, philosophy meant specifically a frank and critical examination of any topic whatsoever – without fear or favour. Any problem might be the subject of philosophy – morals, religion, politics and the state, the arts and sciences – but if the discussion was to remain 'philosophical', it had to proceed on general lines of theory and principle, without mentioning names or institutions, for philosophizing could be a perilous pastime, depending on the constitution of the country where it was practised, and a careful eye had to be kept on the ecclesiastical, as well as the civic powers-that-be in so far as they were not themselves philosophers.

It was possible to philosophize, too, on more modest and mundane topics, such as human virtue and vice, their absurdity and their real value. This is where we find ourselves on the

161

threshold of modern psychology. Philosophical discourse was guided by rational criteria, without bias and taking any number of different aspects into account. It was to be conducted with due reverence for Creation, with a proper regard for ethical principles and with the aim of improving the world. It had room for the malicious satire of a Swift, a Voltaire or a Lichtenberg, as well as for the sentimentality of a Shaftesbury or a Rousseau.

In the final analysis – as in classical times or in the age of humanism – philosophy dealt with fundamental issues: What constitutes knowledge? Are evidence and intuition intelligible modes of communication? What exactly are our sources of knowledge, what lies behind that which we call emotion, and what we call intelligence? The range of topics might be very wide: for example, the French statesman, Henri-François d'Aguesseau, writing at the end of the seventeenth century and the beginning of the eighteenth century, reflects on: man's knowledge, magnanimity, the love of simplicity, the independence of lawyers, the dignity of magistrates, political censorship . . . while the Scottish writer David Hume published brief essays in philosophical terms on the dignity or depravity of human nature, polygamy and divorce, eloquence, passive obedience, the British political parties, national characters . . .

Philosophy, however, had always also been a strict academic subject. University study invariably began in the Faculty of Philosophy, where the professors drummed logic into their students, teaching them mathematical reasoning and geometrical precision. With the Enlightenment, however, this mechanical knowledge was seen in terms of its practical application in the interests of methodical thinking, and was consequently transmitted to a rather wider public.

This was an age when many countries produced eminent philosophers. France began with Descartes and Pascal, England continued with Newton and Locke, Germany had Leibniz, Thomasius and Wolff, Italy had Vico and Muratori, Spain could look back on Gracián.

When people spoke in the middle of the century of the 'philosophers', they meant mainly the group of French writers who took part in the production of the Great Encyclopedia. This enterprise had begun as a project for a French edition of an English encyclopedia, but this had foundered because of disputes between the publisher and the editors. In 1746 publication was entrusted to Denis Diderot. In him the project had found an extraordinarily versatile intellectual, whose interests were truly encyclopedic. His parents had meant him to be a theologian, but he very quickly broke away from the church and became a keen disciple of the Enlightenment. Diderot rapidly brought the *Encyclopédie* project under his personal control and secured it financially through subscriptions from potential users. He was aided by d'Alembert, a level-headed mathematician and moderate philosopher, who was well aware of the limitations of human knowledge and who took his stand on the ground of experience and reason.

The first volume appeared on 1 July 1751: *Encyclopédie ou Dictionnaire raisonné des sciences, des arts et des métiers*, edited by *une société de gens de lettres*. It was an instant success, although (or perhaps because) clerical circles, and the Jesuits in particular, fell upon this 'Satan's Bible' and even contrived to have it banned. The ban had no more than a temporary effect, however, because leading politicians, Madame de Pompadour especially, took the project under their wing. In spite of a host of problems, it was completed after 29 years, in 36 volumes, of which 13 contained plates and illustrations of superb quality. Henceforth a reader could be informed under competent guidance on any topic under the sun, in up-to-date, rational and enlightened terms, with something of an anti-clerical, but by no means anti-religious, bias.

The association of intellectuals or 'philosophers' that backed the *Encyclopédie* in the years after 1751 included the leading minds of the French Enlightenment. The following five individuals, from just two generations of the French Enlightenment, are the best known of those who collaborated in the production of the *Encyclopédie*. They are quoted here simply as examples of the part played by 'philosophers' in the world at large.

A few years before the appearance of the first volume of the *Encyclopédie*, Montesquieu, erstwhile president of the *Parlement* (the supreme court of Bordeaux), had published his *Esprit des*

Lois, a critical account and classification of European legal systems as they had evolved historically.

Voltaire, who cavorted brilliantly through every field of literature, history and philosophy, was much feared on account of his mordant wit. Five years after the publication of the first volume of the *Encyclopédie*, he was to surprise the public with a history of the world on totally new lines.

Rousseau, who had just begun to astonish the world with his revolutionary views, published his critical treatise on inequality in 1754.

Baron Holbach, a sworn enemy of all mere speculation, evolved a purely mechanical scheme of the cosmos and of mankind, which he published in 1770 under the title, *Système de la nature*.

Turgot, with interests in economics as well as in literature, was destined ultimately to make his name as a leading politician in the reform movement. In 1766 there appeared his *Réflexions sur la formation et la distribution des richesses*, enquiring into the creation and distribution of wealth, a topic that was beginning to interest an increasingly wide public.

Soon there were countless 'philosophers': 'philosophy' had become a fashionable ideology. It had ceased to be a scholastic subject couched in Latin and dispensed by Roman Catholic and Protestant divines of an equally orthodox persuasion, no longer the humble 'handmaiden of Theology', but proclaimed as occupying an independent, indeed the leading, place among the arts and sciences. It no longer aimed to offer only theory, but claimed to be utilitarian – practical reason and common sense. Descartes had opened his *Discours de la méthode* in 1637 with the words:

> Common sense is something that is widely distributed throughout the world, for everyone reckons to have his fair share of it. The ability to make correct judgements and to distinguish between true and false is precisely what we call common sense or reason . . . it is not enough to have the right kind of mind, the main thing is to employ it aright.

That had been stated back in the seventeenth century, and it had proved possible to build on the exact mathematical foundation laid down by Descartes. Half a century later Leibniz observed that the existing world was the best of all possible worlds, because it had been conceived through God's reason. Man had been endowed with reason as his essential feature; he was capable of analysing the world and comprehending it as a whole or in its parts.

By virtue of a system of thought such as Descartes had evolved on the basis of identifiable mathematical and logical factors, philosophy had now become the equal of theology. It was taken as a matter of course when, in the second half of the century, a Catholic theologian declared: '. . . it stands to reason that a man has no judge of what he does or fails to do other than his own reason, so that he is answerable to no one but himself.'[3] In 1783 Immanuel Kant struck a balance in his celebrated reply to the question: What is Enlightenment?

> If the question is put in the form: are we living in an enlightened age?, then the answer is no, but we are indubitably living in an age of enlightenment. As things now stand in the main, we have a long way to go before men may be fit to employ their own reason in matters of religion confidently and justly without the guidance of another. But there is manifest evidence that a field has been opened up to them where they may freely use that faculty, and that the obstacles to universal enlightenment or the emergence of mankind from its self-imposed minority are gradually diminishing, and in that sense this is an age of enlightenment . . .[4]

As far as Kant was concerned, philosophy was an autonomous science of reason and wisdom.

The increasing prestige of philosophy in the eighteenth century had repercussions that affected the European mentality, culture and education, including teaching at the universities. Philosophy had outgrown its humble station as a mere prelude to study; it was now the foundation for all the other faculties – law, medicine, philology and the natural sciences. This ideal pattern of education had been devised in Germany by Humboldt, and it was ultimately to influence every university in Europe. But the period during which philosophy thus occupied pride of place was to be relatively brief. Soon positivism, which discarded metaphysics as a philosophical foundation, triumphed, and philosophy once more became a purely academic subject, losing its pre-eminence in university and grammar school as the twentieth century advanced. But that point had still not been reached in the eighteenth century, when a fundamentally philosophical mentality prevailed. The professors teaching at the universities had a philosophical training, although they were using up-to-date textbooks.

Academies and other learned bodies outside the universities were hard at work devising ideal models of a philosophical nature. Particularly interesting in this connection was the secret society Phi Beta Kappa at the American William and Mary University in Virginia. Phi Beta Kappa is an abbreviation of the Greek motto, philosophìa bìou Kybernètes – 'philosophy is the guide to life'.[5]

Philosophy virtually monopolized the French *salons*: the rational mode of philosophical thought became the leading subject of debate, and the entire company thought of themselves as 'philosophers'. Freelance authors were increasingly successful with books on philosophical topics, so that the output of books on such subjects doubled, while the number of books dealing with theology declined sharply.

But all this philosophizing was not limited to airy speculation: it was not only scientific problems that might be solved philosophically. There was a growing conviction that, if causes could be identified with the aid of philosophy, then action might be taken on rational principles. That was one reason why philosophical modes of thought had to be communicated to the people as a whole: such ideas had to be 'popularized'. The language of the great thinkers, which was often hard to understand, had to be translated into simpler terms by popular philosophers. It was mainly French and English authors who best knew how to convey philosophical knowledge in a style that was both elegant and straightforward, precise without being pedantic. According to Voltaire, a good book ought to be *'curieux, amusant, moral, philosophique'* – intriguing, entertaining, moral and philosophical.

In this way a vast readership was able to become familiar with philosophical arguments. It became known that metaphysics could offer answers to questions about mental and spiritual faculties and relationships in general, about knowledge and belief, about ideas and their logical validity. Ethics – now often called moral philosophy – offered guidance on right action and behaviour and the obligations of a human being, whatever his creed, race or nationality. Philosophical thinking meant thinking for oneself: there was no need to appeal to or to trust traditional authorities. Hitherto, dogmatic pronouncements by the church or the absolute wisdom of the ruler had sufficed to ensure instant obedience. Now, however, people were prepared to accept authority only if it had been validated by philosophical standards. What now counted was utility and morality, clarity and naturalness of expression.

3

Rational Christianity

Protestantism and Enlightenment

More than any other age, the seventeenth century had been governed by theological issues, and theology continued to be the main faculty in universities into the eighteenth century: as we have seen, it was largely the clergy who sustained intellectual life, so that we are justified in looking first at the effects of the reform movement in the ecclesiastical and theological sector.

Protestant theology was still rooted in interpretations laid down by the rigid orthodoxy of the Reformation. If a faculty of theology was to be extended in the seventeenth century, then a chair of controversial theology was established, i.e. a professor was appointed with special responsibility for defining distinctions in the dogma of the church. These distinctions were of four kinds: first, in relation to Rome; secondly, in relation to the other established Protestant churches; thirdly, as a defence against heretics in the church's own ranks, for ever since the Reformation there had in fact been groups who took a more liberal view of Christian doctrine – for instance, the Socinians, who even went so far as to deny the divinity of Christ; fourthly, distinctions had to be drawn which would exclude from the church all manner of sectarians, i.e. the descendants of the Anabaptists and the more recent pietists, that group which aspired to a more fervent and personal piety than they found in the lukewarm approach of the established church.

168

The ultimate epitome of Protestant orthodoxy was expressed in 1675 in the so-called *Formula Consensus* promulgated by the Swiss Reformed Church, in which once again an extreme form of Calvinism culminated in the assertion that every single syllable of the Bible, down to the Hebrew accents, must be considered as inspired by the Holy Ghost, and that Christ had died on the cross exclusively for an elite, the so-called elect, i.e. only for the benefit of Calvinists. It is true that the *Formula* provoked outside (and to some extent, inside) Switzerland an astonished and indignant response, because that kind of statement even at that time seemed oddly archaic.

Fourteen years later, a less rigidly dogmatic country, England, was to pass a Toleration Act relating to all the Protestant confessions: that proved to be a turning-point. The world was tired of theological hair-splitting: if theological arguments were to be conducted rationally, it could not be done within such a system as that offered by the orthodox faiths. Latent humanist traditions began to come to the surface once again. The Enlightenment movement began to shun the representatives of the Reformation to some extent, for it seemed that there were still remnants of the Papacy there, from which the great men of the Reformation had been unable to free themselves in the last analysis. People had had enough of confessional disputes which had brought them nothing but misfortune – the Thirty Years War in Germany, the Civil War in England, the expulsion of the Huguenots from France.

The change took place first in England with the Anglican Church. It was there that Richard Cumberland, subsequently Bishop of Peterborough, proposed in 1690 that Christ's teaching should be reduced to *summa benevolentia aut amor universalis*, i.e. to the love of God and one's neighbour, the Ten Commandments and the Gospels. In 1695 John Locke went even further in his *Reasonableness of Christianity*, in which he claimed that Christianity conformed to the requirements of man's reason. Finally, Jonathan Swift, Dean of St Patrick's Cathedral in Dublin, published his *Tale of a Tub*, in which three sons, Peter (the Catholic), Martin (the Lutheran or Anglican) and John (the Calvinist) argue over their father's (God's) will, although this will (i.e. the Bible) enjoins them to live together in peace, love and harmony.

Following their bitter experience of the confessional feuds in Great Britain, the Anglicans were at last prepared to offer the hand of reconciliation to the various other Protestant sects: in fact, they even began to build bridges linking them to Lutherans and Calvinists outside their own country. The Catholics were left more or less in peace, as long as they were not Irish. The Anglicans had adopted a policy known as *latitudinarianism*, based on a tolerant theology. At that time, it was said, the Anglican Church was prepared to christen, marry and bury anyone at all – albeit a little expensively – without too many awkward questions that might merely disturb the peace. The Anglicans believed that conscience was a matter for God alone. In the case of the Calvinists and Puritans, on the other hand, traditional zealotry tended to be replaced by 'the cauld clapper of morality'.

It was not long before repercussions began to be felt on the Continent, where Huguenot emigrants had already prepared the ground. Having themselves suffered much from persecution, they were disinclined to practise the Calvinistic kind of bigotry. Even before the revocation of the Edict of Nantes they had been suspected of being theologically too liberal.

As early as 1709 a theologian in Basel had made the point, *Nullum pondus habent argumenta nostra, si vita non doctrinae respondet*,[6] 'our arguments will carry little weight, if our life does not match our doctrine': a Christian mode of life mattered more than dogmatic convictions.

Hesitantly and cautiously, theologians began to submit even the Bible to scholarly scrutiny. They took up suggestions thrown out by an Oratorian monk, Richard Simon, who had written a *Critical History* of the Old Testament (1678); a second edition of the work, however, had to be printed in Rotterdam in order to safeguard its author. The writer Johannes Clericus, who came originally from Geneva but who had settled in The Netherlands, suggested that the Old Testament ought to be regarded as literature in the same way as the Greek classics. Although even progressive critics still clung to the notion of revelation, revelation was now reckoned to be nothing more than the perfected form of 'natural religion'. Every individual, it was argued, had a natural need for religion, and it was simply a matter of refining this innate propensity through Christian doctrine. The way was thus opened for a reduction of the concept of revelation, for its ultimate elimination, in fact – a path to deism, which did acknowledge divine laws of nature, but not a personal God. It might turn out to be a path to free thinking, or even to atheism. There were indeed a good many deists in this century, and even atheists here and there, but by and large people tended to retain their religious affiliations, and to stay loyal to the church into which they had been born. It was somewhat risky to profess deism or atheism openly. Although there was no longer much risk of being burnt alive as a heretic, there was always the danger of being exiled. It was only in England, in Holland and in Frederick II's Berlin that a man might openly admit to such irreligious beliefs.

For a Protestant clergyman the new trend might in fact entail a conscientious struggle, since he was still called upon to subscribe to the traditional articles of faith. Views that were too liberal – or inclined too far in the direction of pietism – might lead to friction with more conservative colleagues, or even to removal from office. Ultimately, however, the more enlightened view prevailed almost everywhere, and proponents of strict orthodoxy found themselves in a minority.

Since the new attitude called for a strictly practical pastoral approach, the parson might be found preaching around Christmastime on the proper storage of hay since, after all, the infant Christ had been bedded in hay, while on Easter Sunday he might be preaching on 'rational rules for the interment of the Christian dead', on Whit Sunday on 'how we may comport ourselves devoutly and prudently in case of thunderstorms'. In 1715 a little book was published in England under the title, *The Parson's Leisure, or the Pleasure and Profit to be Gained from Horticulture*. Nowadays we may make fun of this sort of thing, or have theological misgivings, but for the parson and his flock, such topics were surely of more practical use than orthodox dogma. Parsons were often to be found as the heart and soul of local charitable and other utilitarian societies.

Somewhat frantic efforts to rescue the idea of revelation were made by offering rational explanations of Christ's miracles. The greatest prominence, however, was assigned to tolerance, which should not simply be passive toleration, but a positive effort at active understanding of other faiths. This was not too difficult *vis-à-vis* the other Protestant congregations, but obviously more difficult – and more important – in relation to Roman Catholicism. However, tentative contacts of an ecumenical kind began to be made, often simply through personal meetings between clergymen in confessionally mixed communities.

The Protestant churches were disposed up to a point to accept the ideas of the Enlightenment. Close reading of the Bible had fostered rational education, and Protestants were used to employing philological methods in their interpretation of the Scriptures; their lay parishioners had reaped the benefit of this. The existence of a number of different confessions might be positively understood as indicating that there were a number of paths to salvation. The equal standing of colleagues in the government of the church – especially in the case of the Reformed Church – ensured that discussion was more or less conducted among equals.

It was not only the Enlightenment – initially in the form of rational orthodoxy – that threatened to upset the old ideas, but also the intensely subjective pietist movement, which entailed a departure from the rigidly orthodox, disciplined and immutable organization and ideology of the Established Church.[7] This new trend had already had its roots in the seventeenth century. In England the chapels of the Dissenters or non-conformists had been set up in the shadow of the cathedrals or the parish churches in the villages. These sects consisted of reformed Presbyterians or Baptists – the latter a throw-back to the Anabaptist movement. Relative newcomers were the Quakers with their highly subjective piety, and the pietistically inclined Methodists. The latter did in fact have an episcopal organization on the Anglican model. In The Netherlands, cheek-by-jowl with the reformed parish churches, but tucked away in courtyards and alleyways, were the *scheenkerken* of the Mennonites – they, too, were descendants of the Anabaptists – and other denominations.

In the Saxon city of Halle, a Lutheran stronghold, a new Christian sect emerged which was noted also elsewhere in Germany. Its adherents came to be known as pietists. Then Count von Zinzendorf founded his *Brüderunität* in Herrnhut from Bohemian Brethren who had fled from Czechoslovakia, a land which had reverted to Roman Catholicism. Pietists began to infiltrate the established congregations everywhere.

The pietists set out to be a brotherhood of common experience and common obligation. They drew a strict dividing line between the converted and the unconverted, evolved a special kind of piety of their own and formed a personal relationship with the 'Lord', on whom they might cast all their cares. They constituted a small congregation of true Christians, living austere and strictly disciplined lives, with their own methodical approach to life that resembled that of John Wesley's Methodists. As circumstances dictated, they might remain within the body of the church, constituting in their own estimation a leaven of piety. Often, however, the established church – whether orthodox or enlightened – had little liking for them. It actually persecuted them, as, for example, in the stiffly Lutheran Swedish Church, where 'our beloved church of God is beset by syncretists, pietists, Quakers, not to mention other heretics . . . In our country we are indeed fortunate, and although this alien swarm has been able to insinuate itself here and there, they are obliged to lie hidden and, like cats, to draw in their claws.'

And so the pietist movement remained apart, clandestine, 'an unseen church, . . . a community of saints, but not unseen by their Lord, not unseen by Him, who tries and tests them and beholds their faith'. It was only in The Netherlands and in England that such sects were relatively free, or else in the colonies of North America, where the Free Church movement was to set its stamp on religion, and indeed on life in general. In those wide open spaces nature had furnished enough room for all; there Zinzendorf's saying held good: 'There are no doubt a score or more religions in the world, but only one family of God.'

This was a vision that enlightened Christians might see in their dreams – the age-old utopia of the 'Kingdom of God on Earth'. The pietists' *ecclesiola in ecclesia*, 'a church within a church', and the enlightened established church were equally dissatisfied with orthodoxy: both were casting round for a new approach. What they had in common was the postulate of individual freedom and moral responsibility. Thus Lessing could state in his *Education of Mankind*:

> It will surely come, the age of a new gospel, which was promised us in the elementary books of the New Testament. It may be that certain mystic visionaries of the thirteenth and fourteenth centuries fleetingly glimpsed a ray of this new gospel and were mistaken only in proclaiming its imminent advent . . . They surely had no evil intent when they taught that the New Testament was bound in time to become as antiquated as the Old. They, too, were thinking of the same design by the same God – or, to have them speak in my terms, the very same plan of the general education of mankind.[8]

In his drama *Nathan the Wise* Lessing expanded Jonathan Swift's idea in the *Tale of a Tub* to embrace the non-Christian religions, Islam and Judaism. In one way or another a trail was being blazed in the direction of ecumenism. This had been evident even at the end of the seventeenth century, when the Protestant Leibniz corresponded with the Catholic Bossuet, and, a little later, when the pietist Count Zinzendorf exchanged letters with Archbishop Noailles of Paris.

The pietist Gerhard Tersteegen concurred:

> I believe and am convinced that in the party of the Catholics, among the Lutherans and in the Reformed congregations or the Mennonites – in spite of differences in the rites and practices of these parties – just as many souls may attain the highest pinnacle of holiness and communion with God as among the schismatic sects.

Catholic Enlightenment

Catholicism found it harder to come to terms with the Enlightenment. The strict orthodoxy enjoined by the Council of Trent

(1563) had led to a radicalization of religious observance. The Jesuits with their efficient organization held the whiphand. However, already in the seventeenth century, the French Jansenists began to criticize the Jesuit Order on the grounds that it was subservient to the Roman curia and that its doctrines departed from biblical principles. However devout Jansenism might be in the spirit of the church, and however remote from the incipient Enlightenment – after all, the movement was ultimately persecuted by Rome and by the king of France – it had an influence not unlike that of the Protestant Huguenots. Jansenism was as much concerned as any of the Protestant movements to practise an undogmatic evangelism within the confines of the church. In the 1720s a Jansenist church in Utrecht even broke away from the main body of the Roman Catholic Church and was accorded the protection of the Republic. As with the evangelical pietists, Jansenism called for serious involvement in Christian life and Christian charitable endeavour. In France the elite represented by the judges of the supreme court and in Austria the aristocratic dignitaries of the church were inclined to embrace Jansenism. This was not Enlightenment by any rational standards, but it was something totally different from the customary Catholicism as it was taught by the Jesuits: it implied a more broad-minded faith and a commitment to Christian action. There was thus a kind of consolidated opposition within Catholicism itself which had its effect in changing the direction in which the church was heading: opposition on the part of the state administration to the church as a kind of state within the state was allied to the new humanistic or humanitarian trend.

The paragon of Catholicism in the eighteenth century was Fénelon (1651–1715), who found himself, as Archbishop of Cambrai, at loggerheads with both king and church. In 1699 he had published his *Aventures de Télémaque, fils d'Ulysse*, a didactic novel featuring the son of Ulysses who is guided through life by the goddess Minerva in the guise of his tutor, Mentor. The hero of the novel is in effect a portrait of the ideal monarch. *Télémaque* became one of the most popular works of the eighteenth century. One of the contemporary authorities on natural law, the

Huguenot émigré, Barbeyrac, wrote of it: 'We cannot but admire the splendid eloquence of the eminent Archbishop of Cambrai, his skill and courage in offering so much excellent advice to our monarchs.'[9] The judgement of a modern historian reads:

> What was the point of Louis XIV constructing his private and personal paradise in Versailles, if this enigmatic bishop was quietly and almost incidentally enlightening the finest minds and hearts of France: do not worry, friends, all that is no more than a façade that will decay; do not be dismayed, dear friends, if we are persecuted and banished, no one can take from us the inner kingdom, our life in God here and now.
>
> In his own way Fénelon even went over to the offensive, openly criticizing and showing how pious foundations established by Madame de Maintenon and the king, the Ladies of St Louis and the nuns of St Cyr, practised a false asceticism in order to mask pride, vanity and aridity of heart through a semblance of piety. Here Fénelon is continuing and carrying to new heights the battle fought by Erasmus and his disciples against the perversions entailed in monastic life. He is primarily concerned to point out to the lay public that a man does not need a strenuous effort of the will or strict disciplinary measures in order to lead a godly life in the world. What really mattered was an open heart, brotherly love and the civic virtues. What counted was not the dubious fraternity of monastery and nunnery, or the closed world of a congregation, but the brotherhood of all men who live in the world – for all men are indeed brothers.

In this century there was even a pope who moved cautiously to follow the new trend. This was the erudite Prosper Lambertini, who reigned as Benedict XIV from 1740 to 1758. He permitted Bible readings under the auspices of the church, he reduced the number of church holidays, he relaxed the church's censorship and revised the index of banned books. Indeed, he even recognized the freedom needed for scientific research in that he initiated the procedure to rescind the ban imposed by the church on the works of Copernicus and Galilei. He was in touch with leading figures of the Enlightenment, and Voltaire spoke of him with manifest respect. No wonder that this intelligent old man was suspected in the curia of being a deist.

A writer as hostile to clericalism as was Voltaire, the Italian, Giancarlo Pilati, wrote of a later pope, Clement XIV: 'He detested bigotry and the mere outward manifestations of piety.' Pilati says of the city of Rome: 'Heretics are not harassed in any way, but allowed to do as they please. They kneel neither to God nor the pope, and no one reviles them for that reason.' Censorship was discreetly handled in Rome, and all manner of books could be bought there.[10]

The greatest public triumph of Catholic Enlightenment was the dissolution of the Jesuit Order. Hitherto, the Jesuits had kept a firm grip on education at the intermediate and higher level. In every Catholic town there was a Jesuit college which served as a well-organized grammar school with a cosmopolitan teaching staff. The Jesuits' influence extended far beyond the schools and reached the courts, where they provided confessors for kings and queens. Their strict allegiance to Rome and their intellectual and economic power, however, gradually came to be regarded as being incompatible with the wish of the courts and their ministers to free themselves from the tutelage of the church. It was unfortunate that the Jesuits showed no inclination whatsoever to adapt themselves to modern scientific trends. Condorcet – himself a former pupil of the Jesuits – pilloried their philosophical teaching in which every rational tenet of philosophy was denied. He denounced their absurd moral code,

> which attempted to teach children that one could not perform a good deed unless one was oneself in a state of grace, that there were two kinds of crime, the first, sins of the flesh for which men had been burned alive for centuries, and the second, mortal sins, for which the sinner was damned in all eternity . . . Humiliation and shame are the natural condition of a Christian.[11]

The Jesuits were still teaching a theological doctrine that had long been discarded by the Protestants. Somewhat less severe, but still damning, is Condorcet's verdict on the Jesuit college in Lucerne, a stronghold of Swiss Catholicism:

> But the sciences will not find disciples amongst us as long as the nature of our schools and the teaching in them remain in their former condition. The schools are in the hands of the Jesuits, their teaching methods are notorious and lack both sound sense and utility, apart from theology, in which they are the best and most accomplished teachers in our country. In Lucerne there are no teachers of the other sciences, which are equally necessary.

When this was written in 1758, the unthinkable had just happened in Portugal: in 1757 the all-powerful minister Pombal had ordered the dissolution of the Jesuit Order in the kingdom and its colonies, and the expulsion of the Jesuits had already begun. In 1764 the same startling development took place in France, in 1767 in Spain and its vast colonial empire, and in 1768 in Parma as well. In 1773 Pope Clement XIV yielded to the pressure of the courts – the combined Bourbon monarchies – and dissolved the entire Order. A veritable persecution of the Jesuits ensued: a ship with expelled Jesuits on board called at all the Mediterranean ports without being able to land its passengers. Under the papal decree of 1773 the Jesuits had to be dismissed in all the Catholic states, including the German states. The order was enforced with varying degrees of harshness in different countries. It was, paradoxically, the most enlightened of monarchs who was prepared to offer the Jesuits refuge, Frederick II; he was only too glad to offer them employment in his newly conquered, mainly Catholic, province of Silesia, although Frederick's successor did ban them after all. In the end, the only escape route left to them was via Orthodox Russia. A mighty system of teaching and administration collapsed in ruins. The final calamity took place in Latin America, where the Jesuits in Paraguay and the other countries of the Andes had built up an efficient economic and administrative structure in the villages of the indigenous Indian population.

The retrograde step represented by the dissolution of the Jesuit Order was not the only feature of the Catholic reform

movement. The organization of the church as a whole was
subject to internal restructuring. The Catholic states now began
to assume some of the controlling functions which Protestant
states had been exercising for some two hundred years: supervision of theological seminaries, subsidies for schools, whether in
the monasteries or outside them, encouragement of the universities through support of their scientific activities.

Enlightenment, however, entailed more than just state intervention in religious and ecclesiastical issues: it also implied an
inner or psychological transformation in the sense of a return to
fundamental Christianity. Inner religious experience was considered more important than superficial and sentimental piety
with its outward manifestations in the form of ritual, saints'
days and pilgrimages. Vernacular languages, for instance, were
to be encouraged in place of the enigmatic Latin used in the
Mass. Here the Catholics had a good deal in common with
Protestant ideas about the practical aspects of religion, and there
was no doubt a hope that in this way Protestants might be
brought back into the fold of a purged and purified Catholic
Church. Toleration began to be taken for granted, and contacts
between Catholics and Protestants were deliberately sought; it
was hoped that such contacts might involve bishops as well as
parish priests.

Voltaire, the most vociferous member of the anti-clerical faction, has left us what is perhaps the finest tribute to the new,
humane Catholicism of the Enlightenment, his *Prière à Dieu*, the
concluding section of the *Traité de la Tolérance*, a work that had
been prompted by his horror at the last notorious heresy trial in
France, the Calas case of 1762. The vital passage of the *Prière à
Dieu* dealing with the confessional issue, runs as follows:

> Thou hast not given us hearts to hate nor hands to strangle
> each other. Make us help one another to bear the burden of
> a fleeting and wearisome life . . . so that the tiny nuances
> that differentiate the atoms called men from each other
> may not serve as tokens of hatred and persecution; so that
> those who light candles in broad daylight to celebrate Thy
> being may suffer those who are content with the radiance

of Thy sun, so that those who cover their garments with a white linen cloth, in order to show that Thou shouldst be loved, may not hate those who say the same thing in a coat of black worsted; that it may be a matter of indifference whether Thou art worshipped in an ancient tongue or in a language of more recent date . . .

Voltaire concludes with the words:

May all men bear in mind that they are brothers, so that they may respond to tyranny of the soul with the same abhorrence as to highway robbery, which lays violent hands on the fruits of peaceful labour and diligence. And if the scourge of war is inevitable, let us at least not hate each other, let us not rend each other limb from limb while peace prevails! Let us use the brief moment of our existence to join in a chorus of a thousand different tongues from Siam to California to praise Thy goodness that vouchsafed us that moment![12]

4

Natural Law, the Path to Human Rights

Changes in theological views were matched by changes in the view of the law, which in turn had an influence on ethics or moral philosophy. These processes were in fact reciprocal: theologians took an interest in theories of jurisprudence, while lawyers were at home in the world of theology.

A system of laws could, of course, be deduced from the Bible, e.g. from the Ten Commandments. There was also the law that had been codified in classical times. Roman law stated: *Juris praecepta sunt haec: honeste vivere, alterum non laedere, suum cuique tribuere*, 'The principles of law are as follows: live honestly, do harm to no man and give everyone his due.' Every educated man had been brought up on Cicero's *De officiis*, where the duties of a man and a citizen were defined in what were reckoned to be universally valid terms. The Middle Ages had contrived to combine the classical and the Christian ideas of the law and to evolve a system that applied to the whole of the Christian world. This system was known as *jus naturae*, the law of nature.

With the coming of the Reformation, however, this universally accepted notion of natural law was replaced by opposing interpretations: Protestant ideas conflicted with the Catholic views. There was an embarrassing absence of rules that might apply to both parties. In 1625 a Dutchman, Hugo Grotius, attempted to lay a foundation for natural and international law in three books, *De Jure Belli ac Pacis – On the Law of Peace and*

War. He began by scrutinizing the current state of legal authorities. There was first of all the law of the stronger party and its
interests, which went by the name of 'reasons of state'. Secondly,
there was common law, which was valid only on a particular
territory. Thirdly, there were philosophical doctrines from all
ages, but these were by no means consistent or uniform. Fourthly, there was Roman law, which had been codified in the period
between late classical times and the early Middle Ages, but
which was antiquated and unsystematic. Finally, there was the
divine law that might be deduced from the Bible.

What Grotius was looking for was a universal foundation
and he found it in the concept of the law of nature. Natural
law issues from man, or rather from the communal life of men,
and is based on historical and logical – nowadays we would say
psychological and sociological – factors. Grotius comes to the
conclusion that man is essentially a rational creature and that
he enjoys moral freedom. He has been endowed by God with
reason and free will, but the law of nature would still be valid
even if there were no God, which is in fact impossible. From
man's *appetitus societatis*, his social instinct, Grotius deduces five
basic laws: first, respect for the property of others; second, the
obligation to return property that has been unjustly confiscated; third, the obligation to honour undertakings that have
been entered into; fourth, the obligation to compensate for
damage; fifth, penalties in keeping with these offences against
natural law.

This simple scheme, which Grotius expounded in the introduction to his *De Jure Belli ac Pacis*, was elaborated by the
German lawyer Pufendorf into an actual legal system in the
form of the 'greater' and 'lesser' Pufendorf: *De Jure Naturali et
Gentium* (1672), on natural law and international law, and *De
Officio Hominis et Civis Juxta Legem Naturalem*, on the duties of a
man and citizen according to the law of nature (1682). *Pufendorf*
became the basic authority used in the training of lawyers in the
eighteenth century. His work was followed by many other textbooks of similar content and tendency: in Germany by Christian
Thomasius and Christian Wolff, in England by John Locke and
Anthony Shaftesbury. Pufendorf became known to a wider pub-

lic through the translation of his work by the Huguenot emigrant, Jean Barbeyrac, which was published in 1706/07.

The school of thought advocating natural law was concerned to create a system of truly international law that would take precedence over the jurisdiction of particular states. The pope had once arbitrated in such matters, but since the *universitas christiana* had been split apart by the Reformation, natural law was required to fill the gap. When diplomats in the eighteenth century convened as the 'concert of Europe' at the peace conferences of Rastatt, Utrecht, Baden, Vienna, Aachen and Paris, they took as their guidelines such precepts of natural law as would enable victors and vanquished to find common solutions.

The concept of a law of nature encouraged the eighteenth century to think of itself as international, cosmopolitan: in 1713, in his treatise on a universal peace, the Abbé de St Pierre had already conceived the utopian idea of a league of nations. In *Télémaque* Fénelon addressed himself to the monarch in the following terms:

> The best safeguard for any state is justice, which guarantees its neighbours security and the confidence that their territory will not be occupied. The strongest of bastions may fall as a result of unforeseen circumstances, the fortunes of war are fickle. But the affection and trust of your neighbours – if they have experienced your moderation – will ensure that your state will never be conquered, that it will scarcely ever even be attacked.[13]

This was another utopian piece of wishful thinking in a century in which Frederick II annexed Silesia and three monarchs proceeded to partition Poland. Nevertheless, people believed that they were on the road to a brighter future: it could hardly be foreseen that the nation states with their imperialist policies would take the place of universal harmony in the course of the nineteenth century.

The proponents of natural law attacked the doctrine of *Staatsräson*, the brutal self-interest of the omnipotent state, as it had been evolved by Machiavelli in his *Principe* (1532) and Hobbes in *Leviathan* (1651). Both these writers fell into discredit in the eighteenth century.

It was from the idea of a man's *duties* as a citizen that the converse notion of the *rights* of man was evolved in the course of the eighteenth century: his right to inviolability of the person, to the undisputed ownership of property and, most important of all, to freedom of conscience. The individual was granted a certain degree of freedom, of which indeed he had to relinquish part in order to make possible any kind of social life. Society – or the state – was obliged in return to respect the residual rights of the individual and embody them in its political constitution. This was in fact what had been done in the Bill of Rights promulgated as a sequel to England's Glorious Revolution, and in the *Declaration of the Rights of Man* embodied in the constitution of Virginia. In this way arbitrary rule by princes was to be curbed. Even in the absence of a written constitution, it was at least the wish of enlightened monarchs and their ministers to see that these unwritten laws were respected, and decrees were issued and other measures taken to this end. The time-honoured idea of respect for one's fellow-man with whom one was bound up in Christ was given a new, more precise, and indeed mandatory form.

During the eighteenth century attempts at real reform were made in an area where inhumanity and injustice were felt to be particularly crass: the criminal law and the penal code as they were incorporated, for instance, in the draconian regulations of the so-called *Carolina*, the Emperor Charles V's Penal Code of 1532. The death penalty in various versions, flogging, slavery in the galleys were meant to act as deterrents to crime. The highwayman, no less than the murderer, had to reckon with the death penalty, confessions were extorted by means of torture, Catholic countries still allowed trials before the Inquisition. Criticism of the traditional system became more and more outspoken, until, in 1764, Cesare Beccaria published his epoch-making book *Crime and Punishment*.[14] Beccaria condemned judicial torture in that it was bound to incriminate a physically infirm individual even if he was innocent. He also attacked the Inquisition, because the accused had no legal safeguards: he might be indicted anonymously and was not in a position to confront witnesses. Beccaria even goes so far as to question the justification of the death penalty: 'What sort of a right is that which men arrogate to themselves: the right to kill one of their own kind?' He was particularly interested in the operation of the penal system, with which he familiarized himself by visits to the prisons of Milan, where the convicts were kept like slaves. Beccaria demanded not only a carefully graduated scale of punishment, but also measures to prevent crimes being committed in the first place.

Beccaria was in fact a revolutionary in the sense that he saw the criminal law and the penal code as the consequences of a maladjusted society: 'What, then, are these laws I am supposed to obey? . . . Who made these laws: the wealthy and the powerful. Let us burst asunder these fateful fetters, let us strike at the root of injustice!'

In 1740, even before the advent of Beccaria, Frederick II of Prussia had abolished torture in his own state. Judges who were guided by common sense no longer prescribed the practice anyway. Towards the end of the century France and Austria followed suit by introducing more humane penal codes.

At least the execution of witches, which had reached epidemic proportions in the seventeenth century, gradually came to an end. The last executions for witchcraft took place in England in 1712, in France in 1718, in the German bishopric of Würzburg in 1749, and in the Swiss canton of Glarus and the German abbey of Kempten in 1782.

5

Politics and Government

When politicians and writers in the eighteenth century, reflecting on the political realities of this age, designed their Utopias and proposed to embark on reforms, they found themselves in a political and constitutional system that was bound to strike them as singularly antiquated. They were living in a world that was bogged down in the late Middle Ages. Everything was jammed tight in an illogical system that could scarcely be seen as a single entity. In the monarchies, which were seemingly simply constructed with their kings at the apex, secure in their absolute power, the political system was nevertheless paralysed. The monarch's will collided with a thousand hereditary factors that were simply taken for granted. Cities and counties, entire provinces, the church, corporations, universities, guilds, ecclesiastical foundations, the minor nobility and squirearchy – all of them were leading lives of their own, in autonomous domains backed up by rights and privileges that had been acquired at some time in the dim and distant past. 'Everything, that is, is right if it can show a charter', they used to say in England.

In this situation it was virtually impossible to rule or to govern, much less to carry out reforms. That is why kings, their courtiers and ministers tried so hard to introduce some order into this confusion, to assert an undisputed central authority over this state of chronic disorder. That was what was called absolutism. Absolutism, however, with all power in the hands of the monarch or of an administration appointed by him, ran counter to the premisses of natural law. The absolute king, as personified in Louis XIV, was no longer the beneficial principle of order in an unjust world of outdated privileges; he had become a despot, a tyrant, who was not there for the sake of his people, but simply for his own sake. Fénelon says in *Télémaque*: 'The king is worthy of kingship only if he forgets himself and sacrifices himself for the common good.' 'Forgetting themselves', however, was hardly to the taste of the kings in the seventeenth, or even in the eighteenth, century. That is why, Fénelon goes on, 'Absolute power in a king ends with him having precisely as many slaves as he has subjects.'[15]

Criticism might be even more drastic and appeal to a time-honoured right of resistance – a right as old as the state itself – the duty, indeed the necessity, to resist, if the ruler neglected his obligations. The natural law theorist, Barbeyrac, contended that the subjects do have such a right *vis-à-vis* their ruler, if by outrageous and intolerable injustice and infringement of his duties towards them he automatically releases them from the loyalty they once owed him.

Throughout the century there was speculation as to the way in which this right might be exercised, if it were not to lead to revolution and anarchy. With its Glorious Revolution, Britain seemed to have found the way – actually a reversion to dualism in government, as it had existed in the Middle Ages, that is, a system of reciprocally controlled powers shared by king and parliament. Parliament consisted of two parties, conservative Tories and liberal Whigs, both of them of an aristocratic complexion, which took turns in governing the country. In a good many countries – a number of German principalities, for instance – similar parliaments still existed under the name of *Landtag*. Was it possible to bring them into line with the monarchical principle of centralism and national unity? Or were they, like the French estates or the Spanish Cortes, so antiquated in their structure that it would be better to let them die rather than have them meddling in national government and claiming their inherited regional or social privileges?

Now, however, the English example had its effect in Europe – less the example of what was after all an old-fashioned and crudely constituted parliament, than the theoretical conclusions drawn in the years following 1688. These theories were incorporated, for instance, in John Locke's *Two Treatises of Government*, which made a timely appearance in 1690.

Locke is a proponent of natural law and proceeds from the assumption that the state rested on a contract between the ruler and the ruled, between a king and his people. If men were allowed unlimited freedom, this would lead to anarchy, the war of all against all. The sensible solution is a contract between the parties, and not subjugation by a powerful individual who brings order into anarchy by the use of force – nowadays we would call that a totalitarian or Fascist solution. In the eighteenth century, people were inclined to quote historical precedents for such contracts between rulers and their subjects. England had its *Magna Charta* dating back to 1215, and it seemed that what was now called for was a modern version of this medieval document!

In Article 95 of his second treatise Locke writes:

> Men being, as has been said, by nature all free, equal and independent, no one can be put out of this estate and subjected to the political power of another without his own consent, which is done by agreeing with other men, to join and unite into a community for their comfortable, safe, and peaceable living, one amongst another, in a secure enjoyment of their properties, and a greater security against any that are not of it.

The implications in the real world of politics are stated in Article 89:

> Wherever, therefore, any number of men so unite into one society as to quit every one his executive power of the law of Nature, and to resign it to the public, there and there only is political or civil society. And this is done wherever any number of men, in the state of Nature, enter into society to make one people one body politic under one supreme government: or else when any one joins himself to, and incorporates with any government already made.

For hereby he authorizes the society, or which is all one, the legislative thereof, to make laws for him as the public good of the society shall require . . .[16]

Society, as the people, is represented by the legislature, which enacts laws on behalf of society, and these laws have to be put into effect by the executive, i.e. by the king and his ministers.

Ideas of this kind, and the political reality which, however imperfectly, reflected them in England became the model for at least some of those responsible for government in Europe. Enlightened monarchs and their ministers were supported by a large number of lawyers and political pamphleteers. Enlightened political thinking reached its climax when it was propounded in terms of natural law – once again in French – by Montesquieu in his *Esprit des Lois* (1748). Montesquieu believed that a proper division of powers had been achieved in the English system, with the king as executive, the House of Commons as the legislature, and – as Montesquieu incorrectly assumed – the House of Lords as the supreme judicial authority. The idea behind the system was the provision of a curb on the machinery of government. Montesquieu wished in this way to guide monarchy back on to the path of legitimacy. In his view the absolutist system – he called it the *despotic* system – was grounded in *fear*. A true monarchy ought to be guided by the principle of *honour*, for its mainstay was the nobility. In the case of republics, he identified *vertu politique* as the basic principle. That already has a distinct bourgeois ring about it.

It was at this point that Rousseau appeared with his *Contrat social* (1762). The work had a revolutionary impact, because it suggested that the republic was the ideal form of government and assumed that all citizens were equal. The *volonté générale* was to be the governing factor, not any criterion of social status. Beccaria, Mably and others seized on these ideas, which were pointing the way to some kind of political Utopia.

Apart from Great Britain, Denmark was the only state which contrived to effect a political transformation by strictly legal means. As far as the motherland was concerned, the kingdom of Denmark had passed a *Lex regia* in 1665 which concentrated authority in the hands of the monarch, who was in a position to rule without anything in the way of parliamentary representation: it was a degree of absolutism that guaranteed equality of all his subjects amongst themselves. Some one hundred years later absolutism in Denmark was progressively dismantled through the legal process. There was no longer any censorship, a freedom of which the Danes took sensible advantage, and the peasantry had gained its freedom from the landowners. It had been a kind of good-natured absolutism: Voltaire had spoken of the Scandinavians generally as *'peuples libres sous les rois'*. Sweden, too, had been modifying its absolutist system – albeit in a less direct fashion.

It was only in the newly created United States of America that it proved possible, both in the individual states and in the federation, to put a modern republican constitution into practice. Later, the American Constitution and the short-lived first French revolutionary constitution were to set the pattern for the liberal state of the nineteenth century.

A constitution based on a guarantee of citizens' rights in terms of natural law remained no more than a utopia during the eighteenth century – but at least the soil had been dug over and prepared for the planting of new ideas.

6

The Economy, Economic Freedom and the Work Ethic

Before the advent of the Enlightenment the world still existed for the most part in a medieval economic system: the farmer grew his crops for his own consumption and, if there was a surplus, he sold it at market in the towns. Grain was exported to more distant markets, as were butter and cheese – the latter being in special demand for ocean-going ships. Farm output was governed as a rule by a traditional system of crop rotation.

Similar conditions applied to trades and crafts, which were subject to regulation by the guilds. However, merchants had breached and infiltrated this rigid system. They had long been transporting their wares by pack-horse, river barge and ship far beyond the confines of Europe. The textile industry moved its productive base into the countryside, where workers were employed at loom or spinning-wheel in their own homes. The cloth they wove was subsequently exported all over the world, a world that was well fenced in with innumerable barriers at city gates and bridges, where all manner of tolls were levied.

Although the pace of life was leisurely, people did work hard – albeit with varying degrees of keenness. This became more obvious once the work ethic enjoined by the Old Testament had been promoted by the Reformers, particularly by Zwingli and Calvin. Both of them asserted that work was a Christian duty, cheerful labour in the Lord's vineyard, and they suspected that

191

the monastic life was nothing but organized idleness in the shelter of monastery walls.

However that might be, it was frequently noted in the eighteenth century that Protestant countries, by and large, were more industrious and consequently more prosperous than their Catholic neighbours:

> The Catholics are poor, even in the same towns where the Protestants are well-off. . . . In Catholic countries the taverns are thronged with folk drinking and dancing, which can rarely be seen in the case of the Protestants. . . . Although they are extremely phlegmatic, German Catholics are a sound race, nobility as well as townsfolk; although the former seldom put in an appearance at the princely courts, they are generally affable in their uncouth fashion and they do the right thing as they see it, i.e. they make sure that there is plenty to eat and drink. The Protestants, however, are more genteel and reserved and a shade distrustful. They are not as much given to conviviality and jollification as the Catholics are . . .[17]

These remarks by an Italian anticipate precisely Max Weber's celebrated proposition regarding *Protestant Ethics and the Spirit of Capitalism*. If this thesis were to be examined in detail, it would transpire that the Calvinists were more prosperous than the Lutherans, while the most prosperous of all were the Mennonites in The Netherlands, who were the descendants of the Anabaptists.

A spectacular demonstration of Calvinist business acumen was provided as a result of the expulsion of the Huguenots from France, from which England, Holland and the Protestant states of Germany all benefited, so that Voltaire could retort indignantly to an English critic: 'The Protestants who left our king's realm took with them industries that constituted the wealth of France. Do the silk and pottery industries count for nothing in your country, then? The potteries in England were perfected by our refugees, and our loss has been your gain.'[18]

The areas where the Huguenots settled were already industrialized when they arrived, but they introduced new methods of manufacture and trade.

This activity by the Huguenots was still being pursued, although it was within the context of the old economic arrangements.

The economic system of mercantilism, known as Colbertism in reference to Louis XIV's finance minister, Jean Baptiste Colbert, had become standard practice in the monarchies during the eighteenth century. The state encouraged industry which mainly met the demand on the part of the courts, the higher nobility, the clergy and the wealthier middle class for luxury articles (e.g. tapestries or mirrors from the royal factories), or which supplied the armed forces via cannon foundries, arsenals and naval dockyards. The aim was to attract capital from abroad through the encouragement of exports and the imposition of heavy duties on imports. It was through bans on imports that a maritime nation like England sought to assert its domination over Holland, which was attempting to exploit the freedom of the seas in the interests of free trade.

Criticism of the prevailing economic system was first voiced by a group of French economic theorists associated with the king's personal physician, de Quesnay, and known as the *physiocrates*. They went even further than the *agronomes*, who had a more practical approach and were mainly based in England. The *physiocrates* adopted this title because they wished to return to 'physis', i.e. nature, and to place the main emphasis on agriculture, which had been criminally neglected under Colbertism, but which, after all, had made the whole system of rule by the court possible through its products and the taxes it paid. Continuing the campaign of the agronomists in England, the physiocrats sought to attract the aristocracy back to the cultivation of their estates, encouraging them to invest their capital in agriculture and thus create a new economic system that was based on the abolition of economic privileges and tariffs, i.e. on the total liberalization of production and trade in general. The theory was startlingly novel and the system not easy to understand. Soon the physiocrats were embroiled in a furious public controversy with their adversaries. They were denounced as 'the Sect' and their publications were ultimately banned in France, since it was very soon realized that their demand for the abolition of freedom from taxation in the case of the clergy and the nobility struck at the very root of the economic order that obtained under the *ancien régime*.

The physiocrats introduced Enlightenment ideas into the farming world with its conservative social order based either on peasant co-operatives or the patriarchal rule of the lord of the local manor. They operated with mathematical, statistical and other rational methods of calculation. Their theory was based on the idea of profit and private property, but they also promoted ideas which nowadays strike us as ecological. For instance, the physiocrats opposed the senseless waste of arable land entailed in the building of new *routes royales*. Ever since the 1730s a relatively extensive road-building programme amounting to several thousand kilometres had been planned, and in the 1750s it began to be implemented. The new *routes royales* were meant to link Paris with all the major provincial cities and seaports; they would reduce travelling time by half and be passable all the year round, even in heavy rain and snow. These highways ran, wherever possible, straight across country; they were 20 metres wide, 27 metres if their flanking ditches and avenues of trees were included. On the causeway, with its solid foundations, ballast and verges, as many as six coaches or carts might travel abreast. 'They were in fact motorways *avant la lettre*, and until that era came to France they did good service for some two hundred years.'[19] The physiocrats' opposition was successful in so far as the responsible minister, Turgot, reduced the extent of the network and modified the width of the roads.

An economic theory not unlike that of the physiocrats was evolved somewhat later in Great Britain, which led the world at that time in almost all economic areas. This theory was incorporated by Adam Smith in a work that has retained its reputation to the present day: *The Wealth of Nations*, published in 1776. Like the physiocrats, he subjected the prevailing system with its privileges and monopolies to a comprehensive critical examination and suggested free trade as the valid solution for the future:

Under such a system of free trade, competition between the nations would prevent profit margins in a new market, or in a new branch of the economy, from exceeding the normal level. The new market would generate new production for its own consumption or in the form of a new supply, without depriving the existing market of anything, and this fresh production would create new capital for the operation of the new trade . . .[20]

It was only to be expected that the idea of freedom propounded by the advocates of natural law would be applied to the economy. The new economic theorists thought in worldwide terms, just as the proponents of natural law did: they saw the world as a whole included in one vast free market which would be self-regulating. The system that had existed hitherto had been static, with one mercantilistic state excluding another; it had led to wars and to mutual destruction. It had to be replaced by something that offered a better future. That, too, was one of the grand utopias that men dreamed of in the eighteenth century.

Like the works of the advocates of natural law and the political philosophers, the economists' books were eagerly read by a select public. And there were even statesmen who tried to introduce the doctrines of the political theorists and economists into the existing system. The absolute despot ought to be replaced by a 'good king' with a modern mentality who would truly be a father to his people, and who would act on the advice of enlightened ministers. There were in fact a good many intelligent rulers who tried to improve their subjects' lot by the exercise of prudent common sense. For instance, there was Kaunitz in Austria, Firmian in Milan, Rosenberg-Orsini in Tuscany, and Ensenada, Aranda and Campomanes in Spain; Hanover had its Münchhausen, France had d'Argenson and d'Aguesseau, as well as Turgot, although the latter had limited success, while, in Denmark, Struensee fared even worse. Their common aim was modernization of the bureaucracy, the abolition of privilege and inequality, and a fairer distribution of resources.

Science, Medicine and Technology

The ideas on religion, politics and economics that evolved in the eighteenth century all have something of a utopian character, whether they are concerned with the Kingdom of God on earth, a monarchy based on civil rights, or an economic system of free production and free trade. Science and technology seem less utopian, for their discoveries and innovations, which began with a rush in the seventeenth century, were after all real. However, science and technology did have a utopian or speculative element, without which indeed the relevant discoveries or inventions might never have been made. As we shall see, a number of utopias remained in the form of problems which could not be solved with the means available in the eighteenth century.

The natural sciences, mathematics and technology had always held a place in the public esteem. Mathematics and physics were numbered among the traditional seven liberal arts which had been taken over from classical times during the Middle Ages. They were taught by professors at the universities, albeit on the fringe of the academic domain, and for a long time only as aids to theology. A number of factors led to the expansion of these disciplines during the fifteenth and sixteenth centuries, especially the demands of ocean navigation, which had become very important. In the seventeenth century theological orthodoxy tended to maintain the status quo and slow down the advance of science in many ways, but science nevertheless continued to develop, almost by stealth, in many cases as little more than a hobby or part-time occupation.

In the eighteenth century the advance of science could once more be resumed. The Zurich physician and naturalist, Johann Jakob Scheuchzer, made a significant note to this effect in 1721. Scheuchzer (1672–1733) is in many ways typical of the naturalists of his era. For one thing, he came of a good family, a middle-class clan with guild connections. In addition, his father had been a doctor. Scheuchzer received his medical training in Utrecht, i.e. in The Netherlands, a country noted for its intellectual freedom, which extended to the natural sciences, and it was there that he graduated as a doctor of medicine in 1694. In his native republic he occupied the position of medical officer of health and later also became Professor of Mathematics at the University of Zurich. He spent his entire career in his native city, and it was there that he started a *Gesellschaft der Wohlgesinnten* or charitable society, which was active from 1697 until 1709 and functioned as a little republican academy. But he was also a citizen of the international republic of letters, a member of the German *Academia naturae curiosorum*, the London Royal Society and the Academy of St Petersburg. It was Scheuchzer who brought Alpine research and Alpine geology into the realm of the natural sciences.

In 1721 Scheuchzer published a fat volume under the double title, *Jobi Physica Sacra* or *Job's Natural Science compared with Modern Science*.[21] It is a work typical of its time: firmly rooted in the world of theology, but seeking to harmonize biblical revelation with the findings of the natural sciences.

The third verse of the twenty-eighth chapter of the Book of Job offers Scheuchzer a welcome opportunity to discuss the progress of the sciences. The verse reads: *'Tenebris posuit (Deus) terminum et ad omnem perfectionem ipse scrutatur lapidem in caligine et densissima umbra abditum'* – 'He setteth an end to darkness, and searcheth out all perfection: the stones of darkness and the shadow of death.'

Scheuchzer inserts *Deus* (God) here, presumably in keeping with the text as he understood it, but as the verse is now interpreted, the reference is to man who puts an end to darkness –

which would correspond more closely to the Enlightenment view. As he points out elsewhere, what Scheuchzer is concerned with is the 'knowledge of God through nature', thus offering important evidence to the enlightened orthodox theologians of his day.

The twenty-eighth chapter of the Book of Job as a whole deals with the true wisdom of God and man in relation to the exploration and exploitation of the treasures hidden in the depths of the earth.

Scheuchzer first discusses the older interpretation, repudiating the view that darkness here means 'nothing' or 'the void'. He goes on, 'I prefer the view . . . that Job is referring to all manner of new inventions which, in keeping with God's wise providence, have been brought from darkness into light to the special benefit of human society.'

The phrase, 'the benefit of human society' anticipates a new view, according to which anything of practical use was more highly prized than purely psychological, intellectual or artistic interests. Scheuchzer goes on to state the typical Enlightenment opinion that the age of darkness is coming to an end and that a new and better era is about to dawn. 'If this interpretation is true and the end of darkness has been ordained for a particular century, then we may claim that no century has been as prolific of new inventions as the seventeenth century just past, in which more has been invented than in all the previous seventeen centuries together.'

There then follows a tribute to the great philosophers of the seventeenth century:

Think of the stature of Cartesius with his new philosophy, and although he may not have long retained the throne to which he was elevated, he at least opened the door to our current *philosophia mathematica*, which has had its effect, not only on the natural sciences, but also on medicine, and even, up to a point, on our moral philosophy, in so far as it depends on a thorough knowledge of human emotions.

Scheuchzer here acknowledges the vital part played by Descartes in the evolution of contemporary thinking. Starting with the principle of doubt, Descartes had postulated the only correct mode of mathematical reasoning. Since his time mathematically logical thinking had facilitated scientific discoveries that would have been inconceivable previously. Man's essential nature as a rational being had been recognized. Later on, voices to the contrary were to make themselves heard, but in Scheuchzer's time, *philosophia mathematica* still ruled, with its mechanical view of the world, a world which had been wound up by God like a clock that ran its course according to immutable laws.

The human organism was henceforth regarded as a kind of machine. Montesquieu wrote: 'My machine is so felicitously constructed that I am affected by every object just sufficiently to experience pleasure without suffering pain.'[22]

In fact it was now possible to examine the human body medically with much greater precision. As a doctor, Scheuchzer begins by looking at the medical discoveries of the seventeenth century:

> We have had new discoveries in medicine . . . The circulation of the blood, which was brought to light by Guilelmus Harveus . . . Numerous new discoveries have been made in anatomy . . . new *ductus salivales* or saliva glands; the morphology of the brain, analysed by Willis . . . of the ear . . . the heart . . . of the most minute glands and veins. *In summa*, the entire anatomy of the human body has revealed completely new aspects.

The eighteenth century was to advance medical science even further and secure for it the prominent place it was to occupy in the twentieth century. The new discoveries very soon brought about changes in the practice of medicine. Modern schools of medical practice sprang up alongside the traditional medical faculties, i.e. in 1724 the Collegium Medico-Chirurgicum and in 1795 the Pépinière clinic for army doctors, both in Berlin.

While human medicine moved into the field of practice, the reverse process took place in the case of veterinary practice, which began to find its way into the field of science. In 1762 the Ecole Vétérinaire was opened in Paris, in 1790 the Veterinary

College in Berlin. This was a development of vital importance
for agriculture.

Scheuchzer then turns to the vast field of mathematics and
mechanics. What had been achieved by Newton and Leibniz was
further developed by the Bernoullis, that unique dynasty of
mathematicians in Basel which produced in three generations no
fewer than eight leading mathematicians. They began teaching
in The Netherlands, then continued in St Petersburg, Berlin and
their native city of Basel. In the fourth generation – by this time
well into the nineteenth century – they had moved into the field
of technology. Scheuchzer writes:

> The whole world is full of new mathematical and mechan-
> ical inventions. I might bring together on one stage Carte-
> sius and his algebra that has lately been carried to the
> supreme point of perfection, Leibniz and Newton with
> their infinitesimal calculus, the Bernoullis with their latest
> graphs and the qualities deduced therefrom, Galileo Gali-
> lei, who successfully revived the theory of Copernicus with
> his new telescopes, that same excellent individual who was
> persecuted by the Roman priesthood.

With his reference to Galileo, Scheuchzer had touched on the
most contentious issue in the context of the new scientific
discoveries, Galileo's elaboration of the Copernican theory,
for which he had been, as Scheuchzer puts it, 'persecuted by
the Roman priesthood'. This was still a burning issue in
Scheuchzer's day.

The thirteenth verse of chapter 10 in the biblical book of
Joshua reads: 'So the sun stood still in the midst of heaven and
hasted not to go down about a whole day' – this phenomenon
had taken place, allegedly, at the behest of the Lord, so as to give
the chosen people of Israel time to accomplish their victory over
the Amorites.

If people came to believe that the earth revolved round the
sun, it followed that the earth was no longer the centre of the
universe – the earth, with its church as the sole source of
salvation and its authorities appointed by God! This opened up
the way for a theory to the effect that everything was relative,

and nothing absolute. It had been in the more liberal era of the sixteenth century that Copernicus had evolved his heliocentric theory of the universe through observation and calculation, i.e. by combining observation of nature and abstract mathematical calculation. Galileo had further elaborated the proof of the theory, but his findings had been condemned by the Roman Catholic Church and he had been ordered to keep his discovery secret. It was not only the Roman Church, in fact, but all the Christian churches in common that still clung to the old astronomical theory.

Scheuchzer was also ordered by the Zurich censors to delete from his *Job* all passages referring to the Copernican theory. He seems to have accepted the demand in a somewhat ironic spirit, deleting those passages that were likely to be understood by a layman. Whether by accident or design, the passage we have just quoted remained. The institution of censorship was one of the last signs of resistance on the part of the old orthodox faction. The Protestant churches proved to be more tolerant in a period when the old theology was giving way in any case to a 'rational theology', or what was called latitudinarianism. The Roman Catholic Church followed suit about halfway through the century.

Scheuchzer singles out Galileo on account of the latter's telescopes, and lists along with him

> Cassini and Huygens with the new planets they have observed round Jupiter and Saturn . . . Leeuwenhoek with his microscopes or magnifying glasses . . . Tschirnhausen with his focal lenses, Guericke . . . and others with their thermometers, Torricelli and Pascal with their barometers . . . Drebbelius . . . with his *navigiis subaquaeis* or ships that travel under water . . .

Scheuchzer has now moved into the sphere of contemporary technology, although some of the inventions he lists still had to wait a long time before they were actually realized. In the seventeeth and eighteenth centuries people were still more or less toying with their discoveries – with electricity, say, or with chemical experiments. A good example was Drebbelius with his *navigiis subaquaeis*, which did not become a practical proposition in fact until the beginning of the twentieth century. The same might be said of airships. The first hot-air balloons, it is true, ascended at the end of the eighteenth century. Goethe wrote at the time: 'Anyone who experienced the invention of the balloon can bear witness to the stir they caused throughout the world, what attention the aeronauts attracted, what longings stirred in thousands of breasts . . . how every successful attempt filled the newspapers with vivid first-hand accounts.'[23] Another century was to pass, however, before the advent of the first heavier-than-air flying machines.

Scheuchzer has a keen eye for the possibilities inherent in the new technology. He gives an enthusiastic account of the great canal enterprises of the day.

> Great princes and kings with their unprecedented projects deserve a place on our stage, Louis XIV, king of France, who joined the ocean and the Mediterranean Sea, Frederick William, Elector of Brandenburg, who linked the river Oder and the river Spree, the Duke of Holstein with his plan to join the North Sea and the Baltic, and Peter Alexiewitsch, Tsar of Moscow, who aims to join the Caspian Sea and the Black Sea, as well as the White Sea and the Baltic Ocean.

This was the period when Europe was first spanned by a dense network of canals that greatly facilitated transport. This in turn was possible only because engineering science had been vigorously developed and relevant schools to that end founded and fostered.

In conclusion Scheuchzer turns once more to the inventors, to 'private persons':

> From consideration of these mighty potentates and their works I turn once again to private persons and call to mind the perpetual motion machines of Becher and Drebbelius, the *antliae pneumaticae* or vacuum pumps of Guericke and Boyle, Huygens' invention of the clock pendulum, the pressure vessel invented by Papinianius, in which bones may be reduced to a pulp . . .

Scheuchzer is referring here to two vital inventions of the eighteenth century. The clock might indeed be elevated to the symbol of the century, on account of its precise mechanism and its ability to mark chronological periods accurately, so that time might be put to profitable use. This meant indeed taking leave of the timeless leisurely ways of the old world. The pressure vessel mentioned here led ultimately to the invention of the steam engine. It was the harnessing of steam in this way that was to revolutionize technology and industry at the close of the eighteenth century. The steam engine was actually developed by the technical team of the Lunar Society of Birmingham as early as the 1760s.

Scheuchzer concludes his list of technical inventions with the words: 'In short, it would take me far too long to speak of all the new inventions which may be found in the *Transactionibus Anglicanis, Mémoires de l'Académie Royale*, the *German Ephemerides*, the *Berlin Miscellanies*, etc.'

This is only one passing hint of the great part played by the scientific academies in the advancement of technology. The publications in Scheuchzer's list relate to the Royal Society, the Académie des Sciences, the German Academia Naturae Curiosorum and the Berlin Academy. Later on, it was the voluntary aid societies and craft societies, as well as agricultural and economic associations which took over the task of promoting, developing and utilizing scientific and technological discoveries and inventions. It was in such societies that the 'private persons' mentioned by Scheuchzer might find encouragement and assistance. They were often parsons with their collections of natural specimens and meteorological observations, or else ingenious craftsmen.

Voltaire, otherwise a hardened sceptic, writes with surprising optimism of the *Progress of the Human Mind in the Century of Louis XV*, i.e. between 1720 and 1770. 'The academies have done a great deal by inducing young people to read and encouraging their talents by awarding prizes. A soundly based science of physics has fostered the necessary industrial processes, so that the wounds inflicted by two ill-starred wars are being healed.' Thanks to the new modern methods of production, textiles could be manufactured more cheaply. Agriculture had also been improved by scientific research, 'and an enlightened minister has made possible free trade in grain, which has been banned for far too long . . . '.[24]

8

Education, Schools and Popular Enlightenment

When people later looked back on the development of technology, they were inclined to ask themselves: which came first, the modern plough or the reading primer?

There is no unequivocal answer to this question, but the part played by the elementary reading book, the school textbook in general, in training the population, especially the rural population, should not be underestimated. The operation of machinery entails a degree of literacy and a certain amount of training, and the same is true of any philosophical or political culture. Education is vital, both for handing on traditional values and for blazing a trail for new ideas.

The Enlightenment inevitably inherited the legacy of the Reformation and Counter-Reformation. The Protestants had everywhere stressed the necessity of an educated clergy, but they were also well aware that education would have to go much further than that: the whole population had to be instructed in the new faith, and that meant universal schooling for children. This was achieved primarily within the religious context by the use of the catechism, a little book of questions and answers instructing the reader in the correct faith and enjoining correct behaviour, a distillation of theological principles derived from the Bible and couched in language that anyone could understand. With the aid of the catechism people learned to read, memorize and recite. They were trained to deal with the

205

questions and answers laid down in their catechism, they were instructed as to what was right and wrong, they learned to identify basic theological concepts, and were familiarized with the world of the people of Israel, an ancient and refined culture that formed one of the bases of European civilization. All this had been complemented by assiduous reading of the Scriptures.

The Roman Catholic catechism was able to achieve similar results, although intensive study of the biblical texts was not encouraged – after all, reading and study were more a matter for the upper classes and the clergy, especially the Jesuits, than for the common people. The latter were more impressed by the sumptuous architecture and ritual of the baroque churches which captivated the emotions and the senses of the faithful.

It was consequently on the work of the Reformation, with its more intellectual appeal, that the Enlightenment tended to build. Certainly, it was necessary to change the emphasis here and there. When Locke wrote *On Education*, his aim was to train free and autonomous individuals. Henceforth there was no end to the flood of educational literature. Rousseau struck an original note when he placed the child, *le petit homme*, at the centre of the educational process and proposed to have him brought up in harmony with nature, as in his *Emile*. Pestalozzi went further in the same direction, calling for education in a spirit of humanism instead of mere drilling in techniques that could be automatically assimilated.

Reform of the schools became one of the main tasks of the Enlightenment. Its protagonists were confronted with an integrated system which they considered to be fossilized and bigoted. They set about changing the existing system in every respect – often against opposition that frequently came from the teachers. At the University of Basel, for instance, there was stubborn resistance to proposals for reform put forward by the great mathematician, Jakob Bernoulli. The old guard's slogan had been: *Limites quos posuere Veteres non moveto*,[25] 'The limits set by the Ancients may not be moved.'

That was a watchword of 1691. But if a university wished to survive in the eighteenth century and make its mark, then it had to consent at least to minimal changes. The two established subjects of mathematics and physics were now supplemented by natural philosophy – the observation of men, animals and plants. Geography provided knowledge of a world full of wonders, where one discovery followed another with breath-taking rapidity. The study of history – once little more than a branch of rhetoric devoted to the greater glorification of the monarchs – was now also being seen as the study of men and their activities throughout the centuries – if not actually as their inevitable advance into a better future. To the study of the classical world, which had hitherto dominated the subject, there was now added the history of more recent ages and of individual countries, *Historia Patriae* as it was called. In the faculties of law, theories of natural law emerged and took the place of Aristotelian ethics.

The universities were nevertheless still dominated by the Latin language, although here and there teaching was conducted in the local vernacular tongue. The path to the university led via the Latin grammar school, where instruction began at about the age of ten. It was not until the nineteenth century that national languages became the medium of instruction pretty well everywhere, and modern foreign languages became part of the curriculum. In many other respects universities and grammar schools were still bogged down in the old system during the eighteenth century: prescribed textbooks, lectures as the mode of teaching, disputation as the method of examination. Discussion of literature in any broader critical sense was a matter for the *salons* and the learned societies, although it is true that professors from the universities were among those who set the tone in such assemblies.

The university prepared its students only for three traditional and specific careers: it trained the clergy, lawyers and physicians – with minimal relevance to the more practical aspects of these professions. It was in practice, in fact, that changes began which ultimately affected the faculties of medicine towards the end of the century. Hitherto the *Doctor Medicinae* had been only an expert diagnostician who identified diseases and subjected them to scientific examination. Treatment was left largely to surgeons without academic training or to apothecaries. Advances in medical practice and treatment inevitably brought

about a change of emphasis, either in the universities themselves, or in medical and surgical colleges and associations. The
way was opened up for the modern medical practitioner.

Now society, and the political states into which it was organized, began to feel the need for new professions with more
exacting technical training. Above all, it was essential to train
engineers, because technical advances were apparent on every
side. Of course, there had always been carpenters, builders,
bridge-builders and architects, but now they began to be trained
intensively in mathematics and geometry. It was France especially that developed schools of engineering: in 1718, the Ecole
des Ingénieurs; in 1747, the Ecole des Ponts et Chaussées; in
1765, the Ecole du Génie marin; in 1778, the Ecole des Mines:
they were all based in Paris and tended to stress military requirements primarily. Mathematics, for instance, was taught with the
needs of artillery officers in mind.

In Germany it was mining academies that came first: in 1770
in Berlin; in 1775 in Clausthal-Zellerfeld; In 1776 in Freiberg
in Saxony. The engineering profession was coming into being,
and in the nineteenth century it was to achieve its rightful
leading place in the great polytechnics.

From the second half of the eighteenth century art schools
began to offer a more liberal education in the crafts and technology. They were the forerunners of the trade schools, industrial
schools, as well as of high schools specializing in mathematics,
and other technical training establishments.

Training for businessmen in commercial schools with a pro-
nounced practical bent came to be seen as the necessary con-
comitant to these developments in technology and industry.
They offered tuition in bookkeeping and the major foreign
languages. For the growing number of civil servants there
were now so-called *Kameralschulen*, institutions which spe-
cialized in law and economics. Cadet schools for future officers
and civil servants had already been established by Louis XIV.
Many rulers in the period of the Enlightenment – not just
Duke Karl Eugen of Württemberg with his *Hohe Karlsschule* –
were concerned to provide more systematic training for their
administrators.

But could the Enlightenment stop there? Professional training was certainly necessary and highly desirable, but was there
not a risk that, in the midst of all this concern for technology
and rational knowledge, the individual might be overlooked?
What was offered here as a remedy was the philanthropic
movement, the first experiments in truly integrated education,
as projected by Basedow in Dessau, Martin Planta and Ulysses
von Salis in Grisons.

Such attempts at philosophically and psychologically based
education affected only a certain elite, however: upper-class, or
at best, middle-class children from the towns. Was that good
enough? After all, one of the essential features of the Enlightenment was that it wished everyone to have his or her share of the
new light – whether from general altruistic considerations, or
from prudent political calculation. Even at the beginning of the
century people had begun to wonder whether quite simple,
everyday problems might not be just as worthy of investigation
as the grand issues of philosophy: 'It is only the art of sound and
prudent housekeeping that everyone seems to despise and think
unworthy of being governed by a few intelligent principles.'[26]

If the people as a whole were to be enlightened, then the first
priority must be the battle against illiteracy. This would be
fought through better, more comprehensive schooling that was
accessible to as many children as possible. This entailed the
establishment of special schools for the lower classes of society,
schools for the poor such as Pestalozzi had set up in the Swiss
canton of Aargau, in Neuhof, or like the schools that Junker
Rochow had opened for peasant children in Rekahn in the march
of Brandenburg.

Existing urban and rural schools might also be reorganized
more democratically, so that they would be open to all children.
If that were to be achieved, patrician families or local lairds
would just have to pay the price of having their children shut up
in the same stuffy premises as the malodorous progeny of the
poor. In fact, many such families preferred to employ as private
tutors theological graduates who were awaiting preferment to a
living. It was not until the nineteenth century that the dream of
rich and poor seated side by side at the same school desk came

anywhere near realization, and even then the situation varied from country to country.

Such measures as were taken applied mainly to children. But what could be done about the adults? After all, whatever modest schooling they had had might have been forgotten in the rigours of their daily toil. What kind of reading matter might they be offered, seeing that what was available on the shelves was mostly intended for the upper classes? Even the vaunted encyclopedias would hardly help, for who could possibly afford those sumptuous volumes? A new form of communication had to be found, literature that offered instruction in a popular guise, especially for the agricultural sector, in which, after all, a large proportion of the population worked. What was needed was not moralizing – that might be found in the catechism – but eminently practical instruction relating to concrete situations.

Such instruction need not necessarily be via the printed word: here there was perhaps a new function for the village parson, particularly in Protestant areas. He might do rather more than just read out from the pulpit various edicts handed down by the authorities. Even his sermons might follow a more practical line, so that he became a teacher of his flock, concerned not only with their salvation in another world, but also with their welfare in this world. Hence the sermons, subsequently so derided, on hay at Christmastime or on lightning conductors that were pleasing in the eyes of God. The parson for his part no doubt derived his knowledge from the publications of voluntary or economic associations. At the same time, of course, care had to be taken not to undermine the existing social order in any way. As far as the landowners and municipal authorities were concerned, what mattered most was achieving a higher yield from the land. Nevertheless, they were bound to have some interest in reducing the number of totally untutored poor.

The function of the clergy in transmitting know-how was soon supplemented by the distribution of popular brochures and pamphlets containing practical suggestions. These were designed to be read by farmers and farm labourers, in so far as they were literate. As late as the 1740s, however, it was still necessary to argue against old, outdated opinions.

In 1749 an attempt was made to refute the prejudice that was derived by many from the curse laid upon the soil following the Fall of Man and that suggested there was no point in seeking to improve farming methods. The relevant comment was that anyone who was so stupid that he could not distinguish between theology and the other sciences was in any case incorrigible. The publications of self-help and economic societies contain innumerable practical suggestions for making everyday labour less onerous and more effective. How may the new discoveries in the natural sciences be put to use in agriculture? How may agriculture – on a large or small scale – be improved to the benefit of all classes of the population? . . . Which new fodder crops are suitable for which type of soil? How may blight in grain be combated? What can be done to ward off cattle diseases? The reader is instructed on the advantages of pig-breeding, a lexicon of fertilizers is intended to help him improve his soil; indeed, there is even discussion on how the poor may provide themselves cheaply with warm beds.

In 1756, the moral weekly, *The Husbandman and his Wife*, wrote: 'Let us strive with all our might to improve the lot of our brothers. Let us not be ashamed to act as teachers to the common man. For, had they but been educated as we have been, they would fain be what we are, and more. The world may well do without us, but it cannot dispense with them.'

Apart from the little instruction manuals which were sometimes in the form of questions and answers, in the manner of the familiar catechism, there were journals and bulletins and, of course, the traditional calendars, which now might incorporate economic or scientific facts. The calendar was a standard item in every farmer's library, which would otherwise not include more than a few books of a devotional or moral character, perhaps a book of psalms or a collection of sermons.

A handbook of medical hints might also have a place there, of course. A start in this area had been made by the Lausanne physician, Auguste Tissot with his *Guide to Our Farming Folk in*

Respect to Their Health, published in 1761 and translated into more than a dozen languages. This *Avis au peuple sur la santé* was followed by innumerable other medical works of a popular kind. By 1768 there were more than 800 items dealing with the prevention and treatment of smallpox in the German-speaking area alone. And then there were naturally hundreds of publications on veterinary medicine. Another aspect of such efforts to enlighten the populace was represented by the campaign against superstition: as early as 1755 a *Register of Superstitious Beliefs and Actions* was published in Leipzig.

Gradually the urban proponents of Enlightenment began to evolve an image of the model farmer. One example came from Zurich, Jakob Guyer, who became world-famous thanks to the *Husbandry of a Philosophical Farmer*, written by the city's Public Health Officer, Johann Kaspar Hirzel, and translated into French as *Le Socrate rustique*. In Zurich, too, the Economics Committee of the Natural Science Research Association organized regular Farmers' Colloquia, in which farmers and citizens alike took part. City-dwellers and nobility slowly began to realize that common sense and the ability to think for themselves might be found even among common people.

Thus the Enlightenment discovered the people and incorporated them into its mainly middle-class world, building bridges from one class to another, in different ways and with a degree of success that varied from one European country to another. We have limited ourselves here to examples from Germany and Switzerland, where the movement was particularly vigorous. What we have observed is one aspect of 'patriotism' as it was understood in the Enlightenment: a rejection of the closed world of segregated social classes with all its mutual suspicions and prejudices. This is perhaps why Goethe, as a young man, once critized a certain writer on the grounds that he was not acquainted at first hand with the common people: 'How very differently his judgement might have turned out, had he deigned to watch the husband with his family, the farmer on his farm, the mother with her children, the craftsman in his workshop, the honest citizen with his stoup of wine . . .!'

9

Virtue and Patriotism

The Enlightenment meant to train not only new men but better men. It was for this purpose and in this sense that it resurrected the age-old idea of a doctrine of virtue, the doctrine of *arete* or *virtus* derived from Greek and Roman ethical systems, a doctrine that had been summed up in the idea of four cardinal virtues: *justitia, prudentia, temperantia* and *fortitudo* – justice, wisdom, moderation and courage – which could still be found emblazoned on fountains, in town halls and churches in many places. The virtues were allegedly of divine origin, but now it was a matter of reformulating them in keeping with the principles of natural law and reason, and of making them valid for all men.

As a rule, writers of the Enlightenment draw a distinction between individual virtues that apply to a man and his own private actions, and those virtues that are valid in society, or alternatively, in politics.

As far as individual virtues went, it was assumed that a man's moral attitude was founded on certain principles. Every individual had an obligation to his own conscience and had to observe ethical principles. For the deist the law of nature was binding, even though he did not acknowledge a personal god. Atheists obeyed some kind of inner voice. Nevertheless, most of those involved in the Enlightenment still felt bound by some kind of religious commitment – not in the sense of any particular orthodoxy, but simply as the 'religious sensibility of the educated class'.[27] They did, in fact, often belong to a church,

213

they attended its services, went to mass or took communion; they might begin the day with an act of worship, in fact the whole household might be gathered together for family prayers. The emphasis, however, would not be on the dogma of the confessional group in question, but more on a generally enlightened kind of piety of a Jansenist or pietistic complexion. Whatever their nominal confession, these people were very much aware that man was made in the image of God. They went in for 'soul-searching' and kept a record of their thoughts and actions, often in writing. A man's conscience would tell him what was right and what was wrong. The German theologian Spalding declared: 'In this way I learned more and more to come to terms with myself, and my conscience became increasingly important.' The conscience might govern the deist or the atheist even, who had renounced allegiance to a church or a personal god: in their case it was conscience that took the place of the religious sense.

The general interest in man as such might emerge as the virtue of philanthropy, the love of one's fellow-men, a notion which occupies a central position in the ethical theory of the Enlightenment as a kind of modified religion. It was the eighteenth century that coined the expression and understood by it the active love of mankind expressed in the tradition of good deeds that figured in all the various Christian confessions and sects. Now, however, philanthropy might be practised outside the confines of a church in the form of works devoted to the common good. It was felt that man's latent egoism, his concentration on his own person and interests, had to be disciplined and brought under control.

Philanthropy was associated with humility, expressed in outward appearance and bearing. A certain puritanism prompted an assault on luxury, opulence, as it was then called, and an effort to reduce personal expenditure.

Related to humility was the virtue of moderation, not only in the satisfaction of personal needs and physical appetites, but also in the form of emotional self-discipline and repression of the passions, which had been allowed free rein in the baroque period – not only in the field of art. Moderation implied the choice of a middle way, as it was put in an English slogan referring to the two political parties: 'In moderation placing all my glory, the Tories call me Whig, the Whigs a Tory.' In choosing a middle way, of course, one ran the risk of being discredited in the eyes of both parties.

Lastly, industriousness, assiduity, was also included among the individual virtues. Indolence was still regarded as a vice and was to be discouraged. The discipline of the nineteenth century with its dislike of leisure and meditation was already looming on the horizon.

The individual virtues – religious feeling, philanthropy, humility, moderation and industriousness – furnished the basis for behaviour in the social context, in family and state. However closely knit the family, however great the concern for children or career, for the maintenance of social standing in the nobility and middle class, it was considered virtuous for a man to devote a certain proportion of his time, effort and money to public causes, especially in cases where he had achieved some degree of affluence by good fortune, inheritance or hard work. Wealth and social position might be put to other, less laudable uses in this opulent century – the nobility were in a position to squander time and money on hunting, gaming and womanizing, men of business might spend their time amassing even more capital or carousing in guildhalls, clergymen might engage in intrigue aimed at the acquisition of profitable livings, in eating, drinking or idly dozing their time away.

If a man occupied some political office or other, as councillor, magistrate, governor, civil servant, mayor or minister, then he was expected to place himself unselfishly at the disposal of the community and to work for the common good. This commitment to the common good might often take place in the context of a voluntary self-help or charitable association. The eighteenth century had a socially committed elite of this kind at its disposal everywhere – with greater or less power to make its influence felt, depending on the country in question and its political situation. The guiding principle was patriotism, and it appeared in a variety of guises. Patriotism was capable of inspiring a king, his minister, noble squires, rural administrators, mayors and councillors, traders and craftsmen, parsons, teachers, medical men and enlightened farmers. It is to be met with not only in republics, but it is experienced particularly strongly there, where fame and honour were essentially local. In the Hanseatic city of Hamburg patriotism was defined as follows: 'It is that powerful inner urge that takes as its object the good of the state and seeks to foster its welfare in every possible way.'[28]

A precondition for effective activity in the community at large was an assurance of the greatest possible freedom for the individual. It was reckoned that every man ought to be able to claim certain basic rights, such as personal freedom, security and a guarantee that his property was inviolable. The state was expected to respect and protect these basic rights, irrespective of what political form it might take, monarchy or republic. As long as the dignity of the individual was respected, then all was well.

The individual virtues now had to be matched by 'patriotic' virtues; in other words, they had to be put in the service of the public, and here the old cardinal virtues were revived in a new interpretation.

Prudentia, wisdom, was naturally of prime importance. The ancient battle against *stultitia*, folly or stupidity, was resumed, now with the polished satirical wit of a Swift and a Voltaire. Erasmus' classic work, *Moriae encomium sive stultitiae laus* (*The Praise of Folly*), continued to be republished, translated and read.

The cardinal virtue of *temperantia*, moderation, now tended to be interpreted in terms of tolerance. One of the first unequivocal statements of this principle is to be found in William Penn's *Frame of Government* for the colony of Pennsylvania:

All those persons living in this province who acknowledge one Almighty and Eternal God and confess Him as the Creator, Sustainer and Lord of the Earth and who feel obliged by their conscience to live in peace and justice in our civil society may not be in any way molested or discriminated against on account of their religious convictions.[29]

This constitutional article absorbed all the bitter experience of many years of persecution of religious minorities in England under the Stuart kings. At the same time, it also contributed a great deal towards the shaping of William Penn's unique policy towards the native Indian population. This article offers more than just tolerance, it offers freedom of religious conviction. The proponents of Enlightenment were thinking on these lines long before the corresponding edicts were issued in Prussia or Austria. Tolerance is itself an expression of a religious mentality.

The cardinal virtue of *justitia* was accepted without question by the representatives of the Enlightenment. In practice it placed the obligation of impartial judgement on all those who bore any kind of political responsibility.

The cardinal virtue of *fortitudo*, or courage, was now construed as the courage to commit oneself to the cause of Enlightenment and the courage to accept setbacks to that cause. One article in the publications of the Berne Economic Society speaks of 'the courage to face the judgement of men':

> Useful undertakings are rarely founded with due foresight: when viewed from afar, objects make only a faint impression. We commonly begin to think of remedies only when some evil begins to make them seem necessary. Even then we are often handicapped by a natural lethargy, if this is not overcome by a powerful determination to deal with an injustice or a defect that grows ever greater in our sight; we lack the will and determination, or else the perseverance needed to overcome various obstacles that are magnified even further by our apprehensive imaginations. This lack of confidence in our own powers may stem from another equally reprehensible source – an all too slavish fear of the judgement of our fellow-men, which is governed by success: our self-esteem is not prepared to run the risk of having made an error.[30]

Determination is needed to overcome inertia, confidence in our own powers must overcome failure. If we are confronted with human distress, with misfortune and catastrophes occasioned by natural forces, such an experience may grieve the philanthropist, 'but it must not weary him in well-doing, this it shall not and must not do'.[31] The supreme example of the virtue of courage, even in classical times, had been represented by death for the fatherland, and it was against the background of the Seven Years War that the German author Thomas Abbt wrote of *Death for the Fatherland*. But this sacrifice was demanded by and large only of officers and soldiers. The view of the Enlightenment suggests that a man's life might be dedicated totally to his fatherland without being involved in war.

And what did 'fatherland' mean? A man's fatherland was the locality where he had been set down and where he had to live and work. Its limits were not simply national, however, for whatever a man did for his home, he also did for mankind in general. If a patriot promoted the welfare of his own country, he also promoted the welfare of mankind at large. Patriotism had not yet turned into nationalism.

There was a 'political patriotism', which might be realized most effectively in republics, where the citizen did his duty and was best able to place himself at the service of the state. But even in monarchies the subject had the possibility of collaborating with the state and loyally exercising the authority allocated to him.

A 'national patriotism' was motivated and governed by a man's image of his own nation. He thus aspired to emulate the heroes who had committed themselves to the cause of their fatherland in the past, whether in peace or in war. This kind of patriotism was concerned to defend the country's supreme values whenever they were threatened.

'Universal patriotism' recognized that the nation state was no more than provisional and that its history would ultimately culminate in a universal humanitarian goal, 'when all nations have become but one', as Lavater expressed his hope in an *Incantation*.

'Ecumenical patriotism' continued the Christian traditions, but in a sense that transcended the various confessions, in the sense of tolerance for all religious convictions – even the non-Christian faiths – in so far as their practices were humane.

When utopia was sought via reform, an 'educational patriotism' was called for to train men in humane values, while a 'social patriotism' concerned itself with human distress and deprivation, and 'economic patriotism' worked to secure a minimum of economic resources for all men.

The ethical doctrine of the Enlightenment saw its task even in the most limited sphere, which might, after all, ultimately be expanded to include wider areas of responsibility.

Any father of a family promotes the welfare of his father-land simply by bringing up his children well; any mother may do the same by running her household efficiently and avoiding luxury and ostentation; young people may play their part by showing respect and obedience; the elderly by experience and good example; the labourer and artisan by their assiduity; the soldier by the employment of his weapons; the scholar through the dissemination of useful knowledge, writing and invention; the clergyman by the purity of his faith and the piety of his life; the powers that be by the administration of justice and the government of the world in keeping with the law.[32]

This was the simple programme of the Age of Reason in rudimentary terms, unencumbered with abstract philosophical or theological concepts, a straightforward ethical code such as had been sought repeatedly over the centuries, a code that had been confronted with evil in the world ever since the distant days of Socrates and Epictetus.

The simple concepts of virtue and patriotism were frequently abused and perverted in the nineteenth century. Virtue might degenerate into hypocrisy, or be reduced to mere propriety or respectability. Patriotism was liable to turn into blind and arrogant nationalism. Besides, the new science of psychoanalysis stripped the virtues of their divine origins and aura and reduced them to mere psychic aptitudes or potentials. National Socialism and Fascism were ultimately to pervert patriotism totally. Nevertheless, the programme of the Enlightenment survived, however utopian the terms in which it was conceived, however severe the demands it made on the individual. Were not the members of the Accademia dei Pugni in Milan right when they called for *belle virtù, doveri – virtù senza noia*, 'comely virtues, duties – virtues without pedantry'?[33] Virtue ought to be cheerful and gay, not boring, the search for virtue ought to be a fascinating quest.

Thus the man of the Enlightenment grew up, with his lucid and logical intelligence, his unspectacular courage and his deliberate, carefully calculated mode of action – sober, objective, no longer governed by traditional ideas, by impassioned orthodoxy and baroque enthusiasm. It was as if the Roman stoics had been resurrected. There was, however, an obverse side to the medal: conservative respectability and chilly rationalism. Shallow, dull, trivial logic-chopping – these were the charges that the succeeding Romantic generation were to hurl at the age of Enlightenment. And yet the portraits of the eighteenth century still preserve the intelligent faces of those men and women with their clear gaze, their upright posture and their friendly smiles often tinged with self-irony.

PART VI

A Window Opened to a Wider World

1

A Window Opened to a Wider World

The Enlightenment was initially centred in Europe. There was so much to be cleared away in Europe, so many new things to be looked at and interpreted, so much that had to be rethought. But Europeans were fully aware that they were not alone in the world. They were already so closely linked with other continents that they were obliged to think in terms of new attitudes and approaches.[1]

When Voltaire began his *History of the World* with a chapter headed *De la Chine* he struck a brand new note, putting classical and Christian ideas into a much wider context. Hitherto, people had been indoctrinated with the history of the peoples of Israel, ancient Greece and Rome as the undisputed basis of all history. They had long been familiar with the Orient of ancient times – that was indeed where light had first come from. But in more recent times the Orient had been compromised: the Turkish wars, the siege of Vienna were still fresh in the memory, and at the start of the century the Venetians were still fighting their last naval battles against the Turks in the Mediterranean.

Ever since Columbus had discovered America there had been widespread knowledge of a vast continent beyond the ocean. Spain and Portugal had divided the New World of the sixteenth century between them. A second Spain extended from Mexico to Chile, while Brazil belonged to the Portuguese, along with parts of Africa and India. Soon the Dutch, the French and the English upset this judicious division of territory. Every European state

223

with an Atlantic seaboard wanted to have its own overseas colonies, even Denmark which set up its Danish West Indies, comprising some of the Virgin Islands, in 1755. Almost all the major ports of Africa and India fell under European influence. Newly discovered territories were promptly fenced off and fortified. Europeans soon began emigrating to other continents: both the Americas were settled by Europeans, particularly North America, which became the classic immigrant country for the European poor, or for those who had left home to escape religious persecution: Presbyterians in Boston, Huguenots in Charlestown, Baptists or Mennonites in Ontario or elsewhere.

In these new continents the Enlightenment thus found a world that had already been infiltrated by European cultures. The trader from Amsterdam felt entirely at home in Batavia on the island of Java, as his London counterpart did in Madras, the French merchant in Pondichéry and the Portuguese in Goa. Spanish viceroys and archbishops had long been resident in cities from Mexico to Lima. Portuguese, Britons, Dutchmen and Frenchmen were busy in their factories or trading stations on the African coast.

The Europeans had come as conquerors, as future masters, as adventurers and traders. What they were looking for was commercial profit and political power, such as they had known in Europe – except that in Europe a man was liable to run up against some barrier or another at every turn. In spite of all the attendant hardships, colonization had been achieved far too easily. For the superior Europeans the indigenous inhabitants were not their equals. They were barbarians, and barbarians were fated by their very nature to become slaves, as anyone who had read Aristotle well knew. The natives had first to be subjugated and then domesticated. This method of colonization was first practised on the Indos of South America, whose highly developed culture, incomprehensible to Europeans, was rapidly eradicated. In 1780/81 the Indians in Peru made a desperate attempt to rebel under the leadership of Túpac Amaru, a descendant of the Inca dynasty who tried to resurrect the myth of the pre-Columbian age. The Indos were converted to Roman Catholicism and were lavishly provided with magnificent cathedrals, even in the remotest mountain regions. The Christian colonists did indeed have qualms of conscience at an early stage. Bartolomé de Las Casas, the Spanish bishop in the Mexican city of Chiapas, devoted himself for the whole of his life to the cause of the Indos and actually achieved a measure of legislative protection for them. In the course of the seventeenth century the Jesuits in the border territories between Spanish colonies in Paraguay and Northern Peru established a theocratic state where the Indos were protected until they were divided between the two colonial powers between the years 1750 and 1776 and hence once more reduced to slavery.

In North America the English Quaker, William Penn, placed himself on the same footing as the Indians with whom he concluded land treaties. In the *Charter* of 1680 he pledged himself to 'instil in the savage natives an affection for civilized society and the Christian faith'. Penn had taken advice from English representatives of the Enlightenment, such as Locke and Shaftesbury. What mattered here, as at home in England, was tolerance. The Jesuits' 'holy experiment' turned out a failure in the long run, and we are all too well aware of the ultimate fate of the North American Indians.

Colonization had a particularly drastic impact on the natives of Africa, who were shipped off to both the Americas as negro slaves – mainly in the eighteenth century. Some ten million were transported overseas in this fashion in the course of three centuries. The slave trade was taken for granted and other African races were only too glad to deliver their hostile neighbours into bondage. Whereas black people could be more or less integrated into the social and cultural environment inherited from their Latin and Roman Catholic masters in South America, a long time was to pass before they could develop their own cultural identity in a North America which had largely been shaped by the Protestant traditions of Great Britain. The development of a separate identity did not become possible until the spread of the evangelical movement at the start of the nineteenth century.

It was not until the second half of the eighteenth century that many Europeans and white Americans realized with horror what had actually been going on: the ghastly slaughter of human beings of a different colour and different culture – not just enslavement and humiliation, but genocide through the importation of lethal diseases, to which the native populations proved to be highly susceptible. Voices began to be raised against colonialism. Voltaire remarked in reference to a report by Las Casas that the latter might be exaggerating here and there, but that on the whole his report was enough to horrify the reader. Now the exploiters' mentality came under fire from the Enlightenment. If the talk in Europe was all of equal rights and self-determination for all, then that should indeed apply to everyone, and hence even to 'savages', whom people were actually beginning to see as good and 'noble'.

Baron de Lahontan, a French adventurer, became acquainted with the North American Indians in the 1680s, and in 1703 published his *Conversation Between the Author and a Savage of Sound Common Sense*. Lahontan carries on a discussion with Adario, an Indian:

> To the Gospels Adario triumphantly opposed his natural religion, contrasting his natural morality with the laws of Europe, which inspire only fear and retribution. He compared European society with his rudimentary communism that guarantees both happiness and security . . . Even Adario's ignorance has its advantages: being unable to read or write, he has spared himself untold suffering, for science and the arts are only a source of corruption. He follows the commands of his kind Mother Nature and is happy. It is the so-called civilized nations that are the real barbarians, in fact: may the example set by the savage peoples teach them to recover their human dignity and their freedom.[2]

That was written long before Rousseau and Voltaire; it was about the middle of the century that they detected a change of sentiment towards primitive peoples – Voltaire in his *Essai sur les moeurs et l'esprit des nations* (1756) and Rousseau in *Discours sur l'origine de l'inégalité parmi les hommes* (1754). Voltaire's voluminous historical study was the first such work to depart from the well-trodden path of a Christocentric universal history, with

Chinese and Islamic cultures eliciting the particular respect of
the author on account of their high level of civilization. While
Voltaire remained committed to the progressive thinking of the
Enlightenment, Rousseau helped to inspire a sense of cultural
insecurity in the European nations that was to have far-reaching
consequences, in that he drew attention to the pre-literate, 'uncivilized' phases of human development. Rousseau's hypothet-
ical fiction of man in a state of unspoiled nature had been
generated by the frustration of this individualist with the absolutist courtly society and culture of the rococo; its counterpart,
the economically independent, politically free and morally innocent *homme naturel*, represented a challenge to everything that
appeared to crib and confine the individual in that age, corrupt-
ing him and alienating him from his true self. That a traveller
through space might simultaneously be embarking on a voyage
of discovery into his own origins and more felicitous early phases
of his evolution – this was a novel and important idea that
acquired great popularity in the works of Rousseau's disciples.

Twenty years later, the president of the Royal Society made the
following recommendation in connection with Captain Cook's
voyage round the world:

> It should constantly be borne in mind that to shed the
> blood of these peoples is a capital crime, for we are dealing
> with human beings from the hand of the same almighty
> Creator, and are obliged to care for them as much as for the
> most polished European, in that they are possibly less
> warlike and more deserving of God's favour. They are the
> natural, and in a strict sense, the legal owners of the various
> territories they inhabit. No European nation has any right
> to occupy any part of that land or to settle there with-
> out their freely given consent. The subjugation of such a
> people cannot confer any convincing title in law, since they
> have not acted the part of the aggressor.

This was an acknowledgement, in terms of natural law, of the
rights of these exotic peoples, and a repudiation in principle of
the spirit and practice of colonization. Individuals of other races
and cultures had to be respected as fellow-men. In this sense

the time-honoured idea of the Christian mission gained an Enlightenment component. The Christian missions had championed non-white people and tried to ensure that they shared the
Christian hope of salvation. Even if the exercise was somewhat
one-sided in that it had to take the form of conversion to
Christianity, the Jesuits and the Capuchins, and later the pietistically inclined Protestants, took the exotic races seriously as
God's creatures. What was said of the pietists' missions applies
equally to the missions of all the other confessions:

> Many of them set out, in spite of great hardships and dan-
> gers, to perform unprecedented pioneering deeds, far away
> from the sheltered ecclesiastical life of their churches at
> home that was secure, ordered and hedged about by tradi-
> tion and convention. Innumerable others in their home
> countries shared the adventures of the missions in China
> and Africa through reports, bulletins and books, and were
> thus made aware of wider horizons – not simply in a literal
> geographical sense, but also in terms of their otherwise
> provincial and exclusively European view of their church
> . . . behind the missions, after all, loomed the grand ideal
> of a universal Kingdom of God encompassing land and sea.[3]

It should not be forgotten, incidentally, that it was the English
Methodists who first took up the cause of the anti-slavery movement in the 1770s.

Interest in foreign cultures did not stem, of course, only from
Christian humanitarian concern: it was prompted also by pure
curiosity and the keen scientific interest of an enlightened age
that was eager to experience anything that was novel or unfamiliar. People were keen to learn as much as they could about the
world as a whole. Travel journals became a highly popular form
of literature, while 'exoticism' was the fashionable trend in the
design of drawing-rooms and gardens.

The book which possibly had the widest influence of any was
Daniel Defoe's *Robinson Crusoe*, published in 1719. Although the
hero tries to turn his Man Friday into a European, he does treat
him as a human being capable of being trained, and not simply
as an inferior and barbarian.

Defoe sets his *Robinson Crusoe* on the island of Juan-Fernandez in the Pacific Ocean, and it was the islands of the South Seas that seemed at that time to be the most fascinating of all the new discoveries. Apart from Indonesia, which had been annexed by the Dutch, these mysterious islands had not hitherto attracted European settlers. It was not until the second half of the eighteenth century that Europeans became aware of them as one of the last areas of the world to be opened up by explorers.

In these decades explorers undertook their voyages in a spirit that was different from that of previous ages: they were keen to make contact with the natives and to learn from them. Round about 1800 the French naturalist de Gérando wrote:

> The main purpose to which the expectation and the zeal of the truly philosophical explorer should be directed ought to be the collection and collation of all those methods which allow him to enter into the minds of the people amongst whom he is living, and thus to explain their actions, in terms of motive and consequences. This aim is vitally important, not only in itself, but also as a preliminary step and an introduction to all other areas of knowledge. How can a man pride himself on his powers of observation, if he does not understand what people say and is unable to converse with them? The best way of getting to know indigenous peoples is to become like them in some sense – if we learn their language, we become their fellow-citizens.

De Gérando goes on to criticize fiercely the manner in which Europeans had hitherto treated other races: 'Columbus sent only greedy conquerors to the New World . . . the cruel Spanish adventurers brought nothing with them but devastation.'

Now even severe self-criticism on the part of Europeans is possible. 'It is devoutly to be desired,' wrote the German naturalist Forster who accompanied Cook on his second voyage,

> that the contacts between Europeans and the inhabitants of the South Sea islands might be discontinued before the corrupt manners of the civilized nations infect these

guileless folk who dwell here in innocence and harmony. It is a melancholy truth, however, that the love of one's fellow-men and the political systems of Europe do not harmonize.

True, Europeans had quite early on come across cultures that proved to be more resistant: ancient and highly refined cultures like those of Egypt, Persia, India, Japan and China, which had mastered the arts of reading and writing at a time when the Europeans themselves were still barbarians. These were cultures in which government and legislation of a complex kind had been evolved, and in which polite social intercourse was taken as a matter of course.

As early as the seventeenth century the Near East had given Europeans much food for thought: the wise Egyptian, *le sage Egyptien* – already foreshadowed in classical times in the works of Herodotus and Strabo – had actually been discovered by Capuchin missionaries in Upper Egypt. The great theologian of France in its classical period, Bossuet, incorporated this figure in his universal history and was at pains to correct errors that were current concerning Moslems and Islam. Further accounts of the Arab peoples followed. In 1730 Boulainvillers wrote his *Vie de Mahomet* showing that the prophet had exemplified in his life the wisdom of the Arabs, just as Christ had embodied the wisdom of the Jews.

But these revelations paled into insignificance compared with what the Jesuits had discovered in China: the circumstances there in no way resembled those in America or Africa. Here the missionaries were not dealing with savages but with cultured individuals who not only had impeccable table manners, but who also took an intelligent interest in Europeans and their ways. Indeed, the Chinese regarded the Europeans as barbarians, but thought they should be treated decently. The Jesuits quickly learned to adapt to the Chinese scene and their acquaintance with this exotic world soon made them a source of information for others. Whereas Rousseau's disciples devoted themselves in one way or another to the cult of the 'noble savage', Voltaire's followers, free-thinkers and enthusiasts for progress as they were, directed their hopes and aspirations to the Empire of the Middle, which aroused utopian notions precisely because it was a long way away and difficult of access. Whatever was critically noted in the Jesuits' reports tended to be put in a positive light. Thus, Leibniz, one of the earliest admirers of China in Europe, linked the alleged military weakness of that country with a widespread predilection for pacifism, while Voltaire saw in its rigidly hierarchical social system and the centralism of the Chinese administration evidence of a prudent concern for the common good as embodied in enlightened despotism. A little later the rococo style eagerly adopted decorative patterns and methods from the art of the Far East, and assigned a prominent place to *Chinoiserie* in the interior decoration of the courts such as had not been occupied by any overseas culture since the days of Islam. This fashionable trend, however, failed to stimulate any serious intellectual approach to Far Eastern culture.

Knowledge of this great variety of remarkable lands was gathered in the first place from missionary reports written by Jesuits and Capuchins, and also from travel journals which were becoming increasingly common as the eighteenth century wore on. Thanks to Anson (1748), Byron (1768), Bancks and Solander (1771), Wallis (1773), Hawkesworth (1773) and Forster (1777) readers were able to find their way about the entire globe; these works gave a fascinating account of the hitherto unknown world of the Pacific Ocean. If one wished to familiarize oneself with Asia, then Choisy offered Siam (1687); Chardin (1711) and Holwell (1766) offered India. Lahontan had described the North America of the 'noble savage' as early as 1683, later came Venegas with an account of California (1757). As for South America, Gumilla wrote about the Orinoco (1738), de la Condamine about the continent as a whole (1743). Africa was dealt with by Kolb, who described the Cape of Good Hope (1705) and Coyer, who wrote about the Gold Coast (1714); Barbot published an account of North and South Guinea (1732). There was a wealth of literature about the Near East: Drummond on the Euphrates (1754), Hanway on Persia (1753), Norden on Egypt and Nubia (1755). Maundrell (1703), Pococke (1745) and Hasselquist (1757) published topical accounts of a Palestine the public had long been familiar with only from the Bible. In 1765

Shaw published an account of the nearer Orient. The extreme north now also aroused fresh interest: Egede wrote on Greenland (1741), Hoegstroem on Lapland (1747) and Horrebow on Iceland (1750). In 1747 Prévost's *Histoire générale des voyages* appeared, a collection of travel journals from every part of the globe.

In the course of the eighteenth century enough became known about the exotic countries for systematic interpretation and analysis to be undertaken. The primary task was the mapping of oceans and coastlines, hydrography, the initial phase in the science of geography. Following Captain James Cook's voyages (1768–79) it was possible to produce an accurate map of the Pacific.

European explorers began to venture more and more into the interior of other continents, where there were as yet no European settlements. Mungo Park, commissioned by the London African Association, reached the bend in the river Niger, Lewis and Clark travelled from the Mississippi to the Pacific coast, Antonio Ruiz de Pavon explored the Andes range in Peru and Chile, Humboldt the Amazon basin. In the nineteenth century it was to be the turn of the interior of Africa and Australia, while overgrown temple ruins in the interior of Mexico began to be revealed as evidence of pre-Columbian civilizations and cultures.

Geography was not simply confined to map-making: it advanced to keep pace with intensive botanical and zoological research. Everywhere a craze for collecting and classifying set in. The pupils of the Swedish botanist Linné began their work: Peter Kalm in North America and Adam Atzelius and Andreas Sparrman in Africa, Karl Peter Thunberg in Japan, Karl Solander in the South Seas. It was their research that brought about a vast increase in our knowledge of plant and animal life.

The most comprehensive single work was provided by Buffon in the numerous volumes of his *Histoire naturelle*, the first of which appeared in 1746. In the preface to the chapter on wild animals we find a passage which indicates how widely zoology had come to be recognized as a science:

In the case of man and domesticated animals we have been able to observe nature in a limited sense only, for here it is rarely perfect, but frequently modified, deformed and always surrounded by extraneous influences and accretions. Now, however, it will appear naked, for all to see, in its original simplicity, but all the more impressive, thanks to its unfettered stride, its unforced manner and all the other attributes of its nobility and independence.[4]

Here we may find European fauna – deer, squirrels, hedgehogs and wolves, side by side with exotic beasts like the rhinoceros, giraffe, lion and tiger. Such exotic animals, it was implied, were capable of being just as noble as, if not more noble than their European counterparts. Buffon was a member of the Académie des Sciences and director of the Jardin des Plantes in Paris. Some time later, Kew was to provide a similar living garden in London.

It was not only animals and plants that aroused serious scientific interest, but man himself: the science of ethnology emerged, not simply as a way of recording curiosities of human conduct and social customs, but as a field of comparative scientific research.

Anyone now intending to write a comprehensive history of mankind could no longer be content to start with the highly developed culture of China (an advance, at any rate, on the Old Testament history of Israel!); now he would have to begin with primitive men and their societies, the manners and customs of which might still be encountered in Africa, America or the South Seas. A history of man was now required to deal with all cultures, primitive as well as civilized. In 1759 Antoine-Yves Goguet published *De l'origine des lois, des arts et de leur progrès chez les anciens peuples*, which was followed in the succeeding year by Nicolas-Antoine Boulanger's *Recherches sur l'origine du despotisme oriental*. In that same year a Dane, Jens Kraft, brought out a *Brief History of the Various Institutions, Manners and Opinions of Savage Peoples*, while in 1761 there appeared Charles de Brosse's *Du culte des dieux fétiches*. In 1764 Isaak Iselin published his *Philosophical Conjectures on the History of Mankind*, the main sections of which are designed on ethnographic lines. He was followed in 1766 by Adam Ferguson with an *Essay on the History of Civil Society* and by Johann Gottlieb Steeb's *General Account of the Condition of the Civilized and Uncivilized Nations with Reference to their Moral and Physical Constitution.* This title seems to sum up the entire programme of the Enlightenment: the spell had been broken.

The world had become universal and had to be understood in universal terms. Thus the great physician, naturalist and philosopher, Albrecht von Haller, was in a position to state in 1755:

> Nothing is better calculated to dispel prejudice than an acquaintance with many different nations and their diverse manners, laws and opinions – a diversity that enables us, however, with little effort to cast aside whatever divides men and to comprehend as the voice of Nature all that they have in common. However uncouth, however primitive the inhabitants of the South Sea islands may be, however remote the Greenlander may be from Brazil or the Cape of Good Hope, the first principles of the Law of Nature are identical in the case of all nations: to injure no man, to allow every man his due, to seek perfection in one's calling, this was the path to honour with the ancient Romans, and it is still the same for dwellers on the Davis Strait or the Hottentotts.[5]

Part VII

Emancipation – A Release from Age-old Restraints

1

Political and Social Emancipation

When Enlightenment goes into action, then it may well be called emancipation, i.e. the release of fresh potential resulting from the abolition of ancient rules and regulations. As used in Roman law, the term *emancipatio* stood for the release of a son from paternal authority, i.e. emancipation from patriarchal relationships, in the sense, say, of a statement from the end of the eighteenth century: 'Emancipation from mere blind obedience which renders superfluous anything in the way of coercion or commands, presupposes at the same time that the guideline for our behaviour is in ourselves.'[1] Emancipation, liberation from a hidebound world, affected both individuals and social groups: the middle class, the monarch's subjects, the lower classes, the serfs, the Jews particularly, and, in a special sense, women.

The middle class sought emancipation above all in the monarchies, where it laid claim to its rightful place alongside the nobility. As businessmen many of its members had actually grown wealthier than many members of the aristocracy, and, even apart from the middle-class representatives in academic professions, they were often better educated than the nobility. The middle class aspired to economic and intellectual freedom and a voice in the government of the state. There were a great many obstacles to be overcome, and sometimes they were simply too formidable. In republics the emancipation of the middle class was already built into the system, all that was needed here was a reduction in the privileges enjoyed by patrician families.

237

Hitherto, the commoner who had grown wealthy had always hoped that he might some day be raised to the peerage. It is this attitude that Voltaire is mocking when he says of the dreams of an ambitious pair of parents:

> When his father noticed that his son had waxed so very eloquent, he was heartily sorry that he had not put the lad to learning Latin, for then he might have bought him some high office in the administrative nobility. His mother, who cherished rather finer feelings, had been preparing to buy him a regiment in the Army.[2]

Gradually, however, the middle class lost its ambition to rise into the ranks of the aristocracy or to be accepted into patrician circles: its members wished to remain middle class and were indeed proud of that status.

Emancipation began to affect the subjects of government in general, whether it was monarchical or republican. The burning issue now was equality before the law. Not that anyone wanted to depose the monarch – only the English had done that in Cromwell's time, or the Dutch in their war against the Governor General or their provincial governors from the House of Orange, who put on monarchical airs. In 'free' Switzerland, nevertheless, between 1653 and 1789, we may count something like a dozen risings by rebellious subjects – all of them, with one exception, being successfully put down.

The aim of the powers that be, as a rule, was to show that their subjects were actually 'happy', thanks to the benevolent concern of their rulers. The majority of the population was in fact generally satisfied with the status quo, the rule of their paternal monarch, or 'our gracious Lord', as they used to call him. It was virtually impossible to organize resistance on a broad front to the kind of arbitrary or tyrannical rule that might be found in certain German principalities. The potentate's police force or his mercenary army were always ready to nip any such attempt in the bud. If a Jakob von Moser or a Daniel Schubart became too outspoken, they were locked up in the fortresses of Hohentwiel or Hohenasperg. In Paris the Bastille served the same purpose.

In Prussia one might still detect a narrow-minded, subservient mentality well into the nineteenth century; the narrow
minds were not those of an underprivileged mob, however, but
of yeoman farmers, businessmen, university graduates . . .

A movement for emancipation might be detected, even in the
case of the mob. For them emancipation had to come from
above, for what could the illiterate, the destitute and the underprivileged do on their own, if they were not driven by hunger to
desperate measures? The champions of Enlightenment were indeed well aware of the plight of the poor, the lowest social class
in general. In every country, not just in the industrialized countries, more and more people were convinced that something
must be done.

We might take the example of Spain, where the voluntary and
charitable societies were particularly concerned with the problem of poverty. Their concern was first manifested theoretically
in research into the problem after the Council of Castille had
turned to the *Sociedades de los Amigos del País*. In 1777 the Society
in Valencia noted that 'the upper classes of society might do
much through the good offices of the Society to encourage sound
Christian and civic manners and put an end to idleness and
vagrancy'.[3] In Valencia there were hordes of beggars, mainly
able-bodied individuals of all ages, including children of both
sexes, 'many of whom call themselves students but can scarcely
read'. It was pointed out that these beggars had simply grown
up in unpropitious circumstances, they would be unemployed
for their entire lives and turn to crime. This was a consequence
of the economic slump of 1771, when numerous silk mills in
Valencia had been closed down and 1,600 families consequently
plunged into destitution. It was noted, too, that the excessive
number of holidays also encouraged idleness. This was a problem throughout the Catholic world that Protestant states had
not experienced since the Reformation.

The random, blind and arbitrary practice of giving alms was
also criticized. The Spaniards had the erroneous and pernicious
idea that the giving of alms was in itself a virtue, a pious act.
The chief minister, Campomanes, estimated the number of beggars in Spain to be 140,000.

Then came the suggestions for improvement. A distinction was drawn, as it had once been drawn during the Reformation, between the deserving poor and the idle and shiftless. It had been observed that an increase in the population without any corresponding increase in available employment inevitably led to impoverishment. As a first step the establishment of more homes for the poor, or workhouses – *Montepios* or *Casas de misericordia*, as they were called – was proposed. But the existing workhouses in fact offered no training and did not possess the technical facilities to provide work. The inmates were confined to the houses and were not permitted to marry. There had to be a campaign to provide jobs, and what was needed for the incorrigibly idle were penitentiaries with forced labour. There should be soup kitchens to feed families in need. In 1779, with the aid of state funds, a spinning mill managed by the local *sociedad* was opened in the royal institute for paupers in Madrid. After three months of employment in Madrid the inmates were to be dispersed throughout the provinces, where further workhouses were to be opened. Problems soon cropped up, however: there was not enough money, and the inmates showed little aptitude for the work they were expected to do. The wages that had to be paid in Madrid were exceptionally high, and the cost of the raw material fluctuated, so that sales were hard to predict. Pestalozzi had experienced similar problems between 1774 and 1780 in his school for the poor in Neuhof near Brugg; eventually the school had to be closed down.

This is why further suggestions were made which would have entailed changes in the existing economic system: changes in the guild regulations, e.g. extended training for apprentices, abolition of the guilds' monopolies, the establishment of a sinking fund to tide tradesmen over slumps, the provision of savings banks for the poor. Above all, the demand was for more extensive industrialization, with employers being encouraged by tax concessions. The *sociedades* were to be increased in number and put in charge of new enterprises. The ultimate aim was *ocupación honesta y útil* – honest and useful employment.

In every country problems emerged which had to be dealt with in the nineteenth and even in the twentieth century; in their acutest form they are still the problems of the developing countries.

A special case was the institution of serfdom, i.e. the system under which an individual might be the property of his master and treated like an inanimate object: the horse, the coach and the coachman constituted a single social and economic unit. It is true that in western Europe serfdom was no more than a relic of the Middle Ages and had in most cases been commuted in the form of a poll tax. In Russia and eastern Europe, beginning with east Prussia, serfdom was still oppressive and largely taken for granted. In these countries the peasants had been expropriated in the course of time, and it was not until the nineteenth century that serfdom was abolished here – at least formally.

The most deplorable humiliation of a man was slavery. It principally affected the negroes in America. As we have seen, their plight became the subject of public debate towards the end of the eighteenth century, but their emancipation did not come until well into the nineteenth century.

2

Emancipation of the Jews

A very special case of emancipation was that of the Jews. Here the emancipation was twofold: first, in the sense of equal co-existence in an alien world of medieval Christian tradition, and, secondly, emancipation from the strict orthodoxy of the Jewish communities themselves. As far as the former was concerned, periods of persecution alternated with periods of peaceful coexistence. At the beginning of the eighteenth century the Jews still found themselves in the same situation as during the Middle Ages, scattered haphazardly in the Mediterranean area and the rest of Europe, either in ghettos, where they were to some extent protected, or pursuing their lonely way as itinerant traders. As a rule they were despised, feared and hated. After all, it was the Jews who had killed Christ all those years ago – and besides they were such astute businessmen, so much more intelligent and so different from those around them. Nevertheless, they were indispensable for wholesale and retail trade, for finance, for balancing the budgets of various states and for supplying the armies. The Jewish communities and their way of life had been best preserved in eastern Europe, where their customs and manners could be retained in archaic form – albeit in isolation and segregated from the community at large. Even in the imperial capital Vienna they were not permitted to pursue their own mode of life – even within their ghetto. They had to pay an extra toll each time they passed through the city gates; they were obliged to pay heavy dues simply in order to be tolerated; they were required to wear distinctive clothing marked with a yellow patch; and they were allowed to live only in houses that had been allocated to them. On Christian holidays they were ordered to stay at home and were not even allowed to look at passing processions from their windows. They were banned from public houses and inns and from concerts and theatres. These restrictions applied everywhere, subject to local variations. As they were normally not entitled to own land, they were forced to earn their living in other ways.

Jews in western Europe had more freedom of movement, although they were still subject to special legislation. Those who had been expelled from Spain since the fifteenth century had been able to settle in The Netherlands, in England and in various commercial centres elsewhere. A typical comment comes from the Italian, Pilati, who otherwise holds modern and enlightened views: 'Only the Portuguese Jews are both honest and hardworking, and hence are apt to bring much benefit to the community without harming it. But they are shrewd enough to settle only in Holland and England.'[4] In both of these countries, especially in Holland with its tradition of liberalism, a wealthy Jewish middle class soon began to emerge.

It was precisely the liberal and cosmopolitan atmosphere in the commercial centres of western Europe that began to have an effect within the closed Jewish communities themselves. General trends and developments no longer passed them by. Various tendencies of a mystical kind threatened to split the orthodox Jewish congregations, individuals began to break away from the communities. The rationalism of enlightened intellectuals attracted many Jews, for their theological tradition, like that of the Protestants, was closely linked to a literal interpretation of texts, and was easily adapted to the rationalism of the age. A breakaway from the orthodox Jewish community had been marked already in the seventeenth century by the *Tractatus theologico-politicus* of Baruch Spinoza – the descendant of a Jewish family that had emigrated from Portugal to The Netherlands. Following the tradition of Descartes, Spinoza had evolved an even more rational psychological and philosophical system which earned him the reputation of an atheist, a charge of which he was acquitted only by the late Enlightenment. As far as the early Enlightenment was concerned, Spinoza was an outsider, which he naturally was in the eyes of the Jews, who expelled him from the congregation. During his own lifetime Spinoza's plea for freedom, equality, tolerance and morality was a voice crying in the wilderness.

Intellectual emancipation did not come until the second half of the eighteenth century. The wealthy and influential Jewish middle class had only then attained a standard of education that enabled its members to assimilate the ideas of the Enlightenment as soon as outward circumstances were favourable. Intellectual emancipation was epitomized by Moses Mendelssohn, descendant of a family of teachers, who was accepted into the liberal circle of enlightened writers and scholars in Berlin, where he was soon regarded as an outstanding philosophical author. As far as he was concerned, the Jews also belonged to a world subject to natural law: 'The truly divine religion needs neither arms nor fingers for its practice, it is pure heart and mind.'⁵ Mendelssohn did not repudiate Jewish traditions, he merely sought to simplify and refine them, himself remaining a devout and practising member of the Jewish faith. His orthodox co-religionists, however, were not prepared to acknowledge that, and for them he occupied the same position as the liberally minded theologians of the two main Christian churches.

As a Jew, Mendelssohn was naturally welcomed with open arms by the proponents of Enlightenment in Berlin. Now they had as an ally a Jew who shared their views and who was their intellectual equal, or even their superior, a man of wit and spirit. And, moreover, a man who set an example in the simplicity and austerity of his life – no wealthy middle-class parvenu, but a modest small businessman all his life, earning an honest living like so many other authors of the day. It was Mendelssohn who appeared as the ideal Jew when the actor Iffland took the stage as the hero of Lessing's drama, *Nathan the Wise*.

Mendelssohn's Berlin became a focal point of Jewish emancipation and its influence was not confined to Germany and eastern Europe. Jewish communities started to modernize their schools and rabbis began to support modern ideas. Frequently, however,

Jews who embraced the Enlightenment would convert to Christianity, since that was the only way in which they could be fully assimilated into the movement. Nevertheless, many of them remained loyal to the synagogue, where interpretation of the Scriptural texts was now more up to date, and where, as with the Calvinists, organ music might now be introduced. Intelligent Jewish women – like Rahel Varnhagen and Henriette Herz – held their *salons* in Berlin as emancipated females and devotees of philosophical discourse. Such enlightened Jews contrived to give a virtuoso performance on two instruments at once, as it were, responding to the middle-class environment and the Enlightenment mentality, while retaining their place in their ancient community in close touch with the ramified Jewish congregations throughout the world. Thus, a German Jew might be sure of a warm welcome in a Jewish congregation in the South of France or in Poland.

In 1781 Christian Wilhelm Dohm was inspired by Mendelssohn to write a work *On the Civic Emancipation of the Jews*. The subject had now become a political issue open to public debate.

But already sixty-seven years before Dohm, in England, John Toland had published a treatise on *Reasons for Naturalising the Jews in Great Britain and Ireland*. The Jews, he argued, ought to be accorded equal status in society, if not identical rights. Emancipation of the Jews in Great Britain came about gradually, without any great fuss, and the relevant legislation followed in the course of the nineteenth century. Jews in the British colonies of North America had been able to acquire civil rights as early as 1740. By 1820 equal rights for Jews obtained in all the states of the Union. In the European monarchies Frederick II of Prussia seemed reluctant to grant equality, but reforms by the Emperor Joseph II in Austria and its dependencies heralded the start of legal emancipation – a marked contrast to the anti-Semitic attitude of his mother – but his initiative was not universally welcomed by a public which was ill prepared for it. Not long afterwards the French Revolution drew the political consequences: in 1787 Abbé Grégoire published his *Essai sur la régéneration physique, morale et politique des juifs*, and Mirabeau wrote an article on *Moses Mendelssohn et la réforme politique des juifs.* Mendelssohn was capable of providing an example for France as well as Germany, it seemed! In the years that followed the Jews were fully emancipated wherever the French exercised political authority, but here, too, the restoration meant a setback – the sorry tale was not yet over. Emancipation remained by and large an unrealized political postulate. In 1823 Heinrich Heine wrote: 'What is the great task of our time? Emancipation. Not merely of the Irish, the Greeks, the Jews of Frankfurt, the West Indian negroes and other oppressed peoples in various parts of the world, but emancipation of the whole world, especially of Europe, which has now come of age.'[6]

3

The Debate on the Role of Woman: On the Way to the Emancipation of Women

When Heine spoke of emancipation he was obviously thinking of oppressed nations, Jews and slaves. Can he have forgotten women? The emancipation of women is something quite different from the emancipation of particular social, ethnic or political groups. It is a problem that affects everyone, a perennial anthropological issue, irrespective of nationality, religion or skin colour. In the final analysis it is more than just a question of politics and legislation.

The century in which – through the accident of succession to a throne – many women ruled over kingdoms or empires of greater or lesser size, as empresses, queens or princesses, was also the century in which the debate on woman's role in society first began. Ever since Poulin de la Barre published his *De l'égalité des deux sexes* in 1673, a theory of the equality of the sexes had existed. This disciple of Descartes was the first to argue, on the basis of the division between mind and body, that the physical differences between men and women could have no influence on their intelligence: *L'esprit n'a pas de sexe*. Up until that point the accepted theory was that it was the male who should lay down the law in keeping with the biblical precept: 'thy desire shall be to thy husband, and he shall rule over thee' (Genesis III, 16). There had indeed always been a realm in which woman reigned supreme: the household. There it was the woman who held sway, as the farmer's wife, say, and she was mistress of all she surveyed.

She was responsible for minor commercial transactions, what with her spinning and weaving and the produce of her kitchen garden, and here she was independent of her husband. Even in business circles, however, a woman might still play a major part, as may be observed from an example from Zurich in the seventeenth century:

> Household affairs were left to the conscientious care of the wife – cleanliness, which was not carried to the point, however, where it was irksome to the family and their friends, thrift, which nevertheless allowed for occasional festive celebrations, arrangements to make sure that everything went smoothly and in good time and good order, that as many jobs as possible were done by the domestic servants, so that expenditure on hired help was spared, that everything that was needed was always available in abundance, and that all the household amenities were provided in due measure: she was knowledgeable and competent in every domestic task, from cooking to the most delicate needlework, and a certain skill in music, to the delight of her husband and herself, was her greatest pleasure. Her greatest ambition was to know that her husband was respected and her children well brought up, to help him in his business, to take his place when he was absent, and to do certain things as well as he could himself. Concern for her children's education she shared with her husband, but in this regard she followed the same plan and principles as he did.[7]

The domains of husband and wife were more or less separated, but the predominance of the male was not disputed: women were excluded from civic activities, which were clearly man's work. At that time an English visitor to Switzerland noted with some astonishment:

> The women are totally absorbed in domestic tasks. Even the wives of the chief municipal officers are involved in all household and kitchen matters, just like the humblest farmer's wife. These wives find so much satisfaction in

their domestic responsibilities and are so disinclined to indulge in flirtation that the 'vapours' – otherwise so common and due, one eminent physician assured me, to idleness and flirtation – are here entirely unknown.

In Zurich 'women do not consort with men, except their close relatives. Even in the street they do not acknowledge the courtesy of strangers who doff their hats to them.'[8] What is here observed of Switzerland no doubt also applied elsewhere in Europe in similar urban, middle-class circles.

At court, amongst the nobility (and the prosperous middle class) things were ordered differently. When Poulin de la Barre was writing about the equality of the two sexes, the 'blue stockings' were just beginning to make their appearance. In Paris Madame de Sévigné had gathered together a company of intelligent men and women who engaged in philosophical debate. Women began to conduct correspondence with like-minded acquaintances, both male and female, and even began to publish books; Luise Kulmus, the wife of the Leipzig literary critic Gottsched, is just one example. By the end of the century the educated woman taking part in serious intellectual discussion was taken for granted in higher social circles.

This new role for woman was, of course, not immune from criticism and ironic or flippant comment: Molière's *Les précieuses ridicules* was performed over and over again. On the other hand, a great many men extolled the intelligence and the discernment of many women – and not only as characters in novels. Pietism developed its own estimation of women based on New Testament exegesis. In every conventicle women, irrespective of their social class, might now play a leading part – the male parson was no longer in sole command.

In Sweden, around the middle of the century, a Mrs Nordenflycht acted as the president of a highly respected literary society. In 1785 an Austrian diplomat was able to report from an allegedly backward country, Spain:

On the sixth of last month the seventeen-year-old daughter of the Marqués de Montealegre passed the necessary examinations at the University of Alcalá for the degrees of

Master and Doctor of Philosophy and duly graduated. In the various examinations the candidate gave evidence of knowledge, not just of metaphysics, physics and moral philosophy, but also of geometry, geography and mythology, as well as of Greek, Latin and French, and of her own mother tongue.[9]

A female president of an academy and a female doctor of philosophy might be nothing more than a couple of exceptions, but they indicate that women were beginning to seek equal rights and opportunities in education. As things were, this could be achieved only outside the official school system – either by private study or by private tutoring. Private tutors already teaching in palaces and mansions were now expected to cater for the daughters of their employers, girls who were often more mentally alert than their noble brothers. By the second half of the century the way was open for the founding of girls' schools which would offer instruction beyond the elementary level. These schools, it is true, had a distinctly feminine character, with a curriculum featuring much singing and embroidery, but they did go beyond that and provided intellectually more stimulating instruction in reading and writing the mother tongue and the learning of a foreign language, normally French.

Towards the end of the century a point had been reached where Condorcet, a member of the Paris Academy, was in a position to write his *Sur l'admission des femmes au droit de cité* (1788), while the Lord Mayor of Königsberg, Theodor Gottlieb Hippel, was able to write an essay on *The Civil Advancement of Women* (1792). Here it was reckoned that women, like negro slaves, could not be counted as full citizens, but that, by virtue of their improved education, they had achieved equality in their own sphere and mode of life and were hence entitled to a voice in public debate. Both authors put forward arguments for the full equality of women, in the private as well as the political sphere. This was evidently a utopian notion, for not even the constitution drafted during the French Revolution went to such lengths.

When Condorcet and Hippel were writing, the burning issue of women's rights had already been damped down to a certain extent: the rationalism of the first half of the century had already reached its limit, and in the meantime the 'natural' constitution of women had been discovered (or invented?). Every human being – that was common knowledge – was indeed a rational creature, but individuals differed biologically according to their sexuality. This discovery of emotional life and of sensuality curtailed the range of pure rationality.

> Women are now indeed credited with rapid intellectual grasp and vivid imagination, but diagnosed as lacking the capacity for profound thought and reasoning on account of the nervous constitution of the female sex. Rational reflection and strenuous mental effort were thus limited to the more robust male organism. This epistemological argument is backed up by the physiological argument: her physiology naturally assigns to woman her social function and role as wife and mother. The ultimate consequence was a sexualization of woman's life and function.[10]

This novel theory was propagated and generally accepted because of Rousseau's *Nouvelle Héloise*. In his novel he harked back to a remarkable female figure of the twelfth century, the mistress of the great theologian Abelard. Rousseau's latter-day Héloise was destined to resurrect the state of nature that had obtained in the Golden Age before it was destroyed by 'male reason'. Given her spontaneous affinity with her fellow-creatures, woman was to become the vehicle of a new morality in a world dominated by competition, violence and militarism. Reason had led to an unscrupulous and unbridled lust for power and sheer utility.

> The identification and representation of woman as the moral sex is a concept that crops up in many accounts of female education after Rousseau's time, but the contradiction inherent in the concept now becomes manifest. On the one hand, efforts to reform women's education were a consequence of the fact that women had at last been granted the right to knowledge. On the other hand, this right to knowledge was simultaneously curtailed by the idea of an appropriate female education which could

achieve its aims only if the pupils were kept at a respectful distance from any effective knowledge. Female education – promptly enlisted in the service of morality – might never be an end in itself. It was accepted as no more than an intellectual exercise, as a useful distraction from the perils of boredom and as a precondition for the moralizing influence that we expected women to have on their families.[11]

Progress now followed two parallel lines of advance. Aristocratic ladies at court and elsewhere, as well as the wives and daughters of the prosperous middle class, might go on taking part in intellectual discussions in their *salons*, but girls of families that were just making their way up the social ladder might well be sent to a girls' school, for their training was intended to fit them only for the family circle and their close friends. Educated mothers brought their sons up to occupy the leading positions they would hold in future, introducing them to an elementary world, in which everything they might expect to encounter in their careers was present in embryonic form. It is she who keeps an eye on the boys as they play at soldiers, for their father has little time to spare for his children; his work is outside the home. It is also the mothers who introduce their children to the world of religion, teaching them to pray and telling them stories from the Bible. Of course, daughters might also have a part to play; they might also play at soldiers, and in the toy-shop they often knew better what they were about than their brothers did. They might read the *Iliad* and the *Odyssey*, *Telemachus*, Richardson's *Pamela* or Defoe's *Robinson Crusoe*, for sons and daughters often read the same books, although there was already a demand for reading matter that would be suitable for girls.

In this connection all that had been propagated and practised in the eighteenth century was perfected in the nineteenth. Women were ultimately excluded from any significant function in the state, the economy or the world of higher learning. The wives of working men, engaged like their husbands in a variety of jobs, tended to aspire to middle-class status: social advancement for them meant that they no longer had to work, and they were glad to leave decisions to their husbands. In the nineteenth century empresses and queens were mainly restricted to their female functions and activities. At the beginning of the French Revolution Condorcet evoked in vain the shining examples of Queen Elizabeth of England, Maria Theresa of Austria and the Empress Catherine of Russia. He pilloried the attitude of male chauvinists – and even the more enlightened males: 'Have they not all infringed the principle of equality before the law in calmly depriving one half of the human race of their right to have a hand in the making of our laws?'[12]

The nineteenth century was determined to divorce the world of man from that of woman. It forced a man – whether he wished to or not, whether he was competent or not – to act as head of the household, the statesman or the officer who gave the orders. How many boys were forced and moulded into shape, and how many of them subsequently failed because they had been so coerced! The female world, however, formed in the image of an innocent young girl, was expected to create a reservation for human values, an oasis of purity – first in a dreamy, Romantic haze, then in a frenzied flurry of Victorian do-gooding. On the other hand there were the wives of pioneers in the American west who were able to turn their hands to anything and, later on, those passionate campaigners for women's rights in Europe, especially in the Anglo-Saxon and Scandinavian countries, taking up a cause that had first been championed by a choice few and now had to be promoted on a vast scale in concrete terms of political rights in a world that had in the meantime become largely middle class and democratic.

Part VIII

For and Against Radicalization of the
Enlightenment

1

Radical Enlightenment

From the end of the seventeenth century onwards, sooner or later, depending on the particular country, it was the early Enlightenment that had summoned up the courage to shake off baroque modes of thought, to promote a more liberal outlook, and to set up the first markers of an age of reason. A change of mentality of this kind was bound to take place within the traditional environment. Individual changes took place quietly and imperceptibly, sometimes it was only the emphasis that shifted.

Towards the middle of the eighteenth century a new generation representing the Enlightenment at its height was able to build confidently on the firm foundations that had thus been laid. They had become familiar with the new spirit of the age while they were still at school. Old prejudices might be eliminated without traditions being arbitrarily destroyed. Governments began cautiously to introduce reforms. The plainest signals came from Frederick II when he ascended the Prussian throne in 1740.

In the second half of the century, the late phase of the Enlightenment, opinions began to differ: many of its adherents remained loyal to the traditional moderation of the movement as it had grown up over the years, but others were impatient and inclined to encourage an escalation of the movement. A certain apprehension arose that this new trend might get out of hand, and there were some who began to prepare to resist any such tendency.

Rousseau's *Discourse on the Inequality of Man* (1754) might be regarded as an early symptom of such radicalization. For some, Rousseau was the great prophet of a more natural, a freer and a juster world, for others he was a muddle-headed idealist, if not actually a dangerous extremist. Soon Rousseau was being stigmatized as a 'Socialist' – initially in an Italian work attacking his views. In the course of the nineteenth century this term came to be commonly applied to anyone who advocated radical equality.

Rousseau's essay on equality was promptly followed by political reactions. The citizen of Geneva found followers in his native city, and accounts in the press of the 'Geneva troubles' inspired similar incidents in North America and in The Netherlands.

Somewhat later a radicalization of the Freemasons through the founding of the secret society of the Illuminati caused alarm in Germany. The Illuminati proposed to follow a more drastic policy than the Masonic lodges, which were now content, it seemed, to confine themselves to vague speculation or mere social intercourse. As a secret fraternity, the Illuminati were determined to gain concrete political influence in the states where they had members. 'The ultimate aim of the Order, then, is to see that Light prevails, we are warriors fighting against darkness, this is what we call the service of fire.'[1]

It was in the electorate of Bavaria that Professor Adam Weishaupt of Ingolstadt University, soon to be joined by Baron Adolf von Knigge, started the secret society of the Illuminati about the year 1760. The Order's aim was to promote Enlightenment and morality in a more clearly manifest way than the Masonic lodges. The new society soon spread throughout the German states, first in the Catholic states, then in Protestant areas. The members it recruited – ultimately some seven hundred – were drawn from the ranks of civil servants, university professors, the clergy and the nobility.

Its organization resembled that of the Freemasons, with a hierarchy comprising novices and minervals (disciples of Minerva) and culminating in the *Illuminatus dirigens*. An Areopagus – identity unknown even to the members of the Order – directed the complex organization. Secrecy extended even to the use of code-names: Weishaupt was known as Spartacus, Knigge as Philo, Duke Karl August of Weimar as Aeschylus, the eminent politicians of the Napoleonic era, Montgelas and Dalberg, were called Musaeus and Baco of Verulam respectively, while Pestalozzi was dubbed Alfred.

A complete system for directing the Order of Illuminati was devised by Baron von Knigge. Germany was divided into provinces, also denoted by code-names. The Bavarian province was called Greece and was divided into prefectures: Achaia (the duchy of Bavaria), Calabria (the archbishopric of Salzburg), Chaldaea (Regensburg, Passau, Ortenburg, etc.), and Delta (the Upper Palatinate). The governing bodies in the provinces were located in the capitals Athens (Munich), Nicosia (Salzburg), Corinth (Regensburg) and Thebes (Freising). The other provinces were Illyria (Franconia) and Pannonia (Swabia). The whole of Germany was divided into four 'inspectorates': Achaia (south Germany), Ethiopia (the Rhineland), Abyssinia (Saxony) and Egypt (Austria) – and so the scheme pursues its fanciful course from Damiata (Stuttgart) via Delphis (Karlsruhe), to Capua (Brunswick). This elaborate organization never progressed beyond the planning stage, but it suggests how wide the potential geographical range of the Order was.

As stated in the Order's statutes as drafted in 1778, its purpose was

> to engage men's interest in efforts to improve and perfect moral character, to promote humane views to the benefit of society, to frustrate evil designs, to come to the aid of virtue oppressed by injustice, to have in mind the advancement of worthy individuals, and finally to reward, both within the society and outside it, exceptionally deserving persons who are able to serve the Order by virtue of their talents, their wealth or their social status, and to accord them an exceptional degree of respect, renown and honour.

The leaders of the Order, however, had more ambitious aims in mind than just the influence of individuals in their own sphere of activity. What they were planning was something like the infiltration of the existing bureaucracy in the interests of more radical Enlightenment. The secret society of the Illuminati had come into existence shortly after the official dissolution of the Jesuit Order, and one of its aims was to counter the continuing influence of reactionary Catholicism. The Illuminati thus represented something like a cross between a middle-class moral improvement association, a learned society and a politically motivated underground movement.

With its supposed strategy of infiltrating its members into the machinery of government, the Order went much further than the other Masonic lodges, which were seeking the common good only in a vaguer philanthropic sense without any intention of transforming society and the state. In the lodges the members devoted their energies to the pursuit of individual moral improvement. The activity of the Illuminati coincided with a period, just before the outbreak of the French Revolution, when political views had become sharply polarized and when the conflict between revolutionary and counter-revolutionary factions was becoming more and more obvious.

The Illuminati were well aware where their chief adversary was to be found:

> In this undertaking, however, we are much frustrated by priests, princes and the present political constitutions. What are we to do, then? Foster revolution, turn the world upside down, drive out force by force, exchange one tyrant for another? That is the last thing we mean to do! Any violent reform is deplorable, because it does not improve the situation as long as man and his passions remain unchanged, and because wisdom has no need of coercion.

The Order had existed for barely ten years before its clerical opponents contrived to have it banned. Widespread and relatively severe persecution of the Illuminati then began in Germany, and also affected the Masonic lodges, although the latter had had only personal, not organizational, links with the Illuminati.

The emergence of the Illuminati is only one piece of evidence to suggest that the Enlightenment did in fact question a good many traditional values. The chilly light of reason was now stripping bare many things that orthodoxy had established so firmly; it was probing into accepted principles, such as the idea of royalty 'by the grace of God', the exclusivity of the nobility and the patrician clans; it had pulled aside the baroque drapery that had so far shrouded the principles of science and philosophy, revealing secular and sacred superstition alike for what it really was. What had cautiously been hinted at by the middle generation of the Enlightenment was now regarded as a cast-iron certainty by many representatives of its latest phase. By the theologian, Andreas Riem, for instance, whose book *On the Enlightenment* caused something of stir when it appeared in Berlin in 1780. As far as Riem was concerned, Enlightenment was 'simply the attempt on the part of the human mind to cast light on every subject in the world of ideas, on all human opinions and their consequences, and, indeed, on anything that has any bearing whatsoever on mankind, in conformity with a purely rational doctrine and to the benefit of the whole human race.'[2] He goes on to cast light on 'the most hallowed of all creeds — Christianity', claiming that it is a rational religion and that its founder can only be rendered more illustrious by the new light shed by the Enlightenment. Any theologian who does not accept the Enlightenment and who does not measure a religion in terms of its rationality, morality and utility is, for Riem, a pestilential affliction on the human race. The Reformation of the sixteenth century and Zwingli's reformed theology are described by Riem as 'Enlightenment'. He is pursuing his argument consistently when he refers to Christ as 'the wise proponent of Enlightenment' and His Gospel simply as 'Enlightenment', thinking presumably of what he terms the 'pure ethical doctrine' of Christ.

Here the 'light' of the Enlightenment is seen in much more dynamic terms than 'the gentle glow of a lovely dawn'. In the history of his church, Riem's position is closely allied to the new rationalistic theology that was beginning to oust the much more cautious orthodoxy of the early part of the century.

There were a good many who went even further, not just trying to make way for a rational Christian doctrine, but actually repudiating the very notion of religion altogether. Of course, the Enlightenment was not the only period of modern history when atheism had occupied men's thoughts, it was an issue that had constantly led to heated argument, but the heresy was now being widely proclaimed in public. In the debate that ensued scientists played a prominent part: in *L'homme machine* (1748) Lamettrie deduced a totally atheistic materialism from the science of mechanics. In his *Système de la Nature* Holbach proposed a natural order that dispensed with the traditional God who had created the universe and who had governed its course ever since.

Condorcet went beyond the cautious formulations of the *philosophes*, openly declaring himself an atheist. The idea of a God, he declared, was superfluous, the institution of a church pernicious, because it perpetuated ideas detrimental to progress. Condorcet is prepared to dispense with the church, and he wages relentless war on the Catholic clergy. In France it was possible to do that, even before the Revolution, but elsewhere militant atheism could be a risky business, in Protestant as well as Catholic countries.

It was easier to undermine traditional historical ideas and images. Rational criticism was not prepared to spare time-honoured myths, sagas and legends. Legends about the origins of monarchs and their peoples were called into question, especially that of the first Romans, Romulus and Remus, and their successors. Voltaire made fun of Joan of Arc and represented her as a superstitious peasant girl. Wilhelm Tell, venerated far beyond the borders of Switzerland, was unmasked as a 'Danish fairy-tale', since evidence of a 'shot at the apple' had been found in the Norwegian figure of Toko at a much earlier stage. The pamphlet with this startling revelation had been written by citizens of Berne and published in that city, but the government of the canton of Uri were able to have it seized and burned, so that the legend of the origins of the Confederation was saved – for the time being at least.

The lawyers' dictum, *quod non est in actis, non est in mundo*, 'whatever is not on record does not exist', became the guiding principle for historians as well. Only what could be proved by reference to written records could be considered as historical truth. The demolition of myths was not to get fully under way, however, until the nineteenth century, at a time when historians were primarily concerned with issues of politics and legislation.

Rational thinking had indeed made great strides in every area. People were very much aware that they were no longer living in the Middle Ages, and everything that was not 'enlightened' was treated with sovereign disdain. The enlightened Protestants now looked down with even more arrogance on the 'backward' Roman Catholics. In France and Italy enlightened Catholics mocked their own backward co-religionists. The whole of enlightened Europe at any rate was agreed that Spain, once the proudest of nations, was no longer in tune with the times. An Austrian report stated:

> In these parts very little progress has been made in the arts, while advances in the sciences are not much more notable. Besides one or two authors who are truly distinguished, there are innumerable others who are scarcely worth reading, and it may well be that the celebrated colleges of Spain are lacking in the basic elements of learning that ought to be inculcated in young people. Nevertheless, from time to time an author makes his appearance with critical works that might in time serve to enlighten those who lack nothing but true judgement and taste. As far as I know, there is little or no talk of new inventions.[3]

Similar judgements would, of course, have applied to the whole of eastern Europe at that time.

2

Enlightenment by Decree

﹨It was in the nature of the Enlightenment to operate with convincing arguments, in the expectation that men would ultimately be guided by their own reason. It was hoped that in time men would free themselves from the trammels of orthodoxy and emerge into the fresh air of the Enlightenment, thanks to their own improved understanding. This would be best and most readily achieved without coercion by the state in Protestant countries and in France, where the legacy of Jansenism and the Huguenots had not been eliminated. How might the aim be achieved, however (even in certain Protestant countries), where a bigoted clergy allied with ignorant authorities still held the local population in thrall? In most cases there was only one obvious solution: to impose Enlightenment by decree for the benefit of a backward populace. In such circumstances the succession of a fresh heir to the throne and the consequent replacement of a reactionary minister might make all the difference.

An initial example was furnished by Frederick II when he succeeded to the throne of Prussia and promptly proceeded to reverse the policies of his father's arch-conservative and patriarchal regime. He flung open wide the gates to admit modern ideas, without in the end actually changing much in the constitution of the state or in its institutions, for he valued the loyalty of his civil service and his officers' morale. Dining in Sanssouci, far away from his subjects, he could well afford to pose as a French free-thinker, scattering witticisms in the form of marginal notes to his decrees – to the effect, say, that everyone in his realm was at liberty to seek salvation in his own fashion, or that newspapers ought not to be censored, as long as they were interesting. Prussia was a Protestant state, and hence in some respects already programmed for Enlightenment. In Roman Catholic and Latin states the situation was rather different; in the kingdom of Sardinia-Piedmont, for example, where it was said of the nobility that they were more pious but more ignorant than the French aristocracy. Nevertheless, in most Italian states a free-thinking element did exist, and the liberal traditions of the Renaissance had not been entirely forgotten. Spain and Portugal, on the other hand, had been indelibly marked by the discipline of the Counter-Reformation.

Portugal was the first of these states to break away from the old order, when, in 1750, with the accession of Joseph I, sweeping powers were delegated to his chief minister, José de Carvalho e Mello, Marquis de Pombal.

He assumed the task of bringing his country up to date through a whole series of radical reforms. He reorganized its finances and its fleet, encouraged manufactures, transport, paper mills, agriculture and fisheries. He also set about rebuilding Lisbon, which had been devastated by an earthquake in 1755. He founded a literary society by the name of Arcádia which supported his reforms. At the same time he curbed the extravagance of the court, reducing the number of royal cooks from 80 to 20. In 1773, slavery was abolished in metropolitan Portugal.

His reforming zeal represents only one aspect of Pombal's character, however: otherwise, he was noted for his ruthlessly tyrannical rule. Thousands of political prisoners were incarcerated in the fortress prison of Junqueira. A number of Jesuits who defied Pombal were kept in prison for over nineteen years, their Order having been banned by the minister in 1759, on the grounds that it had been implicated in the Duke of Aveiro's attempt on the king's life – an allegation that was never proved. On 20 September 1761, the aged Jesuit Father Malagrida was garrotted and burned, so that, paradoxically, the last occasion on which a victim was burned at the stake in Portugal is associated with the name of a man who considered himself a leading champion of the Enlightenment.

Pombal fell from power in 1778, when Pedro III, brother of Joseph I and his successor, dismissed him.[4]

Pombal had shown the world that Enlightenment imposed from above might have two very different faces: on the one hand, progress, reconstruction and modernization; on the other ruthless and brutal tyranny.

In Spain, under King Charles III, various enlightened reforms were also proposed by a succession of ministers — but without Pombal's brutal methods. One issue was 'merely' that of hats and cloaks when Count Squilace, Italian by origin but known in Spain as Esquilache, attempted to deal with organized brigandry by imposing a ban on long cloaks, under which weapons might be concealed, and on the sombreros that concealed the wearer's features. Officials armed with shears were authorized to cut offending garments down to regulation length. Less potentially dangerous garb in a French style should be worn instead! Popular fury, inspired by this ordinance, as well as by steep rises in the cost of living, burst forth in the so-called Esquilache Riots on 23 March 1766. Charles III thereupon rescinded the clothing regulations and dismissed Esquilache. The cape and the sombrero had become symbols of resistance to officious interference with a tradition dear to the hearts of the people — the freedom to dress as one pleased in defiance of police regulations, even when the regulations were in the public interest. The measures introduced by Count Squilace had been part of a programme aimed at modernizing the city of Madrid; they included the installation of street lighting and garbage collection — merely some of the reforms and proposed reforms put forward in the interests of Bourbon centralism.

Centralism was in itself a welcome feature of the Enlightenment. It was no doubt a good thing for a strict national administration to give a lead in the introduction of modern methods and services: whether the populace at large was prepared to follow the lead thus given did not matter so much in a society governed by an elite.

What had happened in Spain and Portugal was noted with mild interest elsewhere in Europe. Reforms introduced by the Emperor Joseph II, when he began to accelerate Maria Theresa's policy with possibly undue haste, caused a considerable stir throughout the Continent. Here, as in any state that wished to keep pace with the Enlightenment, a whole catalogue of reforms was proposed: for example, the abolition of serfdom, the encouragement of manufacturing industry, the reduction of domestic tariff barriers, road-building and the introduction of an up-to-date administrative structure.

It was above all the radicalism of Joseph's policy towards the church that caused astonishment: it involved not just toleration decrees for Protestants and Jews, but also far-reaching intervention in the organization of the Roman Catholic Church, which was the predominant confession in the Austrian domains. The Jesuits had already been banned, and now an offensive was launched against the innumerable convents and monasteries. Only those that were of service to the state as schools or agricultural undertakings were to continue in existence: 'useless' institutions were to be wound up. This is where the Enlightenment's lack of understanding for the practice of prayer and devout meditation was most obviously manifested. Only work, industriousness, counted. The monasteries and their reform was only one item in the programme of the Austrian Enlightenment, which was equally concerned with the emancipation of the Catholic layman and the radical reform of the structure of the church. Even the pope himself, who made a special journey to Vienna, was unable to restrain Joseph and his advisers. It was not until several years later that the Belgians and the Hungarians expressed their opposition to Joseph's measures through rebellions.

We might take the dissolution of the Carthusian monastery of Valsainte in the Swiss canton of Freiburg as a case in point. It was nearly five hundred years old, and the Republic of Freiburg was reckoned to be a stronghold of Swiss Catholicism. But the patricians who governed the capital of the canton were enlightened, just as the city fathers in Milan, Paris and Vienna were. A Carthusian house was numbered among the 'useless institutions', and monks who were disinclined to talk were an unnatural anomaly in this garrulous century. In 1778 the Valsainte monastery was dissolved and its assets transferred to more utilitarian ecclesiastical institutions. But then there was a popular rising, prompted among other things by complaints about the 'enlightened' policies of the patricians who governed the city. The unrest spread throughout the canton and culminated in a siege of the capital which was raised only with military assistance from the neighbouring Protestant canton of Berne. Valsainte remained dissolved until 1866, when it was restored to the Carthusians in the context of a general Catholic revival in the canton.

It was not only religious convictions that were liable to be affected by governmental radicalism: the language of a country might also be affected. All over Europe the scholars of the Enlightenment waged war on dialects or minority languages, which, they believed, should be replaced by the language of the central government. The tendency to think in terms of national unity was allied here with a contempt for popular idiom, which might be looked upon as a relict of barbarism.

In this case, too, Joseph II set the example when he contrived to have German established as the official language throughout his realm. The languages of other autonomous cultures, such as Hungarian and Czech, were consequently forced into second place. The populace received their orders from the imperial centre as often as not in a foreign language. The languages of small minorities were threatened with extinction, as was the case with the Rhaeto-Romance inhabitants of the Upper Inn Valley, where the 'Ladin' dialect of this Latin tongue had been spoken from time immemorial. The Austrian authorities were eager to ensure than nothing but German was taught in the village schools, and within a matter of decades the valley had been totally Germanicized. Ladin was able to survive, however, in the Engadin, the Swiss part of the Inn Valley, because there was no central authority there to dictate which language should be used: the language issue was a matter for each parish to

decide, so that in the canton of Grisons Rhaeto-Romance preserved its own political, literary and religious culture.

In those nations, however, where absolutist government
had long held sway, radical Enlightenment swept through the
land like an iron broom, lending its powerful arm to postulates
of rationality, philanthropy, openness and discipline at work,
and – for all its philanthropic intent – taking no account of
ancient custom and tradition, for such things were the darkest
barbarism.

True supporters of Enlightenment – such as Isaak Iselin – felt
obliged to call for 'toleration for superstition', and Condorcet
was moved to declare: 'Error has just as much right to freedom
as truth has.'[5]

3

Early Romanticism: The Reaction
against the Enlightenment

Radical Enlightenment saw in the unenlightened world nothing but error, superstition, darkness and barbarism. But for many people it was gradually becoming difficult still to feel in the Enlightenment the genial warmth of the sun. The German poet Novalis was moved to speak of the 'harsh, chilly light of the Enlightenment', which seeks 'with mathematical conformity to dismiss all that is miraculous and mysterious.'[6]

A dreary kind of rationality began to take over everywhere, the world had been stripped of its magic, and for the younger generation it was growing tedious. Radical Enlightenment was after all superficial; it lacked profundity, spending itself in barren criticism or shallow moralizing that failed to fertilize the dormant powers of the soul. Following the philosophical demolitions and clearances of the rationalistic era we may detect in the 1770s and 1780s a pre-romantic movement marked by revived interest in occultism, alchemy and magic. We might adapt the maxim, *chassez le naturel, il revient au galop*, to read, 'drive out magic, and it will come back at the gallop'.

The first breach in the rationalistic front was made at an early stage – in England of all places, a country seemingly so enlightened, so level-headed, so given to moralizing. As early as 1708, Shaftesbury, a disciple of Locke and strongly influenced by English neo-Platonists, wrote his *Letter Concerning Enthusiasm*, professing a new kind of enthusiasm – for divinely ordered, harmonious nature. A generation later, in the 1740s, an Anglican clergyman, Edward Young, recorded meditations of nine successive nights – nights spent in a churchyard, not bright days filled with activity, but nights that enshrined the mystery of nature, the sublimity of the divine, love, death and immortality. This was not the triumphant champions of Enlightenment speaking, but a suffering generation. Young's *Night Thoughts* made their greatest impact in Germany, initially via Klopstock, who moved a whole generation to tears with his *Messiah*. To Klopstockian sentimentality, Rousseau added his pessimistic view of culture:[7] 'Everything that comes from our Maker's hand is good, in the hands of man everything degenerates,' even thought itself: 'Of all the past centuries there has been none in which more was read than in this age of ours – and none in which man was less cultured.' Lichtenberg expressed his view of the banal age even more drastically: 'A surfeit of reading has induced in us a kind of learned barbarism.'[8] People began to sense that they were living in a debilitating age.

During the 1770s Germany's youth had had their riotous fling in the so-called *Sturm und Drang* (Storm and Stress) movement, when everything was crazy, unbridled and, if possible, eccentrically brilliant – not boringly average, sound and respectable, as with the more elderly representatives of the Enlightenment. Young men were – literally and metaphorically – intoxicated, carousing through dreamy nights, glorifying in ancient folksongs the charms of unspoiled village maidens. Dramas peopled with medieval knights and robbers banished from the stage the sentimental moralities of the early Enlightenment. The nations found their way back into the Middle Ages – this was the German reaction against exaggerated rationalism, and it was later to spread its influence throughout Europe. In her book on Germany, published in 1810, Madame de Staël noted in astonishment:

The spirit of chivalry still prevails among the Germans . . .
They are incapable of deceit, and their loyalty shines out in
all their relationships . . . If we except a handful of courts
which are determined to ape their French models, Germany has not been seized by the conceit, the immorality

and the lack of faith that have changed the face of France since the time of the Regency. Among the Germans feudalism has still preserved some of the principles of chivalry.[9]

However exaggerated this tribute may sound, it does make clear the reaction against a France that had committed itself totally to reason. Thus came the return to castle and cloister, a nostalgic glorification of a medieval age seen through romantic eyes.

It still has to be said that the change in attitudes and taste associated with pre-romanticism and romanticism was not necessarily reactionary and opposed to reform. It was only in the period of political restoration following the Napoleonic era that it became so – and then only in certain respects. In the closing years of the eighteenth century there were many individuals, both men and women, who were capable of reading Voltaire's scathing satires as well as Young's *Night Thoughts* – the former with lucid intelligence, the latter with sentimental abandon. It was possible, evidently, to sense an affinity with the Enlightenment together with romantic sentiment, while repudiating radical Enlightenment as well as reactionary romanticism. It was in fact thanks to the Enlightenment that the century had grown so liberal that it was able to assimilate in its pluralism all manner of ideas and suggestions, from whatever quarter they might come.

4

Traditionalistic and Governmental Reaction

The Enlightenment introduced a sense of unease into the stable world of the churches, the monarchs and the social hierarchy. Like every other movement, it had its sworn enemies. In its early stages, however, and in its heyday, it was more of a fashionable trend than a political or intellectual movement, by no means unwelcome as a novel alternative. It manifested itself more in theoretical and philosophical pronouncements and seemed unlikely to shake the foundations of the established social and political order. In certain circles, nevertheless, there was a distinct sense of unease. Even the coterie of reformers round the popular periodical, the *Hamburg Patriot*, was suspect in the eyes of conservative fellow-citizens as 'that unholy *Patriot* crew' with their senators and syndics, 'who were possessed by the spirit of Thomasius and infected with the free-thinking plague'.[10] It was not only Hamburg's leading parish priest, it seems, who was upset by free-thinking, especially in matters of religion.

The fate that befell that celebrated philosopher of the Enlightenment, Christian Wolff, might well befall others. On the recommendation of Leibniz, Wolff had been appointed Professor of Philosophy at the University of Halle in 1707, only to be promptly denounced by prominent pietists as a determinist and an enemy of religion. In 1723 King Frederick William I of Prussia dismissed Wolff from all his offices and sent him into exile. But the Calvinist University of Marburg in Hesse welcomed this Lutheran, who was thus able to go on teaching successfully in an enlightened environment until 1740, when, as one of his first official acts, Frederick II recalled him to Halle.

It was not everyone who had the good fortune to find congenial refuge, as Wolff did. Forty years later, Jean-Jacques Rousseau was banished from France following the publication of his *Contrat social*. He sought refuge in his native city of Geneva, but was banished from there and from the principality of Neuchâtel and the republic of Berne before ultimately being able to settle in London.

Ten years after Rousseau's dramatic flight the enlightened world was shocked by the case of Pablo de Olavide. As governor of Seville in 1778 he had just embarked on the planning of a large new settlement when he was arraigned before a heresy court. All his property was confiscated and he was sentenced to eight years' detention in a monastery. The accused was charged with possessing lewd pictures – he owned paintings by Boucher – with having Jansenist books in his library, with being a disciple of Rousseau and Voltaire and with propagating the Copernican theory of the universe. Olavide succeeded in escaping to France, where he remained until returning to Spain in 1798.

Wolff, Rousseau and Olavide were only three examples. It made a great difference in which country a man taught or published his work. There were, of course, also bans on societies and associations, especially on the Freemasons. In Great Britain they were free to do much as they pleased, but their organization was actually illegal in Catholic countries. The prohibition was in fact a papal ban, and the Freemasons were able to continue their activities here and there, even in Catholic countries, depending on the policy of the local government. The century ended, however, with the dissolution of the Order of the Illuminati when, in 1784/85, reactionary circles succeeded in persuading the Bavarian government to outlaw the organization: the ban led to virtual persecution, with known Illuminati being dismissed from the service of the state. The Elector's decree imposing the ban declared:

We have been most exactly informed, and there is irrefutable evidence to confirm the charge, that in their conclaves they are wont to hatch the most dire conspiracies against religion, the state and the government, endeavouring as best they may to extend their abominable system, both by word of mouth and in libellous writings secretly printed and published, slandering our holy religion, the rites of our church and all that pertains to them, seeking indeed to destroy them entirely, and having recourse to every conceivable means to encompass these and similar evil ends, in keeping with the principles they have embraced.

The ban was extended to include all the Bavarian reading societies, and even Joseph II felt obliged under the circumstances to place the Freemasons under state surveillance. Since the Masonic societies represented nothing but 'trickery and fraud', the Freemasonry Patent of 11 December 1785 stated, they

> must be controlled, lest they fall into excesses detrimental to religion, good order and morality, especially as they affect senior officials, who may be liable to behave in an improper manner towards those of their subordinates who do not share their social connections, so that in the end there may be at the very least some kind of financial impropriety.[11]

Even the liberally disposed prince-bishops of Mainz and Cologne felt constrained to follow suit with bans on any society that was suspected of being infected with the ideas of the Illuminati. Such campaigns were part and parcel of the generally reactionary climate that may be detected during these years and that was continued in the form of resistance to the French Revolution. Bans affected reading societies – for instance, in Trier (1783), Düsseldorf (1794), Stäfa on the Lake of Zurich (1795) and Siebenbürgen (1798). Societies in Cologne and Erfurt were placed under surveillance by the authorities of the Electorate in 1792 and 1795 respectively.

As we see, the right of association, the right to found and run a society free of control by the state was by no means taken for granted. Freedom of the press was even less a matter of course; the censorship authorities were everywhere still a regular feature of the political and ecclesiastical establishment – the long-established free states of England and The Netherlands being, as always, exceptions. In many places, it is true, the censorship offices were staffed by enlightened officials. What a historian in Berne wrote in 1786 applied equally to many other places:

> To be sure, we have more freedom to write as we wish than we used to have. A number of arch-ignoramuses who were wont to persecute the Enlightenment have died in the interim. There are people writing now who are not easy to meddle with and who are not dependent on their writing for a living . . . Our censorship, which was never all that severe at the best of times, is now being gently lulled to sleep, *requiescat in pace.*[12]

Nevertheless, we should not overlook in this account the implication that those who lacked influence or who depended on their writing for a living might not always find life easy because of censorship or interference with publication of their work.

If freedom of the press was not taken entirely for granted, even in Protestant or allegedly 'enlightened' countries – where the 'incorrigibly ignorant persecutors of the Enlightenment had departed this life' – then the situation was even more problematic in certain Catholic countries, such as Spain.

How difficult the situation was, is illustrated by the banning of a Spanish translation of Beccaria's celebrated work on criminal law. A diplomatic despatch to Vienna reads:

> The Inquisition is determined not to be stopped in the pursuit of its policy. Regardless of opposition from the Council of Castille and its defence of a number of books which the Council had approved, Marquis Beccaria's book on 'Crimes and their Punishment' has recently been condemned, along with a number of other works, and its publication banned on pain of the most severe punishment. Abbé D. Alvarez de Caballeria, who translated the work into Spanish and long defended it in the courts and in

writing, . . . has found it prudent to forestall the impending storm and has retreated to Rome.[13]

The fact that someone should seek and find refuge from the Inquisition in Rome of all places indicates how circumstances differed in different parts of the Catholic world and how controversial the situation in Spain was liable to be.

But not only in Spain. People had no doubt begun to think they were living in an enlightened Europe, but they were rudely awakened time and time again by some step taken by a reactionary authority.

That heresy trials were not yet a thing of the past was shown all too clearly in 1762 by the execution of the Calvinist Jean Calas ordered by the *parlement* or Supreme Court of Toulouse. Calas was condemned because he had allegedly murdered his son to prevent him from converting to the Catholic faith. His son had in fact committed suicide. In France it had been thought that the age of heresy trials was past. Vigorous protests by Voltaire did in fact lead to a revision of the verdict by the Supreme Court in Paris, and Calas was posthumously rehabilitated in 1765.

As late as 1782 a maid-servant was executed as a witch in the Swiss canton of Glarus, because she was alleged to have cast a spell on her employer's child.

Two years earlier, in Zurich – also a Protestant area – a troublesome enlightened clergyman, Heinrich Waser, had been executed for high treason, because he had published abroad certain facts detrimental to Zurich and had failed to return secret files taken from the state archives. The Waser case was an extreme instance of populist political justice.

Ten years before that, all of Denmark had been shocked by a horrifying affair which culminated in the execution of the kingdom's first minister, Johann Friedrich Struensee. In 1770, as a friend of Queen Caroline Mathilda, he had become chief minister of the crown: it was well known that the king was of unsound mind. Struensee had promptly introduced a wide range of enlightened reforms: abolition of torture, freedom of the press, financial reform, reduction of tariffs, elimination of trading privileges and monopolies, support for farmers and agriculture. All this was in the spirit of the Enlightenment; it was, indeed, anti-mercantilistic, physiocratic, but it had all happened too rapidly and encroached too radically on the preserves of those who had held power under the old dispensation. The court, i.e. the dowager queen and the aristocracy, brought about Struensee's fall after only eighteen months in office, and – since there were doubtless personal motives involved – their vengeance took the exceptional form of the execution of this minister of the crown who had grown too powerful.

It was in fact generally the case that ministers who interfered too drastically with traditional practices were liable to be summarily dismissed. Nevertheless, the dismissal of Louis XVI's finance minister Turgot in 1776 occasioned something of a stir. Turgot had boldly declared freedom of trade and the abolition of guild privileges to allow the free practice of trades and crafts. After barely two years in office Turgot succumbed to a combined assault by the privileged of all classes: the *ancien régime* had demonstrated that it was still there in spite of the Enlightenment and all it stood for and that it was determined to frustrate any serious reform.

If reforms did in fact succeed, if a modern government came to power as a result of changes within a country, the old order, where it still prevailed, had no hesitation in resorting to military intervention. During the second half of the century this came about on at least three occasions.

The attempt on the part of the British crown to suppress the American independence movement may be regarded as military intervention by a conservative power. With the aid of a mercenary force – consisting mainly of German soldiers – an attempt was made to bring to their senses the colonies, which had adopted liberal constitutions; it failed in the face of determined resistance by forces of the Enlightenment in America. It should not be forgotten, however, that many settlers who had remained loyal to England left America and later turned up as emigrants supporting the conservative cause in Europe.

A further conflict between conservative and progressive factions had raged for decades in the republic of Geneva. When ultimately liberal forces gained the upper hand in 1782 and set about introducing relevant reforms, the oligarchy of Geneva called on the protecting powers for help. The three powers, France, Sardinia-Piedmont and Berne, were only too pleased to comply and launched a military intervention to restore the patricians' ancient rights by force. The frustrated liberals emigrated and some of them later played a not insignificant part in the French Revolution.

Some five years later, in similar fashion, reactionary forces in The Netherlands appealed to the conservative governments of Great Britain and Prussia to overthrow the patriotic party, which had been in power for a number of years. Thanks to intervention by Prussian troops and the diplomatic support of Britain, the conservative party was able to return to power and revive the anti-republican regime of the House of Orange.

The ecclesiastical reaction in Prussia which set in after Frederick II's death seems like a fitting conclusion to these reactionary triumphs. Frederick the Great's successor, Frederick William II, meant to wreck the enlightened policy of the great king when he appointed Johann Christoph Wöllner as his minister of religious affairs. In 1788 Wöllner issued an *Edict on Religion*. All three major confessions – the Lutherans, the Calvinists and the Roman Catholics – were to be protected by police regulations against the 'unbridled licence' of the Enlightenment. It transpired, however, that the Enlightenment had taken firm root, even in Prussia: resistance to Wöllner's measures was so fierce that the king had to repeal the edict nine years later, in 1797, and dismiss Wöllner from his post. But Wöllner's edict was a sign that reactionary forces were active everywhere. The king and his minister were both members of the Rosicrucian Order, that syndicate of reactionary forces in the background of the Enlightenment that sought a return to an authoritarian mentality and authoritarian government.

Throughout Europe during the second half of the century other authoritarian or repressive measures might be observed which suggested that governments in various parts of the continent were pursuing policies hostile to the spirit of the Enlightenment. A great many proposed reforms in government, in the churches and in economic matters that were not in themselves controversial nor in any way radical were wrecked on the cherished prejudices of snobbish aristocrats, conservative civil servants, prelates, hidebound professors, old-fashioned artisans and illiterate peasants.

Part IX

The Way Ahead into the Nineteenth Century

1

Nationalism versus Cosmopolitanism

Although nationalism did not become a political force to be reckoned with until after the French Revolution, and although it was not until the romantic period that the concept of an integral national identity began to acquire some substance, the first discussion of these ideas took place in the eighteenth century and may be regarded as one aspect of a reaction against the Enlightenment.

In the eighteenth century a man lived in his native village, lorded it in his manor, or else dwelt in a town, perhaps in a capital city. His domicile was located in a particular state or country, and he consequently belonged to a particular nation. He was not simply a subject of his king but also a member of a national community – although that community might, admittedly, be more imaginary than real. From the moment of his birth the individual was integrated into a larger whole that might actually cross the political frontiers of different states. There was a Europe of different nations besides a Europe of different states. The concept of a nation or a people was inherently vague and appealed more to the political intellect than to the emotions. And yet people had a feeling that they were embedded in something archaic and primeval.

A schematic list of nations[1] from the middle of the eighteenth century tells us about the 'European peoples'. It comes from the Austrian province of Styria and reflects the image of Europe as it was seen by ordinary people. The Spaniards are haughty,

283

virile, clever, wise and generous. The French are careless, talkat-
ive, changeable, cautious. The Italians are underhanded, shrewd,
they pass their time in trivial gossip. The Germans disingenu-
ous, witty, spendthrift, prone to copy everyone and everything,
they spend their time drinking. The English are handsome,
charming, worldly wise, restless, serving now one master, now
another, they spend their time working . . . and so on, via the
Swedes, Hungarians and Russians to the Turks and the Greeks.
This is the simple view from the Styrian vantage-point. As far as
these unsophisticated people were concerned, there were some
ten nations in Europe, and their features were common knowledge. This collection of clichés was current not only among
ordinary people; Rousseau, for instance, states that the English
are given to pride, the French to vanity.[2]

Up to a point, the nations of Europe coincided with its states,
although this was not the case with the Germans, the Italians
and a number of other peoples. The concept of a nation is more
than just a synonym for 'state'. It incorporates a bewildering
multiplicity of meanings. 'People' in the sense of 'nation' did
not refer, of course, just to the lower social class but embraced
every social class and caste. A nation is primarily a country, a
territory that, in the minds of its inhabitants, and even more so
in the minds of its neighbours, has always constituted an entity
ruled over by king or emperor and having a religion of its own.
By this reckoning, for example, the 'people' of Sweden might
be defined by their king and by the Lutheran religion; the
people of Portugal by their king and by Roman Catholicism;
the people of Russia by the tsar and their Orthodox faith. A
common language seemed to be merely a secondary consider-
ation – or else was taken for granted. The common language
might in any case consist of a number of dialects that were
barely mutually intelligible. Besides, the court and the upper
classes spoke a different language from the common people,
either a literary standard idiom, or else French, while academics
and lawyers still often communicated in Latin. The kingdom of
Denmark, for example, included people who spoke Danish, Low
German, Norwegian or Icelandic. Until well into the eighteenth
century they lived peaceably together: after all, they used to say,

God and the king knew all languages. And integration into one state was possible without a common language. This was manifestly the case in Switzerland, with many linguistic minorities in eastern Europe, with the Bretons in France and the Catalans in Spain . . .

In the eighteenth century, a century of the natural sciences, it seemed more appropriate to seek an understanding of a given nation in terms of its natural environment, especially its climate. Even religions seemed to be governed by the climate. Count Zinzendorf of the Herrnhut community believed that God had created the different nations so as to communicate

> the truth and love of his Son to men according to their understanding, and according to the local temperature and climate. The religion of the English is exactly suited to their climate, the Catholic religion is suited to the climate of Spain and Portugal, but it does not match the climate of France, whence comes the *ecclesia gallicana*, a jumble of Catholic and Reformed believers . . . In Germany the climate is quite well suited to Protestantism, and in the Nordic countries even more so, and that is why these religions prevail in those countries.[3]

As states began to bring their subjects increasingly under their control, interest grew in the *esprit des nations* and in specific 'national characters' – in states such as France, for instance, that were aspiring to national unity in the interests of centralization. *La nation* meant the people of France as a whole, who had long since been moulded into one state under a single king. Medieval images of the Frankish people were revived and transposed into the seventeenth and eighteenth centuries. All Frenchmen, it was claimed, were children of one fatherland, protected by the king's government and his army from the ambitions of other nations and from foreign competition. The model copied by the French was England, whose people had already formed one united nation protected by their insularity.

Henceforth it was expected of every nation that it would think and feel as one. The idea of patriotism became increasingly important – not merely loyalty to a king, but a sense of identity with a fatherland. Herder summed up this idea in one sentence: 'Every nation has within itself a centre of well-being, just as every sphere has its centre of gravity.'[4] If a nation was to have its centre of gravity within itself, then it must display certain characteristic features; it must be different from other nations.

Then, all of a sudden, it was the language that took over this unifying and constitutive function. For the French, for example, this presented no difficulty: with them religion had been progressively in decline, while the language of Paris, as the cultural centre of the nation, had more and more become the commonly accepted form of expression. The kingdom of Sweden founded an academy expressly to cultivate the national language. The Swedes had been forestalled by The Netherlands, which had evolved a uniform written idiom and had thus become more than just a political federation. It is significant that, at the beginning of the nineteenth century, Huguenot émigrés in Germany abandoned French for German, so as to be more effectively assimilated into their new environment. But it was not only native speakers of foreign languages who were involved in this process of assimilation. In the course of the eighteenth century educated people began to adopt a standard literary language. If a man wanted to make his way in society, then he had to get rid of his dialect speech. It was thus mainly the upper classes who were affected by linguistic nationalism. Educated Italians, for example, had long enjoyed the boon of a standard literary idiom, whereas untutored Sicilians and Lombards were no more able to communicate with each other than south Germans speaking a Swabian dialect were able to converse with villagers from Lower Saxony who spoke Low German. It was the standard literary language that would free the people from their bigotry and mental lethargy. This was at least the ideal cherished by the Enlightenment. On the other hand, there were romantic enthusiasts who believed that it was actually among the people, the common folk, that the nation's treasures were to be found – and this was where in fact they were unearthed by the poets, who now began to extol their fatherland – in the literary idiom, of course – its uniquely sublime nature and its heroic history.

The further back in history the national heritage lay, the more authentic it was thought to be. The Germans found their historical identity in the tribes as described by Tacitus. It was for the benefit of Great Britain and Ireland that the Scotsman James Macpherson created his *Ossian* cycle of heroic lays modelled on ancient originals. The Nordic nations sought their heroes in the *Edda* and in sagas that survived, phantom-like, only in Ireland. The world of the gods Wotan and Donar and the goddess Freya arose once more, and the ancient heroes, Dietrich von Bern, Hildebrand, Siegfried, Brunhilde and Kriemhilde were reborn. Alongside the universally acknowledged mythology of the Greeks, a new autonomous, national past took its place.

What was more, it was now possible to gain a better understanding of the historically documented past, thanks to new methods introduced by the Enlightenment. Denmark even founded a Royal Society for Nordic History. Much that had been obscured during the Reformation and Counter-Reformation once more became a focus of historical interest: the Frankish kings in France, the Hohenstaufen emperors, or the heroic battles of the Swiss in the past, or – nearer in time – the naval triumphs of the Danes and the Dutch, Swedish exploits in the Thirty Years War. The British could look back with pride on their mastery of the seas, which they blatantly proclaimed in their anthem, 'Rule Britannia, Britannia rules the waves'.

Soon, every nation had been furnished with its specific image that had some claim to historical authenticity and was not just legendary. This image invariably conjured up the idea of a great, virtuous and powerful people triumphing repeatedly over its dastardly foes. The nation was more than just the present age; it was a community embracing the dead as well as the living.

This glorified, regressive vision of the nation would seem to have little in common with the Enlightenment. If, however, it was possible to portray one's ancestors as virtuous men, equable rulers, self-sacrificing warriors, public-spirited citizens, then this was a way of providing the Enlightenment idea of patriotic virtue with a historical prototype. Besides, a nation sharing a common mentality implied a powerful state with the political will to realize the modern aims and principles of the

Enlightenment. The nation would be a much more effective instrument of policy than a mere monarch.

But did not the ideas implied in nationalism conflict with the original cosmopolitanism of the Enlightenment? Did they not represent a relapse into the sixteenth and seventeenth centuries – if not into the late Middle Ages? Did they not evoke the images of foes from earlier ages that the Enlightenment had been trying to eradicate? After all, the Enlightenment had tried, through notions of natural law and a moral philosophy applicable to all men, irrespective of their nation, to lay new foundations for the whole human race. Mankind, as a universal phenomenon, was meant ultimately to supersede the various national states with their separate ideologies.

It might be possible to preserve cosmopolitanism, if a nationalistically coloured love of a man's fatherland could be combined with its cosmopolitan equivalent, which the Enlightenment termed 'patriotism'. It was necessary only to guide man into the cosmos – as Montesquieu and others had done. The primary sphere of a man's activity is then his home in the most immediate sense, his family, his village, the town where he lives. The broader context for this 'patriotic' activity in the family circle, as it were, is the nation, which can inspire energies and initiatives that far transcend the individual in his immediate social setting. But the nation in its turn is seen as just a part of mankind as a whole. A nation is a plausible entity only if it places itself in the service of humanity. These are the aims that the enlightened patriot pursues. In this connection we might quote two statements from the late Enlightenment: 'Is it enough for an enlightened individual to know his own neighbours, or ought it not to be equally important for him to know mankind in general?'[5] Or: 'True patriotism is nothing but the outpouring of the pure love of mankind – and that is not confined to the narrow bounds of a single country or nation.'[6]

2

From the Enlightenment to the Revolutions

The likelihood of a revolution in Europe was already in the air during the second half of the century. We have frequently quoted that Italian observer, Carlantonio Pilati, whom we may regard as our guide through the century of the Enlightenment. In the year in which the United States of America declared their independence, he wrote from Paris: 'But just as events in the world change from one condition to another, as soon as they have achieved perfection, they begin to deteriorate. Foreigners sense all too keenly that the revolution has already begun, and that in France it is already far advanced.'[7]

People had imagined that the revolution would be a more or less peaceful transformation of society, much like England's Glorious Revolution. A dozen years after Pilati had written his letter, the expected event actually happened. The initial phase did offer the appearance of non-violent change, but the process rapidly escalated in 1792, with the reactionary governments of Great Britain, Prussia and Austria playing their part in the radicalization of events. The issue became a matter simply of revolution versus counter-revolution, and this schism affected every nation and every class of society. The same polarization was to mark the nineteenth – and to a large extent even the twentieth – century. It still tends to colour our judgement of the Enlightenment, even down to the present day.

Conservatives placed the blame for the Revolution on the

Enlightenment, at any rate on its radical phase in the second half of the century. Probably the responsibility lies more with the opposing forces of reaction, yesterday's men, panic-stricken ultra-conservatives who had failed to realize in time that radical reforms would have to come in the end. It was they who drove the proponents of Enlightenment and the potential reformers into the radical camp: it was not only in France that patience had reached breaking-point.

A striking example of the strength and the tactics of the Counter-Revolution is the polarization of the Catholic world. At the height of the Jacobin revolution, when Catholic France began persecuting priests, and ultimately abolished the church and religion altogether, then such excesses might have been blamed generally on the Enlightenment. A liberal trend did indeed persist for some decades, but the Jesuits were back, their dissolution had been merely temporary. Following the ban in 1773, they had been reconstituted, mainly in Fraternities of the Sacred Heart, while in many places they had gone on teaching in the schools as ordinary secular clergy, since there was no one to replace them. They had thus continued to exist underground. After some thirty years the Order was reinstated: in Russia in 1801, in Naples in 1804, and in 1814 throughout the world, by Pope Pius VII – unregenerate and under its old constitution. Now the work of restoration might begin everywhere, with its implacable thirst for vengeance on the Enlightenment in all its forms, but especially in its Catholic form.

Even so, during the nineteenth century, there remained in the Catholic Church a relatively liberal minority that carried on the traditions of the Enlightenment, albeit in a more strictly un-compromising spirit than in the Protestant churches – where there was actually a liberal *majority* – or than had been mani-fested by the humanitarian clergy of the eighteenth century. It was left to the second Vatican Council to establish some kind of natural and unforced relationship with the Enlightenment and its Catholic component.

On the other hand, it was actually in the smaller European states – in Scandinavia, Belgium, The Netherlands and Switzer-land – that it proved possible, at the time of the 1848 European revolutions, to put into practice some of the experiments that had been initiated at the beginning of the nineteenth century under the shadow of the French Revolution and the Counter-Revolution as represented by the governments of Austria and Britain. It was only after this lapse that reforms could be introduced across the board – and democratic conditions created, even in monarchies.

The Enlightenment seemed to have come to an end when the French Revolution gave way, in its death-throes, to Napoleonic imperialism, and when, in 1815, the Congress of Vienna rang in the restoration of the old pre-revolutionary regimes. But there were still a good many gains that could not be undone. Moderate conservatives as well as moderate radicals were agreed in accepting as self-evident certain principles of religious toleration, basic human rights, the moral and political autonomy of grown men, the critical mode of thought. Some other beliefs or principles had to be retracted: the one-sided cult of reason, as well as naive faith in the inevitability of progress. Two world wars, Fascism, National Socialism and Stalinism brought about a rude awakening, but in spite of these setbacks hope remained. And where there is hope, it is still possible to look back to the Enlightenment of the eighteenth century, to the world of our forebears, whose portraits we still possess and whose books we can still pick up and read. That age that gave birth to so many hopes is not all that remote. The Enlightenment is still 'a dynamic element of the modern world and a challenge to us to observe humane standards in dark days'.[8]

Basically, the Enlightenment asked too much of men. Its brilliant new light dazzled men and often burst too abruptly and unexpectedly into the gloom of the baroque. An elite of thinkers and aristocrats subscribed to the often naive belief that a simple appeal to *ratio* would suffice to make useful but unpleasant truths palatable. There were indeed countries and whole regions where this appeal was heeded and where it was possible to prepare the way for, and to introduce, necessary reforms – especially social reforms – without incurring an unduly painful break with the past. Elsewhere, however, the task was much harder, and in their impatience for change the elite were not fully aware what degree of resistance they were liable to provoke. Nevertheless, we cannot fail to be impressed even nowadays by the sheer volume of intelligence that erupted in this one century. Without that intellectual explosion, human existence might have gone on vegetating in, to put it bluntly, a state of brute ignorance. That there were risks of exaggeration inherent in the movement was something realized by many individuals, not just by Swift in his *Gulliver* or Voltaire in *Candide*. Both of these authors, however, together with many others, had opened up new horizons, claiming a new liberty which had to be won over and over again and constantly defended against fresh setbacks. Even Lavater, in spite of his religious affiliations and sympathies, remarked, when confronted by the neo-pietism of the Christendom Society in Germany, 'Perhaps they mean well, but light is lacking, and the spirit of free enquiry.'[9]

To liberate the 'spirit of free enquiry' was indeed the prime task of the Enlightenment, a task intended to benefit the whole of mankind. This is what Montesquieu meant when he concluded his autobiography with a succinct statement of the relationship between a man, his family, his nation and mankind in general. These three sentences are a statement of his total commitment to the moral philosophy of the Enlightenment:

> If I knew of something that would be of benefit to me personally, but which would harm my family, then I would dismiss it from my mind. If I knew of something that would benefit my family, but not my country, then I would try to forget it. If I knew of something that would benefit my country, but harm Europe, or benefit Europe, but be harmful to mankind, I would consider it a crime.[10]

Notes

The present work is based in part on my study, *Das gesellige Jahrhundert. Gesellschaft und Gesellschaften im Zeitalter der Aufklärung (The Sociable Century. Society and Societies in the Age of the Enlightenment)*, published by C.H. Beck, Munich, 1982.

Part I The Age

1 Cf. Im Hof, *Enlightenment*, pp. 119–21.
2 Willey, *The Eighteenth Century Background*, p. 5.
3 Lope, *Das kulturelle Leben in Madrid zur Zeit Karls III*, p. 38.
4 Montesquieu, *Caractère*, in *Pensées et fragments inédits de Montesquieu*, vol. 1, p. 7.
5 Vierhaus, *Aufklärung als Prozess*, p. 6.

Part II A Changing Society

1 Cf. Im Hof, *Das gesellige Jahrhundert*, pp. 17–68.
2 Pilati, *Voyages en differents pays de l'Europe*, I, p. 62.
3 Goethe, *Venezianische Epigramme* (1790).
4 G. Maugras, *Le Duc et la Duchesse de Choiseul*, Paris, 1903, pp. 108–9.
5 Lope, *Das kulturelle Leben in Madrid zur Zeit Karls III*, p. 36.
6 Maugras, *Le Duc et la Duchesse de Choiseul*, p. 106.
7 Pilati, *Voyages en differents pays de l'Europe*, I, p. 2.
8 Ibid.
9 Voltaire, *Le siècle de Louis XIV*, p. 1,048.
10 Braunbehrens, *Mozart in Wien*, p. 12.

11 Im Hof, *Das gesellige Jahrhundert*, p. 38.
12 Ibid., p. 68.

Part III Europe and its States

1 W. Altwegg (ed.), *J.P. Hebels Werke*, Zurich, 1943, vol. 2, pp. 80–1.
2 H. Davenson, *Le livre des chansons*, Neuchâtel, 1943, pp. 218–20.
3 Pilati, *Voyages en differents pays de l'Europe*, I, Preface.
4 Broadsheet *Politisches Barometer im Jahre 1785*, in W. Killy (ed.), *Zeichen der Zeit* I, Frankfurt/Hamburg, 1962, p. 25.
5 Pilati, *Voyages en differents pays de l'Europe*, I, p. 201.
6 Ibid., II, p. 45.
7 Ibid., I, p. 74.
8 P. Coulmas, *Weltbürger, Geschichte einer Menschensehnsucht*, Hamburg: Rowohlt, 1990, quoted from U. Bitterli, 'Zur Geschichte des Weltbürgertums', *Schweizerische Monatshefte*, September 1990, p. 786.
9 P. Ochs, *Geschichte der Stadt und Landschaft Basel*, Basel, 1822, vol. 8, p. 6.

Part IV The Champions of Enlightenment

1 Cf. Im Hof, *Das gesellige Jahrhundert*, pp. 216–25.
2 *The Spectator*, No. 68, 18 May 1711.
3 Lope, *Das kulturelle Leben in Madrid zur Zeit Karls III*, p. 38.
4 H.H. Müller, *Akademie und Wirtschaft im 18. Jahrhundert*, Berlin, 1975.
5 Cf. Dierse, *Philosophie*, pp. 826–31.
6 Bödeker, Aufklärung als Kommunikationsprozess, pp. 93–4.
7 Braunbehrens, *Mozart in Wien*, p. 167.
8 Cf. O. Dann, *Lesegesellschaften und bürgerliche Emanzipation. Ein europäischer Vergleich*, Munich, 1981.
9 J. Dierauer, *Die toggenburgische moralische Gesellschaft*, St Gallen, 1913.
10 Im Hof, *Das gesellige Jahrhundert*, pp. 134–57.
11 J. Meenan and D. Clarke (eds), *The Royal Dublin Society 1731–1981*, Dublin, 1981.
12 R.E. Schofield, *The Lunar Society of Birmingham*, Oxford, 1963.
13 Shafer, *The Economic Societies in the Spanish World*.
14 N. Chomel and de la Mare, *Dictionnaire oeconomique*, 1767, p. II.
15 J. Meyer, *La noblesse bretonne au XVIII siècle*, Paris, 1966, pp. 576–85.
16 K. Guggisberg and H. Wahlen, *Kundige Aussaat, köstliche Frucht*.

Zweihundert Jahre Ökonomische und Gemeinnützige Gesellschaft des Kanton Bern 1759–1959, Berne, 1958.

17 von Zinzendorf, *Bericht des Grafen Karl von Zinzendorf*, p. 303.

18 Im Hof, *Das gesellige Jahrhundert*, pp. 164–6, 249.

19 L. von Köchel, *Chronologisch-thematisches Verzeichnis sämtlicher Tonwerke Amadeus Mozarts*, Wiesbaden, 1965–67, pp. 724–6.

20 M. Brecht (ed.), Die Basler Christentumsgesellschaft, in *Pietismus und Neuzeit*, 7, Göttingen, 1982.

21 Im Hof and de Capitani, *Die Helvetische Gesellschaft*.

22 *The Spectator*, pp. 882–97.

23 Pilati, *Voyages en differents pays de l'Europe*, II, p. 327.

24 H. von Greyerz, *Nation und Geschichte im bernischen Denken*, Berne, 1953, p. 24.

Part V Utopia and Reform

1 J. Huizinga, *Naturbild und Geschichtsbild im 18. Jahrhundert*, in *Parerga*, Basel, 1945, p. 160. Cf. also Im Hof, *Das gesellige Jahrhundert*, pp. 75–102.

2 Ibid., p. 245.

3 Canon F.Ph. Gugger in Solothurn (Switzerland), quoted from Im Hof and de Capitani, *Die Helvetische Gesellschaft*, I, p. 145.

4 I. Kant, 'Was ist Aufklärung?', *Berlinische Monatszeitschrift*, December 1783.

5 M. Vorhees, *The History of Phi Beta Kappa*, Washington, 1946.

6 S. Werenfels, *Opuscula theologica, philosophica et philologica*, Basel, 1782/3, II, p. 376.

7 Cf. A. Lindt, *Pietismus und Ökumene*, pp. 146, 152, 158.

8 G.E. Lessing, *Erziehung des Menschengeschlechts*, sections 81–91, in Rille (ed.), *Lessings Werke*, vol. 8, pp. 611f.

9 J. Barbeyrac (ed.), *De Juri Belli ac Pacis de Grotius*, Amsterdam, 1729, Preface, p. XXXIV.

10 Pilati, *Voyages en differents pays de l'Europe*, I, p. 302, II, p. 37.

11 Badinter and Badinter, *Condorcet*, p. 19.

12 Voltaire, *Traité de la Tolérance*, Lausanne, 1959, pp. 152–3.

13 Fénelon, *Télémaque*, Book 10, p. 165.

14 Venturi, *Settecento riformatore, vol. I da Muratori a Beccaria*, p. 709.

15 Hazard, *La crise de la conscience européenne*, II, pp. 66–7.

16 J. Locke, *Two Treatises on Government*, Art. 95, Art. 89. Everyman Library, 1924, pp. 160, 164.

17 Pilati, *Voyages er differents pays de l'Europe*, I, pp. 77, 82, 83.

18 Voltaire, *Le siècle de Louis XIV*, pp. 610–11.

19 P. Hersche, 'Die französischen Physiokraten – Vorläufer der Grünen oder Bahnbrecher des Agrobusiness?', in *Zeitschrift für Agrargeschichte und Agrosoziologie*, 38 (1990), pp. 147–8.

20 Im Hof, *Das gesellige Jahrhundert*, p. 94.

21 Ibid., pp. 96–102.

22 Montesquieu, *Caractère*, p. 7.

23 J.W. Goethe, *Maximen und Reflexionen*.

24 Im Hof, *Das gesellige Jahrhundert*, p. 102.

25 A. Staehelin, *Geschichte der Universität Basel 1632–1818*, Basel, 1957, p. 437.

26 H. Böhning, 'Vielfalt der literarischen Formen. Alltag und "Volk" in der Publizität von Gebrauchsliteratur der deutschen Aufklärung', in *Weimarer Beiträge*, 11, 1990, pp. 1,745, 1,758/1,759, 1,759/1,760, 1,763.

27 H.E. Bödeker, 'Die Religiosität der Gebildeten', pp. 114f.

28 Kopitzsch, 'Die Hamburgische Gesellschaft zur Beförderung der Künste', p. 98.

29 Bitterli, *Alte Welt – Neue Welt*, p. 132.

30 *Abhandlungen und Beobachtungen der Ökonomischen Gesellschaft zu Bern*, year 3, Berne, 1762, Preface, pp. XXVII–XXVIII.

31 Kopitzsch, 'Die Hamburgische Gesellschaft zur Beförderung der Künste', p. 193.

32 Ibid., pp. 72f.

33 Im Hof, *Das gesellige Jahrhundert*, p. 159.

Part VI A Window Opened to a Wider World

1 Cf. Bitterli, *Alte Welt – Neue Welt*, pp. 130, 167, 177, 190, 193.

2 Hazard, *La crise de la conscience européenne*, I, pp. 17–18.

3 Lindt, *Pietismus und Ökumene*, p. 154.

4 Buffon, *Histoire naturelle*, Paris, 1756, vol. 6 (Introduction).

5 A. von Haller, Review of *Sammlung neuer und merkwürdiger Reisen zu Wasser und zu Lande* (1750), in *Göttinger Gelehrte Anzeigen*, 1755 (no page numbers).

Part VII Emancipation – A Release from Age-old Restraints

1 G. Forster (1792), quoted in Vierhaus, *Aufklärung als Prozess*, p. 10.

2 Voltaire, 'Jeanot et Colin', in F. Deloffre, J. van den Heuvel (eds), *Romans et contes*, Paris, 1979, p. 274.

3 Shafer, *The Economic Societies in the Spanish World*, pp. 88f.
4 Pilati, *Voyages en differents pays de l'Europe*, II, pp. 98–9.
5 Greive, *Die Juden*, p. 141.
6 Ibid., p. 150.
7 Im Hof, *Das gesellige Jahrhundert*, p. 49.
8 G. Burnet, *Some Letters Containing an Account . . . of Switzerland, Italy and Some Parts of Germany*, London, 1724, pp. 21, 51.
9 Lope, *Das kulturelle Leben in Madrid zur Zeit Karls III*, p. 48.
10 B. Schnegg, 'Weiblicher Geist und Moral', in *Reformatio*, 1 February 1990, p. 72.
11 Ibid., p. 74.
12 Badinter and Badinter, *Condorcet*, p. 296.

Part VIII For and Against Radicalization of the Enlightenment

1 van Dülmen, *Der Geheimbund der Illuminaten*, pp. 41, 34–5, 212.
2 Stuke, *Aufklärung*, pp. 274–5.
3 Lope, *Das kulturelle Leben in Madrid zur Zeit Karls III*, p. 38.
4 Ziechmann (ed.), *Panorama der Fridericianischen Zeit*, pp. 834–5.
5 Badinter and Badinter, *Condorcet*, p. 85.
6 Im Hof, *Enlightenment*, pp. 116, 131.
7 Rousseau, *Emile ou l'éducation*, pp. 145, 826.
8 Quoted in R. Vierhaus, 'Leseerfahrungen – Lebenserfahrungen', in *Euphorion*, 81, 1987, p. 13.
9 G. de Staël, *De l'Allemagne*, 1810–14, pp. 43, 48.
10 Kopitzsch, 'Die Hamburgische Gesellschaft, zur Beförderung der künste', p. 47.
11 van Dülmen, *Der Geheimbund der Illuminaten*, p. 93.
12 H. von Greyerz, *Nation und Geschichte im bernischen Denken*, Berne, 1953.
13 Lope, *Das kulturelle Leben in Madrid zur Zeit Karls III*, p. 42.

Part IX The Way Ahead into the Nineteenth Century

1 *Völkertafel* (Styria), Österreichisches Museum für Völkerkunde, Vienna (no date).
2 Rousseau, *Emile ou l'éducation*, p. 828.
3 Lindt, *Pietismus und Ökumene*, p. 157.
4 Bitterli, *Alte Welt – Neue Welt*, p. 197.

5 Rousseau, *Emile ou l'éducation*, p. 827.
6 Isaak Iselin, quoted in Im Hof and de Capitani, *Die Helvetische Gesellschaft*, p. 21.
7 Pilati, *Voyages en differents pays de l'Europe*, II, pp. 330–1.
8 Vierhaus, *Aufklärung als Prozess*, p. 7.
9 A. Lindt, 200 Jahre Christentumsgesellschaft in Basel, in *Basler Stadtbuch*, 1980, p. 146.
10 Montesquieu, *Caractère*, p. 15.

Bibliography

Baczko, B., *Rousseau, solitude et communauté*, The Hague, 1974.

Baczko, B., *Lumières de l'Utopie*, Paris, 1978.

Badinter, E. and Badinter, R., *Condorcet (1743–1794), un intellectuel en politique*, Paris, 1988.

Balács, E. et al. (eds), *Beförderer der Aufklärung in Mittel- und Osteuropa*, Berlin, 1979.

Berlin, I., *Wider das Geläufige. Aufsätze zur Ideengeschichte*, ed. by Henry Hardy, Frankfurt, 1982.

Bitterli, U., *Alte Welt – Neue Welt. Formen des europäisch-überseeischen Kulturkontakts vom 15. bis zum 18. Jahrhundert*, Munich, 1986.

Bödeker, H.E., 'Aufklärung als Kommunikationsprozess', *Aufklärung*, 2, 1987.

Bödeker, H.E., 'Die Religiosität der Gebildeten', *Wolfenbütteler Studien*, 1988.

Böning, H., *Die Genese der Volksaufklärung und ihre Entwicklung bis 1780*, Stuttgart/Bad Cannstatt, 1990.

Borghero, C. (ed.), *La polemica sul lusso nel settecento francese*, Turin, 1973.

Braunbehrens, V., *Mozart in Wien*, Munich, 1986.

Brunner, O., *Adeliges Landleben und europäischer Geist*, Salzburg, 1959.

Bury, J.B., *The Idea of Progress. An Inquiry into its Origin and Growth* (1920), New York, 1987.

Cassirer, E., *Die Philosophie der Aufklärung*, Tübingen, 1932.

Chartier, R., *Les origines culturelles de la révolution française*, Paris, 1990.

Chaunu, P., *La Civilisation de l'Europe des Lumières*, Paris, 1971.

Crampe-Casnabet, M., *Condorcet, lecteur des Lumières*, Paris, 1985.

Dann, O. and Dinwiddy, J. (eds), *Nationalism and the Age of the French Revolution*, London, 1988.

Darnton, R., *The Business of Enlightenment: a publishing history of the Encyclopédie, 1775–1800*, Cambridge, MA/London, 1979.

Daz, F., *Voltaire storico*, Turin, 1958.

Dellsperger, R., 'Frauenemanzipation im Pietismus', in *Zwischen Macht und Dienst. Beiträge zur Geschichte und Gegenwart von Frauen im kirchlichen Leben der Schweiz*, Berne, 1991.

Dierse, U., 'Philosophie. Institutionelle Formen', in *Historisches Wörterbuch der Philosophie*, vol. 7, Basel, 1989.

Duchet, M., *Anthropologie et Histoire au siècle des Lumières*, Paris, 1971.

van Dülmen, R., *Der Geheimbund der Illuminaten. Darstellung, Analyse, Dokumentation*, Stuttgart/Bad Cannstatt, 1975.

van Dülmen, R., *Die Gesellschaft der Aufklärer. Zur bürgerlichen Emanzipation und aufklärerischen Kultur in Deutschland*, Frankfurt, 1986.

Ehrhard, J., *L'idée de nature en France dans la première moitié du XVIIIe siècle*, 2 vols, Paris, 1963.

Ehrhard, J., *La politique de Montesquieu*, Paris, 1965.

Erne, E., *Die schweizerischen Sozietäten. Lexikalische Darstellung der Reformgesellschaften des 18. Jahrhunderts in der Schweiz*, Zurich, 1988.

Fabvre, J., *Stanislas-Auguste Poniatowski et l'Europe des Lumières*, Paris, 1952.

Fénelon, *Les aventures de Télémaque, fils d'Ulysse*, Toulouse, 1804.

François, E., *Sociabilité et société bourgeoise en France, en Allemagne et en Suisse (1750–1850)*, Paris, 1986.

Frankel, C., *The Faith of Reason: The Idea of Progress in the French Enlightenment*, New York, 1948.

Furet, F. (ed.), *Livre et Société dans la France du XVIIIe siècle*, 2 vols, Paris/The Hague, 1975.

Gagnebin, B. and Raymond, M. (eds), *J.-J. Rousseau. Oeuvres complètes*, vol. 4, Paris, 1969.

Gay, P., *The Enlightenment*, New York, 1967–9; vol. 1: *The Rise of Modern Paganism*, 1967; vol. 2: *The Science of Freedom*, 1969.

Gershoy, L., *From Despotism to Revolution 1763–1789*, New York/London, 1944.

Godechot, J., *La Contre-Révolution, doctrine et action 1789–1804*, Paris, 1967.

Goulemot, J.-M. and Launay, M., *Le Siècle des Lumières*, Paris, 1986.

Granger, G.G., *La mathématique sociale du marquis de Condorcet*, Paris, 1956.

Granger, G.G., *Condorcet mathématicien, économiste, philosophe, homme politique*, colloque international, ed. by P. Cripel/Ch. Gilain, Paris, 1989.

Greive, H., *Die Juden, Grundzüge ihrer Geschichte im mittelalterlichen und neuzeitlichen Europa*, Darmstadt, 1980.

Hall, A.R., *The Scientific Revolution 1500–1800. The Formation of the Modern Scientific Attitude*, London, 1954.

Hammerstein, N., *Aufklärung und katholisches Reich. Untersuchungen zur Universitätsreform und Politik katholischer Territorien des Heiligen Römischen Reichs Deutscher Nation im 18. Jahrhundert*, Berlin, 1977.

Hampson, N., *The Enlightenment. An Interpretation*, vol. 4, Pelican History of European Thought, New York, 1966.

Hazard, P., *La crise de la conscience européenne (1680–1715)*, 3 vols, Paris, 1935.

Hazard, P., *La pensée européenne au XVIIIe siècle de Montesquieu à Lessing*, 3 vols, Paris, 1946.

Hoffmann, P., *La femme dans la pensée des Lumières*, Paris, 1977.

Im Hof, U., *Das gesellige Jahrhundert. Gesellschaft und Gesellschaften im Zeitalter der Aufklärung*, Munich, 1982.

Im Hof, U., 'Enlightenment – Lumières – Illuminismo – Aufklärung – Die Ausbreitung eines besseren Lichts im Zeitalter der Vernunft', in M. Svilar (ed.), *'Und es ward Licht'. Zur Kulturgeschichte des Lichts*, Universität Bern, Kulturgeschichtliche Vorlesungen 1982/3, Bern, 1983.

Im Hof, U. and de Capitani, F., *Die Helvetische Gesellschaft. Spätaufklärung und Vorrevolution in der Schweiz*, Frauenfeld/Stuttgart, 1983.

Jacob, M.C., *The Radical Enlightenment. Pantheists, Freemasons and Republicans*, London, 1981.

Janson, T., 'The age of associations. Principles and forms of organisation between corporation and mass organisation. A comparative Nordic survey from a Swedish viewpoint', *Scand. J. History*, 13.

Kaufmann, E., *Architecture in the Age of Reason. Baroque and Post-Baroque in England, Italy and France*, Cambridge, MA, 1955.

Kopitzsch, F. (ed.), *Aufklärung, Absolutismus und Bürgertum in Deutschland*, Munich, 1976.

Kopitzsch, F., 'Die Hamburgische Gesellschaft zur Beförderung der Künste und nützlichen Gewerbe (Patriotische Gesellschaft von 1765) im Zeitalter der Aufklärung. Ein Überblick', *Wolfenbütteler Forschungen* 8, Munich, 1980.

Laufer, R., *Style rococo, style des Lumières*, Paris, 1963.

Lindt, A., 'Pietismus und Ökumene', *Pietismus und moderne Welt*, 12, 1974.

Lope, H.J., 'Das kulturelle Leben in Madrid zur Zeit Karls III (1759–1788) im Spiegel österreichischer Gesandtenberichte', *Spanisches Kulturinstitut in der Residenz*, 8, Munich, 1987.

Lough, J., *The Contributors of l'Encyclopédie*, London, 1973.

Mauzi, R., *L'idée de bonheur dans la littérature et la pensée française au XVIIIe siècle*, second edition, Paris, 1965.

Meylan, Ph., *Jean Barbeyrac (1674–1744) et les débuts de l'enseignement du droit dans l'ancienne Académie de Lausanne. Contribution à l'histoire du droit naturel*, Lausanne, 1937.

Montesquieu, 'Caractère de M.', in *Pensées et fragments inédits de Montesquieu*, vol. 1, Bordeaux, 1899.

Moravia, S., *Il tramonto dell'Illuminismo. Filosofia e politica nella società francese 1770–1810*, Bari, 1968.

Pilati, C.A., *Voyages en differents pays de l'Europe en 1774, 1775 et 1776 ou Lettres écrites de l'Allemagne, de la Suisse, de l'Italie, de Sicile et de Paris*, 2 vols, 1778.

Pomeau, R., *La Religion de Voltaire*, Paris, 1956.

Pomeau, R., *Politique de Voltaire*, Paris, 1963.

Pomeau, R., *L'Europe des lumières. Cosmopolitisme et unité européenne au XVIIIe siècle*, Paris, 1966.

Proust, J., *Diderot et l'Encyclopédie*, Paris, 1963.

Reinalter, H. (ed.), *Freimaurer und Geheimbünde im 18. Jahrhundert in Mitteleuropa*, Frankfurt, 1983.

Roche, D., *Le siècle des lumières en province. Académies et académiciens provinciaux, 1680–1789*, 2 vols, Paris/La Haye, 1987.

Roger, J., *Les sciences de la vie dans la pensée française au XVIIIe siècle. La génération des animaux de Descartes à l'Encyclopédie*, Paris, 1963.

Roger, J., *Buffon: un philosophe au Jardin du Roi*, Paris, 1989.

Rousseau, J.-J., 'Emile ou de l'éducation', in B. Gagnebin and M. Raymond (eds), *Oeuvres complètes*, vol. 4, Paris, 1969.

Rykwert, J., *The First Moderns. The Architects of the 18th Century*, Cambridge, MA.London, 1980.

Sarrailh, J., *L'Espagne éclairée de la seconde moitié du XVIIIe siècle*, Paris, 1954.

Shackleton, R., *Montesquieu. A Critical Biography*, London, 1961.

Shafer, R.J., *The Economic Societies in the Spanish World (1763–1821)*, Syracuse, 1958.

The Spectator, complete in one volume, London, 1832.

Starobinski, J., *Jean-Jacques Rousseau. La transparence et l'obstacle*, Paris, 1958.

Starobinski, J., *L'invention de la Liberté*, Paris, 1987.

Stuke, H., 'Aufklärung', in *Geschichtliche Grundbegriffe. Historisches Lexikon zur politisch-sozialen Sprache in Deutschland*, vol. 1, Stuttgart, 1972.

Trevor-Roper, H.R., *Religion, Reformation und sozialer Umbruch*, Frankfurt, 1970.

Venturi, F., *Settecento riformatore*, 5 vols, Turin, 1969–90.

Venturi, F., *Utopia e Riforma nell'Illuminismo*, Turin, 1970.

Vierhaus, R. (ed.), 'Deutsche patriotische und gemeinnützige Gesellschaften', *Wolfenbütteler Forschungen* 8, Munich, 1980.

Vierhaus, R. (ed.), 'Aufklärung als Prozess', in *Aufklärung* 2, 1987.

Voltaire, 'Le siècle de Louis XIV', in R. Pomeau (ed.), *Voltaire oeuvres historiques*, Paris, 1957.

Vyverberg, H., *Historical Pessimism in the French Enlightenment*, 1958.

Willey, B., *The Eighteenth Century Background. Studies on the Idea of Nature in the Thought of the Period*, London, 1950.

Ziechmann, J. (ed.), *Panorama der Fridericianischen Zeit: Friedrich der Grosse und seine Epoche – ein Handbuch*, Bremen, 1985.

von Zinzendorf, K., 'Bericht des Grafen Karl von Zinzendorf über seine handelspolitische Studienreise durch die Schweiz 1764', O.E. Deutsch, *Basler Zeitschrift für Geschichte und Altertumskunde*, 35, 1936.

Zurbuchen, S., *Naturrecht und natürliche Religion. Zur Geschichte des Toleranzbegriffs von Samuel Pufendorf bis Jean-Jacques Rousseau*, Würzburg, 1991.

Table of Dates

304

Index